THE
MANIPULATORS

THE MANIPULATORS

JEFFREY ROBINSON

A Conspiracy to Make Us Buy

SIMON & SCHUSTER
A VIACOM COMPANY

First published by Simon & Schuster Ltd, 1998
A Viacom Company

1 3 5 7 9 10 8 6 4 2

Simon & Schuster Ltd
West Garden Place
Kendal Street
London W2 2AQ

Simon & Schuster Australia
Sydney

A CIP catalogue record for this book is available from the British Library.

ISBN 0-684-81767-5

Typeset by SX Composing DTP, Rayleigh, Essex
Printed and bound in Great Britain by
Butler & Tanner Ltd, Frome and London

Contents

*This book is for
Gladys, Maryse, Joelle, Pat,
Christian, Alain
et leurs bandes de momes*

If advertising speaks to a thousand in order to influence one, so does the church. If it encourages people to live beyond their means, so does matrimony . . . Christ would be a national advertiser today.

Bruce Barton, ad man

Acknowledgements

I am particularly appreciative of the time, insights and efforts on my behalf made by: Larry Adelman of California Newsreel; Dean Ayers of the Entertainment Resources Marketing Association; Jeremy Bullmore of WPP; Lee Clow of Chiat/Day; the inimitable Jerry Della Femina; Jim Durfee of Messner Vetere; Phil Dusenberry of BBDO; Donald Kaufman of Donald Kaufman Color; Bob Kuperman of Chiat/Day; Paul Losee of M+; Burt Manning of J. Walter Thompson; John Morton of Total Research; Shirley Polykoff; Professor Anthony Pratkanis; Professor Stuart Rogers; Leslie Savan of the *Village Voice*; Martin Sorrell of WPP; and Paco Underhill of Envirosell.

Additionally, I am grateful for input from: *Ad Week*; *Advertising Age*; American Association of Advertising Agencies; American Marketing Association; Benetton; Bijan Fragrances; Bloomingdale's; Calvin Klein Inc.; Chanel; Dior; DKNY; Duke University Hartman Center; Estée Lauder; Harrods; Hermes; Hertz Corporation; Macy's; National Infomercial Marketing Association; National Retail Federation; Point of Purchase Advertising Institute; Radio Advertising Bureau; Ralph Lauren Polo; Saks Fifth Avenue; Schweppes Europe; Selfridges; Tiffany's; Tommy Hilfiger Inc.; University of Texas Advertising Research Resource Center; and YSL.

And, as always, heartfelt thanks to Nick Webb and Ingrid

Connell at Simon & Schuster, the ever-sharp Liz Paton, the ever-wonderful Milly Marmur and, of course, La Benayoun.

JR
London

Prologue

He was more human than the ones who came before him.

More approachable.

More like one of us.

He allowed the Berlin Wall to come down and refused to put the state system on life support when Communism gasped for its final breath, and so we crowned Mikhail Gorbachev 'the man who put an end to the Cold War' and awarded him an honoured place in our history books. And even if he dismantled the old system before putting a new one in place, and even if, because of that, he is not a hero in his own land, who cares? Certainly no one seems to at Pizza Hut – because he is also the man who brought deep dish to Moscow.

So, they filmed him sitting in their restaurant with his 10-year-old granddaughter for 40 seconds, never saying a word, never eating a slice – she's the hungry one – just being more human than the ones who came before him, more approachable, more like one of us. And sales went up.

We shall venerate the man by revering his pizza.

One *glasnost*.

One *perestroika*.

Extra pepperoni.

CHAPTER ONE

Alfred, Ernest and James

At one of the largest advertising agencies in America, psychologists on the staff are probing sample humans in an attempt to find how to identify, and beam messages to, people of high anxiety, body consciousness, hostility, passiveness, and so on.
Vance Packard, *The Hidden Persuaders*

It all comes down to this.

Casting spells.

Filling our heads with some catchy tune or neat slogan that will throb gently in the hidden layers of our brain.

Touching buttons. Parcelling intellect and emotion together. Finding ways of saying one thing on the surface and something else beneath it. Targeting our hopes. Remoulding our ambitions. Allaying our fears. Helping us mascara the face we put on to meet other faces. Selling us back ourselves.

Priming us for that singular moment when we spot their product somewhere and find ourselves reaching for it, almost uncontrollably, dropping it in our shopping basket, paying for it and bringing it home.

Making that product an integral part of our lives, without us ever wondering, why?

—'Aren't you glad you use Dial? Don't you wish everybody did?' Don't worry, if you use Dial no one will think you smell bad, the way you keep running across people who smell bad because, obviously, they don't use Dial.

—'The best a man can get. Gillette.' You're too manly to use another brand because that would make you less manly.

—'The best tyres in the world have Goodyear written all over them.' If Goodyear isn't written on your tyres, it's like announcing to the world that you're the sort of person who is willing to settle for less than the best.

—'Promise her anything but give her Arpège.' You no longer have to tell her what she wants to hear, she's yours for just a bottle of perfume.

—'Bring out the Hellmann's and bring out the best.' Dare you risk having your family think you're giving them anything less than the best?

—'We don't sell any size smaller than XL . . . maybe it's time you tried one on' – Harley-Davidson Motorcycles. Are they referring to the bikes or guys who ride them?

—'Ronson, since 1896 – eyewear, wristwear, fashion accessories for the life you live.' If you liked our lighters it's only logical that you'll love our sunglasses. It is?

—'Image Is Nothing' – Sprite. Gee, let's create an image by saying image is nothing.

—'Helps control dandruff' – Head & Shoulders. So does soap!

—'Anacin – Twice as much pain reliever.' Than what?

—'You can be sure if it's Westinghouse.' Sure that Anacin has twice as much pain reliever?

—'All you need to know about paint' – Sherwin-Williams. You probably don't know anything about paint but are you going to admit that to the world by purchasing another brand which will only highlight your ignorance?

—'If it's got to be clean it's got to be Tide.' Of course it's got to be clean, so if you put your trust in another product, everyone will see that your clothes are dirty.

—'You've come a long way baby' – Virginia Slims Cigarettes.

If you're a woman who needs to believe that you can do more than just vote, drive and smoke in public, you can tell the world how far you've come by smoking these in public.
—'You're not fully clean until you're Zestfully clean' – Zest Soap. And you thought you were fooling them with Dial!
It all comes down to this.
Getting us to spend.

Advertising is not a science. It is an art form. And as an art form, at least in its purest sense, it has gone as far as it can go. The end of the road was reached in January 1984.

As purveyors to the uncertainties of any art form, the men and women who run today's advertising agencies – no longer the creative types but, instead, managers and accountants and lawyers – have been confronted with these inevitable truths: that they cannot yet manage the quantum leap from making us salivate to making us buy; that it won't happen until something spectacular comes along to move them closer towards some sort of quantifiable science; that until someone invents a magic black box with lots of shiny buttons which they can push to trigger in us uncontrollable urges to buy things – stuff we didn't plan on buying, or didn't know we wanted to buy, or, in fact, never wanted to buy at all – there is little else to do but globalize.

Copywriters and art directors had long ago proved they knew everything there is to know about making us laugh, cry, sit up and take notice, so the corporate suits have had to be content with turning ad agencies into serious businesses, spreading the gospel and cashing in on commissions from Madison Avenue to the far reaches of the rest of the world.

That's not to say, however, they've ever given up hope that the magic black box might arrive on the next morning's stage. The ultimate quest is to turn this art form into science, somehow getting it to the point where results can be predicted, even guaranteed. They've been anxious for it to happen ever since the 1950s when a man named James Vicary falsely claimed to have tamed subliminal perception.

In spite of Vicary's subsequent confession, and flying in the face of proof that subliminal perception doesn't work, legions of people are, even today, convinced that what he claimed to have stumbled across did work. That it does work. Or, that given the proper set of conditions, it could work.

They believe this with religious fervour because a magic black box – no matter what form it eventually takes – is Madison Avenue's Holy Grail.

These otherwise-enlightened have, for nearly half a century, argued that the mind most definitely does respond psychologically and physiologically to secret messages; that there are ways of broadcasting messages which can make us, unknowingly, act and think in a preprogrammed manner.

Because they want it to be true, they forever actively fuel those fires, leaving stalwarts convinced that there is a massive conspirational cover-up to keep the general public from knowing the truth. They exalt Vicary as the first shot in a war of invisible and inaudible stimuli, unconsciously perceived, by which we are, today, constantly bombarded. They insist that modern-day hidden persuaders are alive and well and manipulating the public at will.

And while there are plenty more on the other side who feel that any explorer in search of hidden persuasion is not merely up against science but also up against a public of consumers more worldly – not to mention decidedly more cynical – than anyone could have dreamed of in 1957, the fact is that both groups are defending the wrong corners.

The question is no longer, can a magic black box happen? But, when will it happen? In that regard, the conspiracy first exposed in 1957 – but which never materialized – is finally real.

The future is not here. But, riding on the back of digital technology, the magic black box will be here tomorrow.

Art cannot guarantee results. Only science can do that. And advertising is not a science.

At least, not yet.

World War II forever changed the economic course of world history, devastating the factories of Europe, lifting the United States out of the Great Depression and bringing full employment to the country. There had never been an industrial power of this magnitude and omnipotence.

Despite recessions and the various oil crises, despite minor depressions, the war in Vietnam and the political upheaval of Watergate, America's position as the world's predominant commercial force would go virtually unchallenged for the next 50 years. The Germans and the Japanese would again become forces to reckon with, but now the weapons of war would be motor cars and VCRs.

Stock markets opened around the world, boomed and crashed and sometimes rebounded. At times, for a time, the balance of economic power tipped towards the Japanese, then the Arabs, then back to the Japanese, before spreading wider, through what is now known as the Pacific Rim. One day, possibly, it might even tip towards whatever form of confederation comes out of the European common market. But throughout the last half of the twentieth century the dollar remained the global currency. And none of that would have happened had Hitler not come to power or the Japanese not bombed Pearl Harbor or the isolationists in Congress somehow prevailed in keeping Roosevelt from declaring war.

America had been caught unprepared.

The guns of World War I had rusted while the country was struggling to keep the banks open and still make butter. Now, to gear up for battle and take the fight to the enemy, the nation focused on the only thing that mattered – marching men off to service and marching women into factories where they would churn out planes and tanks and rifles.

Five years later, when the war was over and the men came home, they took up their places in those factories and re-geared, this time to satisfy the pent-up demand for consumer goods that had come with victory and a national reserve of accumulated wealth.

Almost as a celebration of prosperity, railroads expanded and so did airlines. The Interstate Highway System was built, linking a continent that had, just a few years before, been connected only by rail and by the fledgling service of a few air carriers. Automobile manufacturers stepped up production – now there were roads on which to drive – and, because Detroit was going full force and, because it used to be true that as Detroit goes so goes the nation, the nation was going full force too.

The post-war baby boom created massive new markets that would have to be satisfied for the next 50 years, as those new roads carried young families in those new cars from the cities to the suburbs, from east to west, from south to southwest. In those suburbs they built homes and schools and shopping malls. At the same time, research and development in electronics led to the mass production of televisions and radios – but especially televisions – which followed those families across the nation, propelled by companies like Procter & Gamble and Lever Brothers with wares to sell. Advertising filled the coffers of the broadcasters, who sold the product, which replenished the coffers of manufacturers, who re-invested some of those profits back into advertising. The feeding frenzy created new products and new markets and new demand. Mass production created mass markets, which in turn created the need for young people with fresh ideas to sell it all.

One answer was called 'in-depth research' and, in the early 1950s, it was all the rage.

The future is now, they told us. Science has become so sophisticated that we can delve into someone's subconscious. Today we can discover more about what someone wants and more about what someone will buy than that person knows himself.

The future is now, they promised; we can finally get inside the consumer's brain.

It wasn't as much a bandwagon as it was a steamroller with music, and among the first people to pull into town on it were Alfred Politz and Ernest Dichter. There had always been research – advertising and marketing men believed there was truth in numbers – but there had never been anything quite like this. Although Politz and Dichter fronted different schools of thought, both claimed star status, both brought with them the mystique of a German-educated scientist, and both were, arguably, little more than snake oil salesmen.

Alfred Politz was born in Berlin in 1902 and trained as a physicist. He escaped from Germany when the Nazis first came to power, spent several years in Sweden where he sold aspirin, and moved to the States just before the start of World War II. For a while, he ran a hardware store in Florida and sold mail order mouthwash. A small but powerfully built man, by the time he reached 50 he'd somehow sold himself to the New York advertising community as America's leading market research analyst. Claiming to have perfected a new approach to psychology- and statistics-based research, he convinced companies like DuPont and Coca-Cola to hire him. His fee was a then staggering $200,000.

Dichter was the pretender to his throne.

Five years Politz's junior – a short, stout man with thinning reddish hair, horn-rimmed glasses and a pronounced double chin which he customarily attempted to hide behind a bow-tie – he arrived in the United States in 1938, claimed to have a PhD in psychology, sometimes said he was German and at other times said he was Austrian, and spent several years bouncing around various marketing firms espousing what many of them considered to be off-the-wall nonsense.

However, on the chance that he might just be ahead of his

time, the Compton Advertising Agency hired him as a consultant to work on their Ivory Soap account. Until he happened along, Ivory's market research focused on what the public thought of soap. Dichter instructed Compton to look elsewhere instead, to find out what the public thought about taking a bath. It was, in those days, a radical departure, no doubt given some *gravitas* by his thick accent. Compton followed his advice, changed their approach and sold more soap.

Self-publicist that he was, he parlayed that success into work for Chrysler Motors. This time he preached that sex could sell cars and convinced them to use the slogan, 'A sedan is a wife but a convertible is a mistress.'

By 1953, Dichter was on his way to capturing Politz's crown. Now demanding fees from clients of $10,000–$75,000, he decided to enshrine his self-proclaimed genius by establishing the Institute for Research in Mass Motivations – later called the Institute for Motivational Research – and moving into a huge mansion on a hilltop towering over the Hudson River in Westchester County, just north of New York City. He boasted a full-time staff of 62, including 45 legitimate psychologists, and 450 part-time interviewers spread around the country.

Simply put, Dichter's doctrine was that manufacturers needed to sell function and emotional security. In other words, for a product to succeed, two things were necessary: it had to work properly; and it had to appeal to feelings deep inside the psychological recesses of the human mind – feelings that only he was capable of unlocking. 'Don't sell shoes,' Dichter advised a manufacturer of women's footwear, 'sell lovely feet.'

The way he saw it, all consumer decisions were based on one of four basic motivations: sustenance, security, status and sex. 'Once a businessman knows where his product stands in relation to the Four-S's,' Dichter maintained, 'he can gauge his selling appeals with maximum effectiveness.'

Although his pitch was seductive enough to sign up General Foods, Lever Brothers and American Airlines, the tools of his 'Four-S' trade were little more than purpose-built gimmicks, such as psycho-drama sessions in his 'Motivational Theater' and a contraption he named 'the shadow box'.

A product to be tested would be put inside the box, unseen by the person being interviewed. That person would then be asked to put his hands through the holes on the side of the box and feel the product. While this was going on, Dichter and his researchers would be studying every facial expression through peepholes and two-way mirrors.

Whether the shadow box analyses actually revealed anything is questionable. Still, when General Foods asked him to conduct studies for Bisquick, he reported back to them that his shadow box enquiries had proved, conclusively, that cooking was more than just a chore for most housewives, that it was, more importantly, a symbol of a woman's status in the family. General Foods supposedly followed his advice and, instead of telling the housewife what Bisquick could do for her, they began telling the housewife what she and Bisquick could do together. Whether sales increased because Dichter was right, or simply because General Foods renewed their enthusiasm for the product and pushed it harder, creating more visibility in the marketplace, no one will ever know.

Next, he advised the Sanka Coffee people that their advertising – then based on how their competitors' caffeine-laden coffees destroyed sleep – was alienating the public. He argued that no one wanted to hear that regular coffee was bad for their health. Purportedly, the caffeine-free Sanka people believed him and changed their slogan to, 'Now you can drink all the coffee you want.' At least according to Dichter, sales increased.

His finest hour, however, came thanks to prunes.

Again pitching the power of his shadow box, Dichter landed a contract with a consortium of California prune growers. Several weeks and a lot of their money later, he apprised them of the news that the general public associated prunes with ill health – specifically, constipation. Claiming that any advertising that reminded people of ill health was a turn-off, he sent them another bill to design an advertising campaign that would get prunes 'rediscovered' – today the word would be 'repositioned' – by highlighting their 'vigorous and masculine' aspects. He dubbed prunes 'The California wonder fruit' and linked them with good health by using pictures in ads of young people at play.

As prune sales rose, Politz fought back, saying that Dichter's brand of motivational research wasn't really research at all. 'It's pointless to concentrate on basic motivations in consumers, when the only important task is to find motives which can be controlled to commercial advantage, basic or not. If a farmer asks, "What makes wheat grow?" and you tell him, "The carbon cycle of the sun", you are giving him the basic cause and probably impressing him. But you aren't doing him much good. A better answer would be, "Fertilizer".'

Unfortunately for Politz, it was too little too late. Madison Avenue ruled that he was yesterday's man. And despite the fact that Dichter attracted clients by bragging that he'd been the brains behind a famous ad for Plymouth motor cars – which no one seemed to have noticed had run six years before Dichter even arrived in America – he'd seized the moment and simply installed himself as king. But, unseen pretenders were lining up to do to Dichter what he'd just done to Politz.

By 1957, in-depth research had become a whopping $12 million industry. Two-thirds of America's top-100 companies admitted they were using motivational researchers to help plan their advertising campaigns. One popular prediction of the day was that, by 1965, no major advertising campaign would be launched before the product and prospective customers had both been thoroughly analysed by motivational psychologists.

Suddenly everybody wanted a piece of the action.

A firm in Connecticut perfected a system where answers to their morning surveys were phoned into their office each afternoon. Over night, questions were narrowed in scope then sent out again the following morning, until they felt they'd uncovered what made someone buy, or not buy, their client's product.

Another company, this one in Chicago, held itself up as a specialist researcher in beer drinking and cigarette smoking. The reason people smoke, they decided, is 'proof of daring'.

Seeing its market share slip, the Elmo Roper Company of New York – one of the original 'nose counting' researchers who simply went out and took large surveys to determine market shares – claimed that their more traditional methods also took into account consumers' motives, and warned that no one should presume that any of these newcomers had staked out as their own, what was, in reality, a very broad field.

To flex his own muscles, Dichter subjected 200 advertising executives to motivational research, concluding that they were more likely to buy media for their clients on the basis of fear and insecurity, than anything logical. Upon hearing that, one ad man immediately fired his agency's staff psychologist, saying, 'I may have butterflies in my stomach, but these guys have butterflies in their heads.'

Now into the fray came a tall, ambitious young man with deep-set eyes and a square face named James Vicary.

Born in Michigan, he said that he was a social psychologist – a lot of people were doing that in those days – and, just in case anyone doubted him, he listed memberships on his CV of the American Psychological Association, the Society for Applied Anthropology and the American Marketing Association. But he never formally trained as a psychologist.

Instead, he'd picked up what he knew working in Detroit for a subsidiary of the George Gallup Audience Research Institute. From there, he'd moved into the advertising business and was, at one point, employed by the agency Benton and Bowles.

Although this was a crowded market, he attracted some minor attention in 1950 by publishing an article in the merchandising trade journal *Printers' Ink* entitled 'How Psychiatric Methods Can Be Applied to Market Research'. Based largely on that, he took a gamble and formed the James M. Vicary Company of New York, naming himself president. For sale, he said, was his singular ability to discover, through consumer testing, hidden meanings in words that could be used to sell products through advertising and packaging.

Taking a page out of Dichter's book, Vicary swayed a cake mix manufacturer into believing that baking was, somewhere deep in a woman's psyche, symbolic of giving birth. He advised them to repackage the cake mix so that the housewife needed to add milk and eggs to it. He said this helped to create in the woman's subconscious the feeling of presenting her family with a special gift. Like Dichter with Bisquick, no one will ever know whether sales increased because Vicary was onto something important or because the cake mix manufacturer believed in Vicary's ebullience and therefore made a concerted effort to increase sales.

For a while, he laid claim to having perfected the science of 'Mass Observation'. He put together a ragtag band of volunteers – school teachers, shop clerks, barbers, estate agents, taxi drivers, plumbers, telephone linesmen, small businessmen and, most notably, children – and got them to keep a diary of everyday events. His idea was that the general public were better qualified to observe the general public than professional researchers because they came to this field with no preconceived notions.

His next ploy was to stalk supermarkets.

On assignment for a small chain of neighbourhood groceries, he observed that American women were changing their shopping habits, abandoning those more traditional, personalized-service groceries in favour of the anonymous shopping offered in large supermarkets. In the old corner shop, you told the assistant what you wanted and he'd fetch the items for you. But that, Vicary decided, meant the woman had to know what she wanted. If she didn't – for example, at the meat counter where the butcher would ask what cut she was looking for – there was an embarrassing moment of having to confess she didn't know. However, in supermarkets where meat was prepackaged, she could choose a cut without knowing the name for it. So he went back to his client and told them to train their butchers to be more sensitive to that moment of embarrassment.

Sometime in late 1954 or early 1955, when a women's magazine asked him to study consumer behaviour, Vicary returned to supermarkets. Now he noticed that women blinked at different rates depending where they were in the store. Walking through aisle after aisle clutching a stopwatch and notebook, he determined that, when faced with canned goods, instead of blinking at a normal rate of 32 per minute, they blinked 14 times a minute. At the checkout, watching the clerk adding up the bill, blinking increased to 45 per minute. His conclusion was that most shoppers were walking through the supermarket in a semi-daze and weren't coming out of it until they were ready to leave the store. He took that to mean that they were somehow vulnerable, and theorized that, due to this vulnerability, shoppers wound up buying stuff they didn't actually need.

Today, modern retailers have become expert at successfully taking advantage of that particular vulnerability. But in those days the message was not yet understood. Mainstream consumer research was still, essentially, a 'yes and no' affair. A manufacturer would ask housewives, 'Do you like our package?' Or they'd test-market their product, head to head, against a competitor's and then wonder, 'Which washes whiter?' The result would be an ad that boasted, 'Three out of five mothers who care about their children's clothes recommend . . .'

Thanks largely to the publicity that Politz, Dichter and a few of their faithful were able to generate, motivational researchers were beginning to persuade manufacturers that consumers' stated opinions about anything and everything, from TV dinners to hair spray, could not be trusted; that those opinions were often so weighed down by emotional associations that consumers were either not capable or simply unwilling to tell the truth; that people, all too often, answer questions with what they think the pollster wants to hear.

The way to get at the truth, in-depth advocates believed, was to conduct commercial mass psychoanalysis which could mysteriously penetrate the subconscious of a selected group. If the study was set up carefully enough, and if they based their focus groups on the proper criteria – age, sex, income, geography, education, marital status and material possessions – and if they could get those people to talk about a myriad of subjects, then they could unlock the public's hidden desires. If they could manage that, advertisers would know what buttons to push in order to sell a product.

Although occasionally denounced as voodoo, by 1956 any number of large companies were swearing by the results that in-depth motivational research was bringing them.

Chrysler Corporation, for example, were said to have changed the design of their car to satisfy some previously hidden inner desires of the potential customers.

It was the same story at Bell and Howell, the camera company. Researchers there discovered that weekend photographers were intimidated by cameras with loads of buttons and dials. They made the camera look too professional and hobbyists felt excluded. So Bell and Howell produced a simplified model. Clearly an idea whose time had come and is still with us. Cameras today promise perfect pictures every time and even advertise themselves as 'idiot proof'.

An airline tried in-depth and were advised – in the face of the common practice then of hiring only young, attractive stewardesses – to hire middle-aged hostesses because, the more matronly the on-board reception, the less fearful the customer was of flying.

The oil company Sacony Vacuum delved into in-depth research and, as a result, changed their name to Sacony Mobil.

The Philip Morris Tobacco Company went that route and came up with a new brand of cigarette in a newly designed 'flip-top' red and white box, called Marlboro.

The Corning Glass Works discovered that one of the so-called 'wonder products' that had come out of World War II, Pyrex, had run smack into the public's fear that glass was fragile and if put on the stove would break. So in-depth experts changed the direction that Corning took in their Pyrex advertising. Ads now confronted those fears and proved to consumers that this wasn't ordinary glass. Here, too, sales took off.

A luggage company using another wonder product, Fiberglas, advertised their suitcases as unbreakable by show-ing them tumbling out of an aeroplane. But the ads weren't selling suitcases and it wasn't until they hired an in-depth researcher that they discovered their customers didn't want to be reminded of anything as terrifying as falling out of an aero-plane. The luggage company changed their ads and sales climbed.

In-depth was the in-thing and even advertising agencies were boasting of researchers on their payroll. When McCann-Erickson hired five for their newly formed Motivational Research Department, one of their competitors, Ruthrauff & Ryan, went one better, stocking their newly formed depart-ment with six psychologists and a hypnotist.

All of this quickly took its toll on James Vicary.

With a staff of six installed in a townhouse office on a fashionable block in the East 60s just off Fifth Avenue, he was a man floundering under the weight of competition. He needed to do something to stay in business. Increasingly desperate, he turned back to supermarkets.

His observations there had led him from blink-times and customer vulnerability to wondering about what the eye could see. Now he wanted to know what the brain could consciously register and what messages could sneak past our conscious defences to be registered subconsciously. Then he heard about a projector that could flash messages one by one onto a screen at up to 1/3000th of a second.

At last, he hoped, salvation.

Tachistoscopes had been around since the turn the century, but it wasn't until 1926 that a professor at Tulane University Medical School in Louisiana had patented one. He'd been hoping to prove that, even though such speed is too fast for the human eye to recognize consciously, the brain would record the messages subconsciously and the person would then somehow act on whatever the message was. For the next 15 years, the professor's patent stayed in his lab. It wasn't until World War II that tachistoscopes found some practical use. Pilots and gunners in the US Army Air Corps were too slow to distinguish between friendly and enemy planes at a distance, and consequently were attacking the wrong aircraft. So the military developed training courses using tachistoscopes which flashed aeroplane silhouettes across a screen. Beginning with large pictures at slow speeds, then gradually increasing exposure speeds while decreasing the size of the image, aircrews learned to recognize up to 2000 different tiny silhouettes correctly at 1/100th of a second.

After the war, a few college football coaches used tachistoscopes to train quarterbacks to spot open pass receivers, and driving school instructors intermittently used them to teach students to spot potential accident situations. Law enforcement agencies also took to flashing images on screens for weapons training, to speed up an agent's ability to distinguish between threats from bad guys and the sudden appearance of other good guys. Before long, an especially fast tachistoscope was built by the Kodak company – it supposedly flashed at 1/60,000 of a second – which they used to take close-up colour photos of bullets smashing through a pane of glass, mosquitoes stopped in mid-air, and that fraction of an instant when a ball-bearing, dropped from above, breaks the surface of a glass of milk.

Vicary now saw another use.

If the human brain could take in the information it needs to build a response from an image below the perception threshold – a message that perhaps directed someone to buy something – he might be able to re-create the shoppers' vulnerability in a myriad of other places. After giving it some thought, he decided the ideal place to test this would be a cinema. And the words to flash on the screen should be 'Drink Coke' and 'Eat Popcorn'.

In the autumn of 1957, he announced that he had installed a tachistoscope in a Ft Lee, New Jersey, cinema and over the course of six weeks – during which some 45,000 people had been unknowingly subjected to his experiment while watching the movie *Picnic* – he'd flashed those words on the screen for 1/3000th of a second every five seconds. He reported that Coke sales had increased by nearly 58%, and that popcorn sales had increased by almost 18%.

Subliminal perception, Vicary bragged, was the most powerful marketing tool yet known to man, and he'd successfully unleashed it.

Madison Avenue was excited. *Newsweek* published several features on it. Even the London *Sunday Times* reported that American ad agencies were experimenting with 'subthreshold effects', which in turn prompted the BBC to do two programmes on it.

But Vicary's windfall was short lived. Almost as soon as he put out the word, streams of criticism began pouring in from every quarter – government, the church, educators and the general public – all of them sharing a common fright and anger. They found it greatly unsettling that someone could, somehow, control our actions with an undetectable, outside force. They worried that, if these invisible messages did indeed cause behavioural change, we could all be controlled and made to do anything by anyone with the force. They remonstrated, this is not permissible.

It was left to psychologists to say that subliminal perception was possible but, in a case like this, only someone who was not otherwise averse to drinking Coke or to eating popcorn would have gone to buy some. As far as they believed, no one could be made to eat or drink something they didn't like.

Not surprisingly, Vicary's most vocal critic was the man with the most to lose, Ernest Dichter. He labelled the technique a kind of hypnotism and denounced Vicary for turning an otherwise respectable science – that is, in-depth research – into a parlour game. 'The American consumer,' he warned, 'will resent and resist any form of subliminal manipulation.'

Vicary struck back, robustly defending his turf. Subliminal perception, he said, is just an instant commercial that happens to be very effective. He accused Dichter of 'subliminal sour grapes', knowing full well that, in weaker moments, Dichter himself had already admitted subliminal perception was real and that 'most ads had some subliminal effects along with their conscious impact'.

He maintained that Dichter's criticism was 'like saying a whiff of a Martini is worse than a swallow', and that subliminal perception was 'simply a new band of human perception, like FM [radio]. It's an innocent band.'

Although Vicary said he understood how some people

might feel uncomfortable with it, he pointed out that opposition to it was by no means unanimous and that many businessmen were anxious to try it. One cinema chain – which he did not name – had already ordered tachistoscopes for their movie houses. Accordingly, he'd formed a company called Subliminal Projection to advise advertisers how best to use subliminal perception. Subliminal Projection had now licensed the Precon Process & Equipment company in New Orleans to commercialize the tachistoscope.

'Subliminal perception,' he bragged, 'has to be unseen to be believed.'

Therein lay the downfall of Mr Vicary.

To appease a concerned public, America's National Association of Broadcasters and the British Institute of Practitioners in Advertising outlawed subliminal perception. At the same time, demands were placed on Vicary to repeat his Ft Lee success.

First he wouldn't. Then he couldn't. Most of the time the machine failed, unable to flash the words on the screen in the suggested time frame. On the few times it did work, no one responded. And when others tried the same experiment, they too failed.

Vicary now began backtracking on his original claims. He contended that only someone who had needs in relation to the subliminal message would respond to it. Then he said that because the message had to be so simple it was really just 'reminder advertising', a means of keeping people aware of a product.

In 1959, the *Journal of Applied Psychology* reported that a group of qualified scientists had attempted to re-create Vicary's results under strictly controlled laboratory conditions. Subjects were shown the subliminal message 'beef', then offered a choice of assorted sandwiches. Beef was not chosen to any greater degree than any other sandwich. Radio-Canada also slipped subliminal messages into a show. Over the course of 30 minutes, they broadcast a phone number 352 times, asking anyone who heard it to ring. No one did. When they later quizzed the studio audience, wondering if anyone there knew what the message was, the responses ranged from 'Drink Coke' to 'Eat Popcorn'.

Eventually, someone actually bothered to trek across the George Washington Bridge to Ft Lee to interview the manager of the cinema, who confessed that he knew nothing about Vicary or his test and, anyway, his cinema was too small to have seated the number of people Vicary claimed had been there during the six-week test period.

In 1962 Vicary finally admitted the whole thing had been a hoax, little more than a fabricated attempt to prop up his failing marketing research business.

Then he disappeared.

The possibility that advertisers could somehow trick us into buying things we didn't otherwise want stayed in the news, along with stories and comments about James Vicary's supposed experiment, not just because this frightened people but also because a former Associated Press journalist named Vance Packard was looking for work.

When Packard heard about Vicary, he contacted several magazines in New York hoping to freelance an article on the dangers of subliminal perception. None of them would have it. He concluded that they were refusing to print anything that criticized the advertising business because ads were their lifeblood, so he went in search of a book publisher. He later explained that he only just managed to get his account of Vicary's work into the first edition of *The Hidden Persuaders*. But it was enough to confirm an image of Madison Avenue many people wanted to believe – that advertising was an evil art; that advertisers could, without our knowledge, inoculate us with a 'buy this' virus that would cause us all, instantly, to break out into a spending rash.

It was, in its own way, as terrifying as the 'beep-beep-beep' of the just-launched Russian satellite, Sputnik.

Packard, relishing his newly found guise of popular alarmist, made speeches around the country in which he reduced everyone to the common denominator of 'consumer', then tagged on all of us, as a group, eight needs or emotions that, he claimed, could be and were being manipulated by the advertising industry. His list consisted of: emotional security, trust, creativity, love, ego gratification, power, family history and immortality.

Supporting his allegations with the then startling announcement that two-thirds of America's largest advertisers were using in-depth research on which to base their campaign strategies – he stressed that Madison Avenue was mass producing customers for manufacturers the same way manufacturers were mass producing goods for the market, a claim many people argue is still valid – Packard raised legitimate concerns about the society they were inevitably creating.

Before long, he had a string of garrulous allies at his side, writers and thinkers who accepted, almost as a foregone conclusion, advertising's role in creating and maintaining a debauchery of consumption.

'History will see advertising as one of the real evil things of our time,' said Malcolm Muggeridge. 'It is stimulating people constantly to want things, want this, want that.'

Added journalist and diplomat Clare Boothe Luce, 'Advertising has done more to cause the social unrest of the 20th century than any other single factor.'

Author Marya Mannes took up a similar theme. 'Advertisers in general bear a large part of the responsibility for the deep feelings of inadequacy that drive women to psychiatrists, pills, or the bottle.'

Author Ernest Van Den Haag observed, 'It does not matter what people want to buy as long as they want to buy enough of the same thing to make mass production possible.

Advertising helps to unify taste, to de-individualize it and thus to make mass production possible.'

Of course, Madison Avenue riposted.

'Anyone who thinks that people can be fooled or pushed around,' said the famous agency boss Leo Burnett, 'has an inaccurate and pretty low estimate of people.'

Wrote the *Journal of Advertising*: 'To be successful, advertising must understand or anticipate basic human needs and wants, and interpret available goods and services in terms of their want-satisfying abilities. This is the very opposite of manipulation.'

Bizarrely, even Alfred Politz came down on advertising's side when he told a reporter, 'The findings of the motivational researchers are interesting, but they don't prove anything.'

The fray was joined, back on Packard's side, by media guru Marshall McLuhan. 'Ads are carefully designed by the Madison Avenue frog-men-of-the-mind for semiconscious exposure.' He claimed that their ultimate aim was programmed harmony – which, oddly, didn't seem quite so obvious at the time as it does now – bringing together all human impulses, aspirations and endeavours. 'Using handicraft methods, it stretches out toward the ultimate electronic goal of a collective consciousness.'

McLuhan then raised the stakes by insisting, 'Ads seem to work on the very advanced principle that a small pellet or pattern in a noisy, redundant barrage of repetition will gradually assert itself. Ads push the principle of noise all the way to the plateau of persuasion. They are quite in accord with the procedures of brainwashing.'

Advertising as a form of brainwashing now became a popular motif.

According to the *Oxford English Dictionary*, the word 'brainwashing' was coined in the United States only in 1950, which suggests that it was in vogue by the time Packard came along. So fashion may account for some of the frequency with which it was used in those days. But it does not explain why the association is still much bandied about today.

The *American Heritage Dictionary* defines brainwashing as an intensive indoctrination to change a person's convictions radically. It defines advertising as the business of calling attention to a product so as to produce sales. Inexorably linking those definitions today – and soaking that bond in credence – are scores of academics. Writing in scientific and social journals, they minutely analyse various techniques – many of them perfected by the Japanese in World War II, the Chinese during the Korean War and the Russians during the Cold War – and superimpose them on what they are able to observe along Madison Avenue.

One obvious similarity is repetition. Running the same ad over and over and over again is the media equivalent of dropping water on someone's forehead until they finally give in. Along the same lines, advertising and brainwashing both rely heavily on emotional approaches, such as playing off fear, creating anger, stimulating excitement and inducing tension.

Given that, comes the argument, isn't the ceaseless recurrence of the words 'Drink Coke' proof positive that manipulation of one mind by another is both the general definition of brainwashing and, at the same time, the transparent ambition of advertisers?

Not at all, comes the answer, I drink Coke because I like it, not because those two words are everywhere.

Here, the response of the otherwise-enlightened is that people who have been brainwashed almost always vigorously deny their own susceptibility to manipulation. Either they have been shown the light, or they have arrived at their own state of awareness all by themselves.

As is often so evident today in the membership of various cults, until they are deprogrammed most people who have been brainwashed refuse to believe they have been brainwashed. By the same token, until we are convinced otherwise, most of us refuse to admit that we are choosing Coke over Pepsi because someone in an ad agency has got inside our head and managed, somehow, to direct that choice.

One popular rebuttal is that brainwashing is evil, and, at least according to David Ogilvy – arguably one of the most legendary of all advertising men and, not by coincidence, also one of Madison Avenue's most adept self-publicists – 'Advertising is only evil when it advertises evil things.'

The counter to that is, does the mouthpiece relinquish any and all responsibility for the message? The editors at *Newsweek* magazine answered that by pointing out, 'In the ad biz, sincerity is a commodity bought and paid for like everything else.'

Having thrown open the shutters and allowed the public to peek inside, Packard earned respect and gratitude, admittedly much of it in the form of royalty payments and large speaking fees. At the same time, he absolutely earned the industry's undying wrath. Not because he wasn't necessarily telling the truth, but for having the sheer gall to challenge their methods and their motives. He, more than anyone else, transformed the image of ad men from suburbanites in grey flannel suits into monsters intent on capturing the minds of an innocent populace, and from there, into dangerous fiends creating a society based on covetousness, consumption and greed.

These days, advertising executives still reel when they hear his name. 'He picked on us because we've always been a soft target,' notes one in New York. 'He did more damage to the profession,' adds another, 'than any person in history.' Comments a British colleague, 'Packard is detested for the injuries he caused.'

Undeniably, Packard stepped on toes and bruised egos. But, most of all, he touched raw nerves. He saw this as a moral issue – logic could never win here – arguing that most people don't know what they want, even if they say they do, and that advertisers take advantage of this.

It wasn't any longer about exposing the likes of Alfred and Ernest and James, it was about lifting up the rock and suddenly uncovering a world of 'them versus us', with thousands of thems wriggling all around, frantically, and plainly winning.

We are alone, he warned, forced to defend ourselves from throngs of men with ominous-sounding job titles – psychometric specialists, psycholinguists, hypno-technicians, message compression technologists, voice pitch analysts, psychographic segmenters, neurophysiologists, operant conditioners.

Now, smack bang in the middle of the Cold War, with visions of Russian tanks crashing through our borders while we cried, 'Better Dead than Red,' we also had to worry about subversion from within, infiltrators who moved amongst us, intent on driving home one and only one religion – Buy!

Packard was telling us to open our eyes and see ourselves as Madison Avenue did – nothing more than one huge Pavlov's dog.

He was saying that Madison Avenue was channelling our unthinking habits, directing our subconscious, manipulating our purchasing decisions.

That they were lying to us when they vowed this was about nothing more than why women use lipstick, and why men are drawn to car showrooms by convertibles but wind up buying sedans, and why kids love cereal that goes snap, crackle and pop.

That neatly concealed behind dancing toothbrushes and singing bananas there was something menacing.

That, by establishing why we behave the way we do, these manipulators were changing our habits and redirecting our choices.

That they could, and would, in effect, pre-ordain what we buy, how we think, who we vote for, the way we live.

Before Packard came along, the world was a simpler place.

We accepted as a fact of life certain tenets: that everyone knew what he or she wanted; that everyone would always tell the truth about his or her likes and dislikes; that everyone could be trusted to behave in a rational way.

The Hidden Persuaders challenged those rudimentary assumptions.

Today's manipulators have long since put the lie to all three.

CHAPTER TWO

Packard's Disciples

The Hidden Persuaders *exposed what he saw as the growing and not entirely benign influence of the nation's advertising industry. Alarmed by new techniques that convinced people to run out and buy things, he detailed advertising's fascination with the school of consumer analysis known as motivational research. 'Many of us are being influenced and manipulated, far more than we realize, in the patterns of our every day lives,' he wrote. He compared motivational research to 'the chilling world of George Orwell and big brother.'*
From the *New York Times* obituary of Vance Packard

Cognitive scientists now agree that the brain can indeed accept messages below the threshold of normal recognition. But it doesn't mean that any of these messages could, or would, in anyway influence us.

We process information outside of awareness, for the most part, to identify information we would otherwise process consciously. Say you're at a party, carrying on a conversation with someone at one end of the room, when someone on the other side of the room quietly says your name. You become aware of it, even though you had not, perhaps, previously been aware of that person. That's processing of information outside of awareness. It does not prove the existence of subliminal influence.

Even if the words 'Drink Coke' were imprinted at 1/3000th of a second on the brains of people watching a movie, or at any other speed for that matter, there's no reason whatsoever for anyone to act on the message. You wouldn't run out for a Coke, any more than you might be expected to follow the instructions of the person on the other side of the party who whispered your name and then added, 'Jump out the window.'

However, all too often, when science declares something has never been proven true, a cottage industry develops to argue the other side – that it has not been proven false.

Out of that gaggle emerged a Canadian university professor named Wilson Bryan Key. 'Subliminal perception,' he said, 'is a subject that virtually no one wants to believe exists, and if it does exist, they much less believe that it has any practical application.'

An early practitioner of the 'Elvis is Alive School of Social Science', Key claimed to be utterly convinced that such techniques were in widespread use by the media, advertising agencies, corporations and governments too. 'Merchandisers,' he said, 'by embedding subliminal trigger devices in the media, are able to evoke a strong emotional relationship between, say, a product perceived in an advertisement weeks before and the strongest of all emotional stimuli – love, sex and death.'

The fact that he alone could see them merely added to his ardour. 'Most national advertising includes embedding. Retail or local ad layouts may not have the facilities, as their artists and writers either do not know about subliminal techniques or they lack the skill and craftsmanship required to do the work well. Every major advertising agency has at least one embedding technician in its art department. The technique is taught in most commercial art schools.'

Instead of worrying about popcorn sales in cinemas, Key asserted that messages – most of them sexual in nature – had been hidden in pictures used in magazine advertising. Among the culprits, he named liquor companies – including Tanqueray Gin, Chivas Regal, Crown Royal and Gilbey's Gin – Betty Crocker's SuperMoist Cake Mix, Wish Bone Salad Dressing, Kent cigarettes, Eminence underwear, *Time* magazine and McDonald's. He insisted that images of breasts and genitalia were common. And when it came to liquor ads, he had a penchant for finding the word 'sex' embedded somewhere in ice cubes.

According to Key, 'Ice cubes likely sell more alcohol for the distilling industry than attractive models in cheesecake poses. The inconspicuous ice cubes often hide the invisible sell – invisible, that is, to the conscious mind.'

In the case of *Time*, he pointed to the cover of the 21 April 1986 issue, which featured the Libyan leader, Muammar Gaddafi. The headline was 'Target Gaddafi', and the story inside detailed the US raids on Libya that had taken place the week before. Key said he found the word 'sex' purposely embedded onto Gaddafi's forehead and the word 'kill' purposely embedded on his right cheek. Looking at it today, you need to squint a lot and stare real hard. And, well, maybe the lines on Gaddafi's face do sort of look like 'sex' and 'kill'. But it's impossible to say if someone put them there on purpose.

Key maintained that the words were embedded 'to increase the emotional support of *Time*'s readers, some 25 million, for the attack upon Libya'. But *Time* doesn't have 25 million readers – actual circulation was then around 5.6 million – and, anyway, why those two words?

Unable to come up with believable answers, Key took the roundabout tack that proof of his allegations was evident for anyone to see because *Time* had used this technique before. According to him, they'd put the word 'sex' into their cover portrait of the Ayatollah Khomeini during the Iranian hostage crisis, and also into the small inset photo of President Jimmy

Carter. What effect, if any, this was supposed to have on us was not something Key dwelt on. Not because he didn't want to but because he couldn't. Not surprisingly, his work is widely regarded as 'quintessential pseudoscience'.

What we see in *Time* covers, cake mix ads and ice cubes, if we see anything at all, almost certainly has more to do with the psychology of perception than enlightenment from Professor Key. Under the accepted heading of Gestalt psychology, embedded images can be generally explained by the fact that the mind needs symmetry and order, and, to provide that, we quite naturally see optical illusions and pictures in random shapes. It is then down to 'the law of similarity' to explain how the brain associates those illusions with familiar objects.

When Key's claims first appeared, creative directors at agencies up and down Madison Avenue admittedly had every reason to hope that this time the Messiah had come to town. Although deep down most of them knew better, still they were more than willing to take a long look at the methods Key described because they wanted them to work. In several agencies, considerable time and money were sunk into further study. However, in every case, the time was written off as wasted and the money was written off as lost. The general conclusion was that people were seeing what they wanted to see.

Key retaliated that subliminal perception was effective only if the ad agencies could convince the public it didn't exist. But he was remarkably stingy when it came to providing footnotes, citations, references or any other documentation to support his pronouncements.

His reputation, nevertheless, held credibility with some people. In 1990, he appeared in a Reno, Nevada, courtroom as an expert witness for the plaintiffs in the subliminal perception case brought against the British heavy metal rock band, Judas Priest.

Five years previously, two teenage boys had attempted suicide, supposedly on the subliminal urging of the band through a track on their 1978 album *Stained Class*. Although one of the boys lived, both sets of parents filed suit against the band. The song in question was 'Better By You Better Than Me.' The words in question were 'Do it.' The band denied having anything to do with subliminal messages, so Key was brought in to help the judge see the light. He explained how subliminal messages were present on ice cubes, in store catalogues, on Ritz Crackers and on the evening news. He also defined science as 'pretty much what you can get away with at any point in time'.

Professor Timothy Moore – a Canadian psychologist who also testified at the Judas Priest trial, but who was there for the defence and helped the band come out victorious – insists, 'There is not now, nor has there ever been, any reliable empirical evidence that subliminal stimulation can produce anything other than fairly brief and relatively inconsequential reactions. Further, there is no evidence whatsoever that subliminal directives can compel compliance.'

That most advertising people and other academics wrote Key off as crazy merely played into his hands – they would say that, wouldn't they?

The more you deny the conspiracy, the more you fuel the fires.

Key had stumbled onto a good game and skilfully turned his ability to see the word sex embedded everywhere into a livelihood. There were enough book-buying adults who believed in the force of subliminal perception, and enough malleable college students who believed in a huge conspiracy that had armies of little men with awls scratching naked ladies' forms into ice cubes, that Key was able to spend nearly 20 years maintaining a fairly popular niche on the campus lecture circuit.

As long as Key had books and speeches to sell, and as long

as Packard's books were in print, and as long as Marshall McLuhan kept coming up with soundbites to justify his support of all this, the subliminal perception peril refused to die.

It continues today.

When *Time* published an article called 'Secret Voices', repeating a claim that major department stores across North America were using subliminal messages in their sound systems, conspiracy buffs had a field day. Reassured about something they'd believed all along, they pointed to messages shrewdly hidden inside string section refrains – messages that whispered, 'I am honest' and 'I will not steal' and 'If you shoplift, you will be caught'. That was followed by a story accusing every major chain store in North America of abandoning the 'I will not steal' message for more sinister sub-audible sounds, including 'Obey', 'Buy more', and 'Spend'.

Most of the stores denied any and all culpability. The few that did admit to trying it swore they'd abandoned it when it didn't work.

The next craze went backwards.

Possibly as a vestige of the supposed hidden messages in the Beatles 1967 *Sgt. Pepper* album – 'I buried Paul' – it was claimed that words were recorded backwards and played at odd speeds, or printed backwards and embedded into ads.

If it didn't work frontwards, that should be reason enough to wonder why anyone would have thought it might work backwards. Still, those people who believe that Vicary and Key were telling the truth seem prone to believe, as well, that governments are staffed by moles who spend their lives working in windowless basements to make certain that we never find out that governments are staffed by moles working in windowless basements.

'We grew up founding our dreams on the infinite promise of American advertising,' wrote Zelda Fitzgerald, wife of author F. Scott, in 1932. 'I still believe that one can learn to play the piano by mail and that mud will give you a perfect complexion.'

Packard and Key wanted us to understand that this was sinister.

And even if most of us now think that naked ladies in ice cubes is more ludicrous than sinister, it is not as easy to dismiss the idea that highly intelligent men and women gather, not in windowless basements but in well-lit conference rooms, to argue the merits and deficiencies of an ad campaign and to plot their product's excursion from storyboards to the public psyche.

As early as 1936, author E. B. White saw advertisers as the interpreters of our dreams. Plotting against us, he likened them to Joseph interpreting for Pharaoh. 'They infect the routine futility of our days with purposeful adventure. Their weapons are our weaknesses: fear, ambition, illness, pride, selfishness, desire, ignorance.'

On the defensive, Madison Avenue continued to insist that, in the end, it's the product that wins or loses, not the ad. Okay, some advertising executives were reluctantly willing to admit that Mark Twain might have touched on a minor truth when he wrote, 'Many a small thing has been made large by the right kind of advertising.' But, they persisted, believability is what really matters.

'And nothing is more believable,' said Leo Burnett, 'than the product itself.'

Rallying to the cause, it was advertising superstar Bill Bernbach who so succinctly summed up the industry's stance with what might well be his most often quoted phrase. 'A great ad campaign will make a bad product fail faster. It will get more people to know it's bad.'

A classic example of Bernbach's argument was still cluttering the landscape in the late 1950s, forever to be remembered as the proverbial lead balloon.

It was called Edsel.

Only a few years before, the American car market was booming. In Detroit, Ford executives believed that their own line – low-priced Fords, mid-priced Mercuries, and high-priced Lincolns – still left room for a car aimed at upwardly mobile young executives. So in 1954 they put into motion a project they claimed would be the first totally new car to be designed in 20 years. To set it apart from their other lines, they created a new division and, to match that excitement, went in search of a thrilling new name.

Normally, there are rules about such things and car manufacturers, even today, tend to follow them religiously. One is to find a name that evokes some sort of immediate positive response – Mustang, Imperial, Continental, Taurus, Panther, are all words that produce images of speed, power, sophistication. Next, they must avoid any name that rhymes with anything that anyone might find offensive – imagine a car called the Renis! And then they should use a word with a first letter that will look good as an initial prominently displayed somewhere on the car – the Mercedes M and the RR of Rolls-Royce being the classic examples. So Ford asked their market research people – who'd recently come up with the highly successful name Thunderbird – to see what they could do this time. And, after conducting polls in New York, Chicago, plus a pair of small towns in Michigan, the researchers returned to Detroit with no fewer than 2000 possible names.

Realizing they needed outside help, Ford turned to Fairfax Cone, president of the agency Foote, Cone and Belding, which had just landed the new car account. Cone polled his employees and duly produced a list of 6000 names.

Now getting slightly desperate, the company decided to seek the help of a professional wordsmith. They hired the renowned poetess Marianne Moore to come up with something that signified 'a visceral feeling of elegance, fleetness, advanced features and design'. She responded with Resilient Bullet, Utopian Turtletop and Mongoose Civique.

By November 1956, the corporate Executive Committee had heard enough and, just like that, decided to name the car after Henry Ford's only son, Edsel.

That it sort-of-rhymed with 'pretzel', that vowels don't look good as an initial on a bonnet and that the word didn't mean anything to anyone outside the company – evoking no visceral feelings, except perhaps confusion – should have been enough to warn them off. Years later, Ford's three grandsons, who were all around when the decision was made, claimed they had unanimously rejected the use of their father's name. But for three fellows with enough stock in the company to have otherwise had their voices heard, it's uncanny that the name was, nevertheless, approved.

Even then, they might have got away with the name had it not been for the car itself. It was totally unremarkable, more or less the same as anyone could expect to find in any other mid-priced car, except for two things: what it looked like and how they promoted it.

With the rest of Detroit having committed to front-end designs that worked horizontally – bumpers and grills going from left to right – the Edsel planners decided to make theirs vertical, creating a front grill that could be mistaken for a horse collar or a mildly uncomfortable toilet seat.

Deadlier still was the hype.

For 24 months, a full two years before the first Edsel rolled off the assembly lines, Ford's public relations people carefully leaked stories into the press to prime the market. And they did a fine job. So fine that, it might be fair to say, more ink flowed about this car than any other non-existent car in automotive history. *Time* magazine and *Life* magazine both heralded the Edsel, in major feature stories, as the result of 10 years' worth of planning and the first brand-new American car in two decades.

The only problem there was that neither claim was true.

Much of the Edsel was borrowed from the Mercury and,

from start to finish, the entire project took a fairly average three years.

By this time, Cone and his associates were going full-steam ahead, planning a massive advertising strategy. Unlike typical automotive ads, showing the new car parked outside some fancy country club, the Edsel would be photographed against a white backdrop, to stand alone, with a few people in the shot to give it size. The copy headline would simply read, 'This is the Edsel.'

A teaser campaign of four ads – never showing the car itself but eventually showing the steering wheel – was scheduled to run in several magazines, leading up to the day when the car would be revealed in national television advertising. But the Ford people, who'd committed themselves to spending $8 million on hype in the first four months, decided that blowing an additional $1 million now in the build-up was too much. So the teaser ran only in *Life* magazine.

When the time finally arrived to show the car to the media, 75 automotive journalists were invited to drive an Edsel from the plant in Dearborn, Michigan, to their local Ford dealer, wherever that was in the country. To be absolutely certain that everything would be perfect, each of the 75 test cars was put through two months of extensive inspection.

And almost all of them failed.

In the end, 7 cars had to be scrapped for parts to get the other 68 ready for the journalists. That little exercise alone cost the Edsel team $10,000 per car, or twice the high-end sticker price.

Photos of the car were released to newspapers in late August 1957, a few days before billboards across the country announced the car's arrival in showrooms. That was followed by local newspaper ads with more photos of the car and show-room addresses.

Oddly, Ford executives postponed Cone's plan to use TV or radio spots, and didn't bother buying airtime until mid-October.

In the midst of all this, September 1957 saw a recession sweeping through the country and racial unrest in the south. A month later, the Russians launched Sputnik. American Motors, who introduced their Nash Rambler around the same time – admittedly it was much further down market than Edsel – had to do it with considerably less flamboyance because they couldn't afford to buy the same kind of hype. Yet they did manage to sell a lot of cars, which means there was a market out there for certain kinds of cars.

Except it wasn't ever going to be an Edsel market.

The advance billing had created extravagant expectations. The promise of Cone's copywriters – 'There has never been a car like the Edsel' – helped draw huge crowds to showrooms. But once they got there all the public could do was yawn. The product was mediocre. Its end was expedited by its own publicity.

For years the Ford people insisted it was the economy's fault. But Rambler kept selling. So did many other cars. Yet within three years, thanks in some part to advertising, Edsel was a name synonymous with failure.

There had once been rules in advertising, just as there had been rules in life, things you did because that's the way it was. One of them was, the more facts you tell, the more products you sell. It meant that an ad's chance of success increased with the number of facts included in the copy about the product. Side by side came the rule, always show the product and the product's name. But just as the rules for life were being questioned – and eventually tossed out – so too were the rules for advertising.

One of the men who helped create an atmosphere in which change would take place was Rosser Reeves, a man with the calculating mind of a superior amateur chess player and a Madison Avenue star long before he became chairman of the advertising agency Ted Bates and Company.

Beginning his career as a 19-year-old copywriter in 1929 – in the days when everyone blindly obeyed the rules – he is remembered today as a great theoretician of advertising and father of the concept 'USP'. Reeves believed that once you identified a product's 'unique selling point', everything else – meaning the advertising angle – was easy. 'If the manufacturer brings you a motor car that can go 500 miles on a gallon of gas you don't have to look far for a campaign idea. If, on the other hand, you have an Edsel that's not very different from any other car, you're doomed to failure in advance.'

He firmly established his concept in 1954 when John MacNamara, then President of M&M's Candies, walked into his office complaining that the candy wasn't selling because the advertising wasn't working. He wanted Reeves to come up with an idea that could turn the product around. The first thing Reeves did was to rip open a bag of M&Ms and pour the candies across his desk. What he saw was the only candy on sale that had chocolate surrounded by a sugar shell.

That was far as he had to go to find his USP.

Next, Reeves put an M&M in one hand and pretended to have a competitor's chocolate in the other. Then he asked MacNamara which hand held the M&M. MacNamara didn't understand until Reeves announced the campaign tagline – one of the most famous ever – 'M&M candies melt in your mouth, not in your hand.'

Reeves was convinced that a campaign based on USP would never wear itself out, unless, of course, the product became outmoded. Once, a client came to him to say, 'You have 700 people in that office of yours and you've been running the same ad for me for the last 11 years. What I want to know is, what are those 700 people supposed to be doing?' His answer was, 'Keeping your advertising department from changing your ad.'

After a time, Reeves set down a list of 'immutable principles.'

'The better product,' he wrote, 'advertised equally, will win in the long run.' Like Bill Bernbach, he believed that '[advertising] stimulates the sales of a good product and accelerates the destruction of a bad product.' However, Reeves warned, 'An advertiser can be running two different campaigns and not know it – the campaign he thinks he's running and the campaign the consumer sees.' At the same time, he postulated, the consumer tends to remember just one thing from any ad. It might be a strong claim. It might be a strong concept. But there is only one take-away. Therefore, '[each] advertisement must make a proposition to the consumer. Not just words, not just product puffery, and not just show-window advertising. The proposition must be one that the competitor either cannot or does not offer. The proposition must be so strong that it can move the mass millions, can pull new customers over to your product.'

Although these were rules he developed in the advertising world he'd known, they formed the basis of the advertising world that was to come – a business where the emphasis shifted away from product and onto consumers.

The emergence of this new world created a huge new vacuum in which a new in-depth would flourish.

Researchers now 'profiled' us – reducing us to our common desires for conformity, security, oral stimulation, reassurance of worth, sense of roots, love of objects, need for ego gratification and the sense of our own immortality – then drew maps of our vulnerabilities, laid out like cities and factories and railroad junctions before World War II pilots on a bombing mission.

'The deeper problems connected with advertising come less from the unscrupulousness of our "deceivers" than from our pleasure in being deceived,' wrote historian Daniel Boorstin, 'less from the desire to seduce than from the desire to be seduced.'

Marshall McLuhan agreed. 'The modern Little Red Riding

Hood, reared on singing commercials, has no objection to being eaten by the wolf.'

So did ad man Ray Locke. 'Next to Christianity, advertising is the greatest force in the world.'

Columnist George Will also concurred. 'Commercial society regards people as bundles of appetites, a conception that turns human beings inside out, leaving nothing to be regarded as inherently private. Commercial society finds unintelligible the idea that anything – an emotion, activity, or product – is too "intimately personal" for uninhibited commercial treatment.'

In the eyes of Madison Avenue, we had become little more than targets to be picked off. Once in their sights, all that was left was to test these new weapons.

Like the old wives' tale that goes, 'You never hear the shot that kills you,' the advertising industry needed to make certain that we should never feel the pain, at least not until it's too late.

And their timing could not have been better.

Ads preached. That's what they did, pretty much from the earliest days of the twentieth century through to the demise of the Edsel. They told us how good something was and what it would deliver if we bought it. They told us about self-cleaning ovens and shoes with heels that didn't wear out, smoother-tasting tobacco and the most comfortable way to get from here to there.

They told us, 'Agreeable recreation is that which least resembles work, diverts the mind and smoothes off the rough edges of life's cares. Bicycle riding is a boon to busy brain workers, in school or office, especially to ailing women – Rambler Bicycles.'

And, 'If cleanliness is next to Godliness, soap must be considered as a means of Grace, and a clergyman who recommends moral things should be willing to recommend soap –

Pears Soap, the famous English complexion soap.'

And, 'Here's spaghetti sauce with meat, the way Italians make it – Franco-American Canned Spaghetti.'

But just as the consumer society was changing the way we lived, ad men were coming to understand that we could be defined by what we bought, and that, if advertising could transform goods into 'communicators of meaning', they could sell us back our own insecurities. So they hired scientists to delve even deeper into our emotions, to diagnose every inch of our motivations, and to rummage through words and symbols in a furious pursuit of switches inside our head that could ignite a sale. They kept us pinned down under a microscope, watching us discover that there was instant gratification in consumption.

Based on what they saw, they began to formulate a new language, not of words, but of symbols of prestige and identity that could be transferred to us through the purchase and use of their product. A language of instant status, instant lifestyle, instant sex appeal through products that mean fashion, popularity, and success. Here was pleasure. Here was glamour. Here was, you can have it all just for the price of admission.

The buzz words became 'triggers of action'.

Until Abraham Maslow came along, most of his fellow psychologists – the original in-depth crowd – reckoned that all the 'buy' buttons anyone needed to push could be found neatly wrapped around our three basic needs: shelter – because we need to protect ourselves from the elements and predators; food – because we need to eat in order to stay alive; and sex – because we need to propagate the human race.

But by the 1950s, Maslow felt he had sufficient grounds to disagree. As the leading proponent of what is today known as 'Humanistic Psychology', he'd come to theorize that we share five general categories of need, which when layered one on top of the other formed his 'Hierarchy of Need'.

His first level was 'physiological' – which included food,

water, oxygen and safe body temperature. Because these needs are life sustaining, when you deprive someone of everything, of all their needs, Maslow argued, these are the ones that they will initially struggle to regain.

Next was 'safety' – meaning shelter and protection from predators.

That was followed by 'love' – because we need to care, to be cared for and to belong, to form tribes and families.

Then came 'esteem' – comprising acceptance by others, wealth creation, recognition and self-respect.

The fifth level Maslow called 'self-actualization' – referring to our need for the spiritual, for aesthetic appreciation, for growth, for learning, for charity. Here, he said, was the need that drives someone to a calling, where one finds the restlessness that makes a musician become a musician, that makes a poet become a poet, that makes a dictator become a dictator.

Building his hierarchy like a pyramid, Maslow went on to say that needs are satisfied from the bottom up. That higher-level needs cannot be met until all of the other needs below it have been. That someone who is hungry cannot have self-esteem and someone who is threatened cannot achieve self-actualization. Accepting his premise, there is plainly nothing to be gained by advertising Rolls-Royce in the barrios of Rio de Janeiro because ghettos are all about food and shelter – first- and second-level needs – and any appeal to esteem or self-actualization when any lower needs have not yet been fulfilled, no matter how cleverly done, is a foregone lost cause.

'Advertising is found in societies which have passed the point of satisfying the basic animal needs,' wrote Marion Harper Jr in 1960 when he was president of the agency McCann-Erickson.

Economist John Kenneth Galbraith reinforced that concept when he wrote, around the same time, 'A man who is hungry need never be told of his need for food. If he is inspired by his appetite, he is immune to the influence of Messrs Batten, Barton, Durstine & Osborn. The latter are effective only with those who are so far removed from physical want that they do not already know what they want.'

Today, further proof is easily witnessed in the emerging capitalist societies of Eastern Europe, where a rising affluent middle class are anything but immune to manipulation. With their first three levels of need relatively secure, they've turned to wealth creation, self-esteem and showing off. What you find these days on the streets of Moscow, Leningrad, Budapest, Warsaw and Prague are locals sporting Rolex watches, Armani t-shirts, Ralph Lauren jeans, Prada hand-bags and Gucci shoes. Former communists have traded in their forced ideology for Mercedes, Jaguars and BMWs. And even if some of the cars have been stolen in the West, and even if some of the brand names are Italian-made counterfeits, and even if those who seek to make a statement haven't yet got enough money to do it properly and must pamper themselves with also-rans – Gap, Benetton, Kookai, DKNY, Guess – it's not really the goods that matter but rather the proclamation that these people believe they are making with those goods. They think they're saying, 'I've arrived.' They're definitely saying, 'Capitalism has won.' They are also saying, 'Greed is good.' At the same time, they're proving Maslow right, in that the higher up the pyramid you go the more shopping becomes a lifestyle activity.

In certain ways, there's an odd quality of *déjà vu*, because some of what we see today in those former communist-bloc countries is what we saw in the USA, and Europe at the end of the 1950s. Although television had a weighty presence, a good portion of the populace – notably those living in rural areas – was still best reached with ads in newspapers and magazines and on radio. We too were flexing our economic muscles and we too were saying greed is good, although in those days the expression was 'keeping up with the Joneses.' It is hardly a coincidence that the message that manufacturers are now sending into Eastern Europe shamelessly echoes the message that scientists brought to ad agencies at the beginning of the 1960s – we can sell stuff simply by giving people permission to enjoy themselves.

They told us then, just as they are telling the Russians now and will undoubtedly someday tell the Chinese – a sitting-duck market of vast wealth and vulnerable consumers – it's okay to surround yourself with products that enrich your lives; it's all right to think first of number one.

While manufacturers answered the call by coming up with more and more 'time-saving' devices – perfecting the doctrine of planned obsolescence so that whatever time we saved could be spent shopping for new things that would wear out sooner – scientists decided that housewives could be, and therefore must be, conditioned to accept time saving as a legitimate concept. But that alone would never serve as a satisfactory trigger of action. They needed to go deeper. They needed housewives to believe that a new washing machine wasn't about clean clothes or having the afternoon to play bridge, it was about having more time to enjoy her family.

The message became, you owe it to your children to buy this new washing machine.

Housewives who believed that bought washing machines.

Just like the light bulb that snaps on over the heads of cartoon characters, everybody on Madison Avenue stumbled onto the bright idea that they were in the business of pre-soothing guilt with absolution. The missive came down from on high: you have our permission to have fun without feeling remorse; it's okay to buy stuff just because you want it; buying what you need is good, but satisfying a craving is even better.

Go ahead . . . just do it!

We believed them. We did it. And while we weren't looking – because we were too busy shopping – they turned us into the 'me' generation and for ever altered our world. Chocolate would never again be a sweet indulgence for children, it would be a prize for something well done, so that kids would slip into adulthood long in the habit of rewarding themselves with Mars and Snickers and Milky Ways. Power tools would be a way Dad could exercise his God-given right to cut off the outside world and build his own fantasies in the backyard. Luggage would never again be just for carrying clothes, it would be covered in designer's initials so that the world would see how successful we were and, at least in theory, treat us accordingly. Petrol was surrogate power which we seized by putting a tiger in our tank. Crest added fluoride to their toothpaste and promised us that by using this 'milestone in modern medicine' we'd spend less time in the dentist's chair, which meant less pain. Then Gleem came along to challenge Crest, saying that their brand was 'For people who can't brush after every meal,' playing off our guilt for not brushing three times a day. Home freezer manufacturers appealed directly to our 'squirrel' syndrome, that inner comfort we get by hoarding. Life insurance was no longer an acknowledgement of our ultimate demise but a restatement of our love for the family we were protecting. Perfumes were no longer sexual magnets, they signified a woman's sense of independence. Cough drops would never again be a substitute for candy, they would have medicinal benefits – like an extra shot of spearmint to keep our nasal passages clear – so we didn't blame ourselves for eating them like candy.

As advertising got better at finding the right buttons to push, manufacturers sold more, which meant they had increased profits to reinvest in advertising. As the agencies made more money, they reinvested some of their profits in better research. As research improved, the scientists moved from more buttons to push to how better to push them.

And all the time advertising became more intrusive in our lives.

It was advertising that taught us to define ourselves by what we consumed – by the products we bought – and, because we found that essentially gratifying, advertisers increasingly invested their products with symbols, images, values and lifestyles. There might have been times when we were right to believe that advertising was about identifying a problem and then being offered a convenient solution: everyone worries about dandruff, so everyone needs Head & Shoulders; everyone has a ring around the collar, so everyone needs Vanish – but not any more.

Or, if we did, it was only to fool ourselves.

It wasn't important what we bought, as long as we bought.

Everyone has their own insecurities, so everyone can achieve self-esteem with Armani suits and Ferragamo shoes and Chanel perfume.

We became what we wore, what we drove, where we vacationed.

L'Air de Temps perfume made us attractive. Levi's jeans made us an individual. Skiing in Klosters or Veil or Aspen made us exotic. A Mont Blanc pen made us successful.

The more goods we bought, the more we bought into this new language and, in turn, the more advertisers sold us who we are, who we wished to be, who we hoped others would think we are.

To keep us buying, to satisfy our fourth- and fifth-level needs, products were redesigned.

They would never again be just trainers, automobiles or ice-cream.

They were communicators. They had built-in values, identity and prominence.

Now they were Nike, Mercedes and Häagen-Dazs.

But none of this could have happened without our complicity.

And we would never have been so sheep-like compliant had it not been for television.

*

Everyone was smitten with the promise of television. Especially the ad men. Here was a tremendously powerful, super-fast, super-efficient, reasonably economical delivery system that could drive a sales pitch straight into the nation's living rooms, dining-rooms and bedrooms and, from there, park ideas inside the public's psyche.

Adding to television's appeal, it quickly became evident that the medium could not survive without advertising. No one seemed terribly concerned then that, once advertising got its claws into television, variety shows, sitcoms and even the night-time news would become fodder – something, anything – to fill the airwaves in between commercials, much the way magazines have never been more than articles and features used to separate ads.

More important, at least to Madison Avenue, was that if a picture was worth 1,000 words, then 30 seconds of airtime was more than worth whatever it cost.

Taking up the cause, the scientists were telling the ad men that the human mind doesn't process images the way it does words. That images are much more persuasive. That the public would be more inclined to follow when they felt an emotional investment in an idea. And that images could more easily invade that part of their emotions than words.

They were saying, consider the fact that some images have become so everyday-familiar to us we hardly have to think of the words they evoke. A red light doesn't have to say stop. A green light doesn't have to say go. But the classic example they cited was a 1935 painting by the Belgian surrealist, René Magritte.

In 'The Key to Dreams' he mixed four objects with words. There is a horse's head, under which he has written the word 'door'; a clock, under which he has written the word 'wind'; a water pitcher, under which he has written the word 'bird'; and a suitcase, under which he has written the word 'suitcase'. The effect, which is almost immediate, is to find the first three uncomfortable and therefore to focus attention on the last one. Because the image and the word match, it is the most comfortable. So Madison Avenue started to think about comfortable images.

In the 1950s, there was a popular American radio programme hosted by a pleasant, folksy, red-haired chap named Arthur Godfrey. But by then radio was being relegated to second place – what you listened to in the bath or while driving the car – because television was taking over. Before long, someone at CBS decided to put Godfrey's radio show on television. But radio personalities didn't automatically work on television, any more than silent-screen stars automatically made the transition to talkies. Because the camera could come in close, there was a startling sense of intimacy with television. We could see him, so we knew that Godfrey had freckles. We could see him, so now it mattered that he looked us straight in the eyes when he sold us something.

Although the concept of the program would remain radio, certain subtle changes needed to be made for the sake of sincerity-on-camera. The way it was done was to portray Godfrey as a congenial father figure. He was dressed that way, his set was designed to be a middle-class living room, his regular guests were symbolically cast as his children, and visiting stars were always treated like company in his home. The only thing missing from the program – again, deliberately – was a mother figure. And that role was to be fulfilled by the housewife at home.

The perfect pitchman, Godfrey personally sold his sponsors' products, like father telling mother what kind of starch he wanted in his shirt collars. Because it worked, all sorts of variations on the 'family through television' theme sprang up, talk shows about as far removed from today's Oprahs and Ricki Lakes and Jerry Springers as could be imagined. And it is not by accident that Oprah and Ricki and Jerry don't sell products themselves, but rather break away for commercials, because we tend to associate the product with the salesman and in today's 'schlock jock' world of talk shows the idea of having Jerry Springer interrupt a discussion with a two-headed lesbian to flog deodorant would be laughable.

Except it wasn't laughable when Arthur Godfrey did it. He pitched us stuff in between gentle conversation and middle-of-the-road tunes played on his ukulele or sung by an Irish tenor – a family of believable people making us believe in the goodness of a product, about its quality, about how we'd save money if we bought two instead of one. After all, Godfrey was family. He reassured us, the way Daddy did, that it was healthy to eat Wonder Bread and that everyone would admire a woman who used Max Factor cosmetics and that all children would sleep better in Dr. Denton pyjamas.

That's what television advertising was all about in those earliest days. Reassurance. Confidence. Comfort. Encouragement. Optimism. About making us feel we are doing the right thing for our family by spending money.

At least that's what it was all about until something strange happened.

The biggest programme on American Sunday night television, also a CBS show, was a variety hour hosted by an especially wooden New York newspaper columnist called Ed Sullivan. Originally entitled 'Toast of the Town' – named after his column – he wasn't a father figure so much as the school principal pretending to be the Master of Ceremonies at the annual talent show. He first appeared in June 1948 and managed to last 23 years, each Sunday night promising everyone 'a really big shue'.

He brought the Beatles to America, the first appearance of the 'Fab Four' drawing a massive 73 million viewers. He also brought the Rolling Stones to America. And he helped to establish dozens of show business careers, not least of which was Elvis Presley's. Although, true to his rather square image,

Sullivan put certain restrictions on his more 'outrageous' guests. He dictated, for instance, that the camera had to stay on Elvis's face so that no one at home could see his hips gyrating. But then, this was mom-and-pop fare, sponsored by a good old American mom-and-pop product, Eastman Kodak.

Sometime around 1960, a viewer got it into his head to send Kodak a bunch of pictures he'd taken of his daughter over the years standing against a wooden door with her height marked off as she got taller. The photos struck a chord with whoever opened the envelope at Kodak and he, or she, had the good sense to pass them along to the company's advertising agency, J. Walter Thompson. When the creative folk there saw the photos, they didn't need scientists to tell them that this was a great way to push buttons, they could feel it. So they put the photos onto film – this was before video tape – and added music to create a lovely mood, coming up with a two-minute movie called 'Turn Around Little Girl'.

It ran on the Sullivan Show a few weeks later. When it did, word travelled up and down Madison Avenue that a lot of people out there in television-land hadn't realized those two minutes were a commercial.

Image was in.

So was mood.

J. Walter Thompson would go on to make hours' worth of 'Those Kodak Moments' – and dozens of companies would follow their lead – setting the tone of the genre, reconfirming that, as the 1960s dawned, the way to get at us was with commercials that didn't look like commercials.

Coinciding with the arrival of 'The Kodak Moment', and also because of the mass proliferation of television, an increasingly restless audience was demanding programming – and advertising too – that aroused curiosity and amused. In response, the lines between selling and entertaining were deliberately blurred.

'It is difficult to produce a television documentary that is both incisive and probing,' said Rod Serling, creator of 'The Twilight Zone', 'when every 12 minutes one is interrupted by dancing rabbits singing about toilet paper.'

Added *New York Times'* media critic Clive Barnes, 'Television is the first truly democratic culture – the first culture available to everybody and entirely governed by what the people want. The most terrifying thing is what people do want.'

The wider use of images reinforced our growing subservience to those symbols. Advertising moved even further away from being a reflection of culture to becoming the preeminent engine that transformed it. Vance Packard was no longer the lone voice in the wildnerness, he was the Mormon Tabernacle Choir.

With so much social data being implanted into products, it was in effect up and down Madison Avenue where our identities were being moulded. And it was on television where they were being paraded before us like menus from which we could choose who we wanted to be.

Suddenly, it mattered less if something washed whiter or smelled better. Everything had to be 'new and improved'. Like the decade itself, everything had to be hip, cool, groovy, irreverent, sexy.

This was Mary Wells painting Braniff's aeroplanes in bright reds and yellows, then bragging in ads, 'When you've got it, flaunt it.'

This was Alka-Seltzer making jokes about heartburn, and giving the world one of those expressions that people were forever repeating, 'Mamma Mia, atsa some spicy meatball.'

This was Benson and Hedges making jokes about how their new 100-millimetre cigarettes were too long to be smoked in an elevator without getting caught in the door.

This was Maxwell House evoking the smell of a freshly brewed pot, on television, to the blip of the percolator.

This was Gunilla Knutson, a former Miss Sweden, selling

Noxema Shaving Cream to the tune of the 'The Stripper', urging men to 'take it off, take it all off'.

We got caught up in it because this was change, and change meant growth, and growth in the 1960s for the 'me generation' had as much to do with navel gazing as it did with rebellion.

We were as receptive to the influences of advertising as advertising was obsessed with trying to invent that magic bullet.

We got caught up in it because it was easy.

Because it was fun.

Because it was psychedelic.

Because life was a great big adventure bundled up for the taking in go-go boots and mini-skirts.

Peace and love, dude.

We got hooked on it because we wanted to.

CHAPTER THREE

Ultimate Expectations

Someone once said that the perfect ad is one which makes a co-conspirator out of the audience. I think that's right. You dig out a stimulus that evokes a response. The buttons are always there. The trick is in getting the people to push those buttons themselves.
                    Burt Manning, J. Walter Thompson

In order for the sixties to become the sixties, a lot of people had to stir the cauldron. Along Madison Avenue, that included advertising's three greatest sorcerers ever – Leo and David and Bill.

For his first 60 years on this planet, Leo Burnett was just another guy in the business, and not a terribly impressive one at that. Short, balding, paunchy, round-shouldered, with a prominent lower lip and, more often than not, cigarette ash all over his clothes, he was born in the Midwest in 1891, studied journalism at the University of Michigan and got his first job as a cub reporter on a paper in Peoria, Illinois. After a couple of years working as a copywriter in the advertising department of the Cadillac Motor company, he moved onto the agency side of the business, and bounced around several until he formed his own in Chicago in 1935.

Borrowing $50,000 against his life insurance and his mortgage to do it, he was warned by friends that he'd taken a huge gamble. They chided him, 'You'll wind up selling apples.' But he responded, 'The hell I will, I'll give them away,' and even today the lobbies of his offices around the world still feature a basket of fresh apples.

Fruit notwithstanding, it wasn't until sometime in the 1950s that anyone on Madison Avenue even considered that there might be intelligent life west of the Hudson River. Then, it happened only because the Leo Burnett Company had invented what would come to be known as the 'Chicago School of Advertising' – faces on products to give them a walking-talking-breathing personality.

Burnett's first, and arguably most lasting, 'face' was the Marlboro Man.

Before he came along, Marlboro was a mediocre-selling woman's cigarette. Deciding that big changes were necessary to keep the brand alive, the Philip Morris Company came up with the famous red and white flip-top box, and hired Burnett to find something decidedly unprissy to help sell it. His answer was a series of ads featuring macho guys with tattoos. From there, it was a logical step to classic American mythology – cowboys riding herd through big country.

A workaholic whose only time off was, apparently, Christmas morning, he used variations on the Marlboro Man concept wherever he could, giving twentieth-century Western culture Charlie the Tuna, the Pillsbury Dough Boy, Tony the Tiger, Morris the Cat, and the Jolly Green Giant.

Taking Reeves' USP to the next logical step, Burnett believed 'there is inherent drama in every product', and the role of advertising is to find it. He was convinced that effective advertising relies not on tricky new words and pictures, but instead on familiar words and pictures put into new relationships in order to create a personality. Many of the faces he gave to products are still with us all these years later, living proof that, when it's done well, we'll fall for it every time.

Ten years Burnett's junior, and born a world apart – in West

Horsley, Surrey, a few miles north east of Guildford along the A246 to Leatherhead – David Ogilvy was educated at Fettes College in Edinburgh and, at least until he was expelled, at Christ Church, Oxford.

Not knowing what he wanted to do, he offed to Paris where he found work in the kitchens of the Hotel Majestic. From there he sold stoves door-to-door in Scotland, was hired as a social worker and, in 1938, opted to try his luck in the United States. He wound up in Princeton, New Jersey, employed by George Gallup's Audience Research Institute. Eleven years later, at the ripe old age of 38, Ogilvy decided to open his own advertising agency in New York. He had one employee and no clients. Today, Ogilvy & Mather have more than 270 offices in 64 countries.

In that French kitchen, Ogilvy learned how to make a perfect soufflé and, he always claimed, how to lead men into corporate battle. In Scotland he learned how to sell. In Princeton he learned that research, properly conducted, could contribute the single most critical element of any ad – the promise.

Ogilvy championed research throughout his entire life, perhaps more so than any other ad man of his generation. 'Research is often misused by agencies and their clients. They use research as a drunkard uses a lamp post, not for illumination but for support. On the whole, however, research can be of incalculable help in producing more effective advertising.'

One of the many things that research confirmed to him was that a totally fabricated personality could make or break a product, and that the public would always be more interested in personalities than in corporations. He proved it in what is generally considered his most famous ad campaign, one in which he used a $1.50 piece of cloth tied to an elastic band to create a personality that catapulted a shirt company, and himself, to fame.

Ogilvy's style was to feature a single photograph with a headline and copy under that. The photo pushed a button that got people to read the headline. That was where he put the first promise of benefit. The headline – he always referred to it as 'the ticket to the meat' – then pushed the button that got the consumer to read the rest of the ad.

'What you say in advertising is more important than how you say it,' he contended. 'What really decides consumers to buy or not to buy is the content of your advertising, not its form.'

Because research had shown that five times as many people read the headline as read the ad – 'When you have written your headline you have spent eighty cents out of your dollar' – he dictated that the headline had to say something the reader would remember. The photo and the headline therefore became the trap.

To set the trap in the ad for the shirts, Ogilvy wanted a photo that would grab the reader's curiosity. He wanted people to say to themselves, what's going on here? But, after 17 attempts, he still didn't have it.

The photo shoot he'd set up featured a debonair-looking chap wearing the product in a sophisticated environment – a gentlemen's club library – and playing bridge with 13 spades unfolded on the green baize table in front of him. Yet, each time, the end result was just that, a cultured fellow hanging out somewhere posh in a new shirt. Finally, in a moment bordering between inspiration and desperation, Ogilvy spotted something in a local drugstore. He bought it, stood the model in front of bales of material – a reference to a high-class tailor's shop – and told the model to put it on.

It didn't make a lot of sense to anyone in his office and, admittedly, had nothing to do with the product. But it made the picture work.

After 116 years of being just another shirt company, a man wearing a $1.50 black eye patch pushed the button that got people to read the copy that turned Hathaway Shirts into a national brand. It became one of the most recognizable images of the decade and made David Ogilvy a living legend.

'What struck me as a moderately good idea for a wet Tuesday morning,' Ogilvy wrote in his autobiography, 'made me famous. I could have wished for fame to come from some more serious achievement.'

Obviously on to a good thing, Ogilvy pushed the same button to sell Schweppes Tonic, this time substituting an eye patch for the exotic face of the company's US-based president in the ads.

Commander Edward Whitehead looked as if he'd stepped right out of central casting after a call for someone to play a British Naval Officer. A dapper man with a wonderful red beard, he was headlined 'The Man From Schweppes'. In order to know who he was, you had to read the ad. While you were doing that, Whitehead told you that it had taken House of Schweppes more than a century to bring the tonic to 'bitter-sweet perfection' and that it was 'curiously refreshing'.

The ad was so potent that Ogilvy used Whitehead to push 'buy this' buttons for Schweppes for the next 18 years, and made him so popular that polls showed Whitehead to be the second most famous Briton in the USA, after Winston Churchill.

Nearly three decades later – long after Hathaway and Schweppes had moved on – Ogilvy was still cheerleading the appeal of promise. In a speech to the American Association of National Advertisers, he reminded them, 'If you focus your advertising budget on entertaining the consumer, you may not sell as much of your product as you like. People don't buy a new detergent because the manufacturer told a joke on television last night. They buy it because it promises a benefit.'

Ogilvy's skill lay in his ability to gift-wrap promise of benefit in memorable ways – among them, what is often considered to be the greatest headline ever written. Under the picture of a brand-new Rolls-Royce Silver Cloud, with a woman at the wheel and two children in riding gear coming out of a shop carrying packages, he put the words: 'At 60 miles an hour the loudest noise in this Rolls-Royce comes from the electric clock.'

Those 17 words touched buttons so deep in the national subconscious that, within a year, Ford acknowledged Ogilvy's virtuosity by running ads that promised their cars were 'quieter than a Rolls-Royce'. Some years after that, in what can only be called a tribute ad, another company paid homage by showing a photo of their car above the headline, 'At 60 miles an hour, the loudest noise in this new Land Rover comes from the roar of the engine.'

Never venturing far from the idea that we, as consumers, will buy image, Ogilvy sold downmarket Guinness as the perfect accompaniment for upmarket oysters, and provided a guide, suitable for framing, to the best oysters available in the United States; sold the old-fashioned quality of Pepperidge Farm bread with a photo of a horse-drawn baker's cart on a misty morning, near a lake, being chased by two children; sold France with photos of a Loire Valley chateau and a headline in French; and sold Puerto Rico with a photo of a sun-drenched room where a cello is leaning against a simple wooden chair and the headline, 'Pablo Casals Is Coming Home.' But most of all Ogilvy sold the idea to Madison Avenue that, if research tells you what button to push, all you then have to do to push it is find the right image.

Bill Bernbach thought much the same way.

Six weeks younger than Ogilvy, he was raised in the Bronx, a quiet, studious boy who, as an adult, stood only five feet seven and never weighed more than 155 pounds. Instead of sports, he read books and wrote poetry. He graduated from New York University in 1933 with a degree in English Literature. But this was the Depression and the only job he could find was in the mail room of Schenley Distillers, a company that made whiskey.

More often bored than not, he decided to try his hand at writing an ad for one of the brands. He duly sent his copy to the advertising manager, who ran it word for word in the *New York Times*. But somewhere between the mail room and the getting published, no one could recall who'd written it. So Bernbach got up his nerve and went to see the president of the company to tell him. It earned him a promotion into the advertising department.

From there he got a job doing PR for the 1939 World's Fair. He followed that with a brief stint at an ad agency. Then came World War II. After two years in the army, he returned to New York to work as a copywriter at Gray Advertising where he was soon named vice-president in charge of copy and art. There, Bernbach hooked up with another Gray vice-president, Ned Doyle. The two of them then joined forces with Max Dane – who'd been running a small agency of his own – and in 1949 pooled what little money they had to set up their own shop.

Madison Avenue had never seen three more unassuming men go into business together. Doyle was the finance man. Dane was the organization man. Bernbach was the creative guy. A coin toss decided the order that their names would go on the door – it worked out to be Doyle Dane Bernbach – and because his name was last the other two decided Bernbach could be president.

The only account they had was one they'd managed to lift from Gray's, a New York discount department store with a branch in Los Angeles, called Ohrbach's.

What Bernbach did for them was what Burnett and Ogilvy were doing for their clients – he gave Orbach's a personality. Instead of selling them as an outlet for cheap clothes, he turned them into a secret place for someone who knew how to find great value. One of his wittier headlines read, 'Our summer sale began October 4, 1923.'

His success there brought Doyle Dane Bernbach to the attention of Henry Levy, a fellow who owned a bakery in

Brooklyn. He needed someone to tell the world just how terrific his rye bread was. Bernbach's first ad for him pictured one slice in three stages of being eaten. The first bite was captioned, 'New York'. The second was captioned, 'Is Eating'. The tiny remaining piece was captioned, 'It up'. That got Levy off the launch pad. But the ad that put the company into orbit was Bernbach's series of ethnic faces – oriental, black, Indian – shown over the caption, 'You don't have to be Jewish to love Levy's real Jewish rye.'

He followed that with two of the greatest ads in the history of the business.

In 1959, at a time when America was buying big, petrol-guzzling cars, Bernbach was hired to sell the funny little Volkswagen Beetle. Instinctively, he knew that he could never push the same power and sex appeal buttons that car advertising usually did. Nor could he go for elegance or status, or the kind of sheer luxury that Ogilvy aimed for with Rolls. So Bernbach invented reverse snobbery. He photographed the car with nothing around it and headlined the ad, 'Think Small.'

That proved to be the most successful ad ever for a foreign car in the United States.

His next VW ad used a single-word headline, 'Lemon'.

To describe a car either way, but especially as a lemon, was risking everything on the power of button pushing. But Bernbach knew what buttons he needed to push, and he proved that he knew how to push them. The copy under the headline told the reader, 'This Volkswagen missed the boat. The chrome strip on the glove compartment is blemished and must be replaced. Chances are you wouldn't have noticed it; Inspector Kurt Kroner did.' The text went on to explain how 3389 men at the factory in Germany inspect every Volkswagen at each stage of production and, in the end, reject one Volkswagen out of every 50. The tagline read, 'This pre-occupation with detail means the VW lasts longer and requires less maintenance, by and large, than other cars. It also means a used VW depreciates less than any other car. We pluck the lemons. You get the plums.'

The trade journal *Advertising Age* summed up Bernbach's prowess by proclaiming, 'Indeed if the '60s were the best of creative times, then the Volkswagen campaign is not merely the best of the '60s, but the best of all time.'

The creative strategy was solid and the copy that came out of it so irreverent that it became indelible in the minds of anyone who read it in print, heard it on radio, saw it on TV or spotted it on posters. Making it even more memorable, the campaign ran for several years without ever appearing tired or repetitive. As one critic put it, 'The car ran out of gas before the campaign did.'

Bill Bernbach had established the Volkswagen Beetle as the cult car of all time and, in so doing, essentially changed the advertising business.

Four years later, he struck again.

The world's leading rent-a-car company has always been Hertz. Bernbach was hired by Avis, then a half-baked operation hoping somehow to steal just enough of a slice from the giant's pie to stay alive. The company had been around for nearly 15 years with a near-unbroken record of corporate failure, and Hertz was so far out in front it was hard to see how Bernbach could find anything that would even remotely put Avis in the same game, let alone the same league.

Again, he opted for 'small'.

To tell the public that the two companies could, indeed, compete, he simply admitted what the world already knew: 'We're Number Two.' To that he added his promise of benefit: 'We Try Harder.'

Despite at least one research report that warned him that the campaign would fail miserably because no one wants to do business with the second best – Bernbach is said to have responded, 'Get other research' – he knew there has always been something deep inside the American spirit that sides with the underdog.

All he did was push that button.

The campaign ran for five years and increased Avis's market share by nearly one-third. The company is still, all these years later, referred to as the number two that tries harder.

Survival, admiration, success, love and taking care of our own, these were the buttons in each of us that he unashamedly aimed for.

'It is insight into human nature,' he wrote, 'that is the key to the communicator's skill. For whereas the writer is concerned with what he puts into his writings, the communicator is concerned with what the reader gets out of it.'

In this case what we, as the readers, got out of it was quantifiable by how much of the product we bought.

'You can say the right thing about a product and nobody will listen,' he asserted. 'You've got to say it in such a way that people will feel it in their gut. Because if they don't feel it, nothing will happen.'

The Marlboro Man and the Hathaway Man and 'We Try Harder' were great campaigns, not because they were clever and broke new ground, but because they sold the product. They touched old buttons in a new way.

However, the research and the savvy of Leo and David and Bill could take the industry only so far. These were the sixties and the stage was quickly filling up with a lot of young gunslingers.

Whatever moral perspective advertising might once have preached, if any, that wasn't what the business was all about now. It's redder than green. It's greener than blue. It's bluer than red. These were guns for hire to the highest bidder who didn't mind which side they took, as long as someone believed them when they claimed their side was the best, and paid for it. These were kids in jeans with the skills, the prodigy, the audacity and the egos, too, to draw faster and shoot better, to rudely shove aside the men in the grey flannel suits and, fundamentally, to change everything for ever.

'We were all having fun in the '60s,' recalls Jerry Della Femina, a then young gunslinger who set the tone by commenting, 'Advertising is the most fun you can have with your clothes on.' Later, he wrote one of the best books ever about advertising, bearing a title he'd suggested for a Panasonic ad campaign: *From Those Wonderful Folks Who Gave You Pearl Harbor.*

'It was a decade of great promise,' he says, 'the first time that young people tried to wrest control from older people. Until then, there was a rite of passage. But in the '60s kids started saying to their parents I'm not going to live the way you live, I have different aspirations, I want a different world.'

Although he reluctantly confesses, 'I'm afraid that everyone in my generation suffers from long term memory loss because the 1960s gets better every year, it improves with age,' he still insists, 'you couldn't see so much freedom around you and not be free. Advertising, which had been as stodgy as the rest of the world, was suddenly filled with young people taking chances. When I first tried to get into the business in the 1950s, I was told by an old guy at J. Walter Thompson that I was making a mistake because there was no place for my kind in advertising. Since I wasn't sure what my kind was, how could he know? By the mid-'60s, I could tell them all to go fuck themselves because there were a hundred people who wanted to hire me. Everything had changed. The world went wild and we did too.'

The fun they were having was reflected in the ads they were making.

'Most of our clients were dragged along by the excitement of the era. Of course, those who were stodgy stayed with a certain type of old-line agency. Everybody else was trying to be different and in many cases they were succeeding. The Alka-Seltzer campaign was funny and successful. But the

Volkswagen campaign, well, that's the best example. That's the campaign that changed the industry. It's the one you can trace back to as the day when the new advertising was really born.'

The kids who were taking over knew all about Leo and David, but most of all they'd seen how Bill had rubbed the genie. Now, they decreed, it is no longer important that the copy be Shakespeare or that the pictures be Picasso. It's image that matters because it's image that will get someone to buy something.

That's what 'We're Number Two' was all about. Bernbach and Avis had drawn a bull's eye on Hertz's back and taken their best shot. They'd created their own image, defining themselves at Hertz's expense. That's why, when Hertz struck back, they also went for image, being 'Number One'.

The Carl Ally Agency was a young gunslinger operation, billing about $11 million. Ally, Jim Durfee, who wrote the copy, and Amil Gargano who handled the art, had earned reputations for themselves as street fighters – three self-confessed pool hustlers from Detroit – who'd come to New York a few years before and changed things with their very first account. They'd been hired by Volvo, then totally unknown in the States and, despite a tiny budget, lifted the company out of the trade papers and into *Life* magazine. They managed it by breaking the golden rule that said, never name the competition.

Durfee remembers, 'What we did was make direct comparisons with all the other compact cars in America, by name. We explained how Volvo outran them in speed and got better gas mileage.'

That first ad was so tough that Ally got a call from an attorney at the Ford Motor Company saying they were upset. He asked, 'What do you think we ought to do about this?' Ally reportedly told him, 'Make your cars go faster.'

Although that was the last the trio heard from Ford, it was

not the last Madison Avenue heard from Ally, Durfee and Gargano.

'Naming our competitors the way we did, making direct comparisons like that, had not been done before.' Durfee goes on, 'So when we got our second account, which was *Women's Day* magazine, we did it again. In those days in the media business, everybody was claiming some sort of number one spot. In our first ad for *Women's Day* I wrote something like, "Since everybody else is number one, we'll be number two." And again, we named names. We took them on head-on.'

Their style attracted attention from the kinds of clients who wanted aggressive button pushing. It also attracted Hertz, which, with hindsight, desperately needed it. The only problem was that everyone at Hertz seemed terribly reluctant to take such a drastic step.

For nearly nine years, Hertz had been running a campaign that proclaimed, 'Let Hertz put you in the driver's seat.' By today's standards it was utterly dismal. Even then it was silly because anybody could put you in the driver's seat, including Avis. But, as the market leader, they never felt they had to do more. Such lethargy opened a window for Avis, driven by Bernbach, to take huge chunks out of their hide. So when they finally approached Ally to ask what his agency could do for them, Ally promised they could get nasty. Hertz went away, solicited pitches from other agencies and heard, from each of the others, that it would be a mistake of mega proportions to acknowledge Avis.

'They talked to all the really big agencies,' Durfee says, 'and all of them told Hertz you can't admit Avis exists. Except us. We argued, it's crazy because there's a dog gnawing on your leg in the middle of the street and everybody can see it and you're saying, what dog? Just as bad, if you looked at the graphs, if you charted Avis's gains and the business Hertz was losing, those lines could have crossed in about five years. Unchecked, Avis and Hertz might have changed positions. So, eventually, Hertz came back to offer us a little piece of the business because they wanted to see how it could work. We told them, you don't have time for that. Give it all to us or we don't want any of it.'

Hertz took the plunge and the campaign that followed was overtly vitriolic.

It began with an ad that was headlined, 'For years, Avis has been telling you Hertz is No. 1. Now, we're going to tell you why.' It was followed by a lot of copy answering all of Avis's claims. It ended with, 'No. 2 says he tries harder. Than who?'

Adding to the effect, the photo in the corner was a man's fist with his index finger pointing up, making the now universally accepted number one sign. Besides all the other ground breaking that Ally, Durfee and Gargano were doing, it was the first time that gesture ever appeared in an ad.

The next barrage was little more than one long headline. 'If you were in the car rental business and you were No. 2 and you had only half as many cars to offer and about half as many locations at which to offer them, and fewer people to handle everything, what would you say in your advertising? Right, your ashtrays are cleaner.'

In all, Durfee wrote six hard-hitting ads before Hertz chose to call a truce with one final well-aimed jab.

'Aha! You were expecting another get tough with Avis ad,' read the headline, above a photo of a young woman in a Hertz uniform hugging a young woman in an Avis uniform. 'After being picked at by No. 2 for four years, we got a little irritated. We felt we had to say something about the things that have been implied about us. Mostly because these things aren't true. And our people who clean, service, deliver and take reservations wanted the air cleared. And now that we've gotten the irritation out of our systems, all future advertising will be devoted solely to acquainting you with how reliable, resourceful, helpful and pleasant we are so you'll come in and rent a car from us instead of our dear friends down the street.'

Avis tried to fight back by handing out red and white 'We Try Harder' badges. And, like the number one gesture, it too became a rallying cry. But Ally, Durfee and Gargano were simply too ferocious.

Ninety days after it all began, Avis had been gunned down, stopped dead in their tracks.

We are not totally rational beings. Nor have we ever been. Great advertising takes advantage of the fact that we see what we want to see, hear what we want to hear, and believe what we want to believe. Great advertising works, at least in part, because we irrationally allow emotion to cloud our judgement.

Totally rational beings would never spend money on many of the products we buy, for instance cigarettes.

Tobacco companies have always been among the most manipulative advertisers because there is no other way they can sell a product that is required by law to warn, in every ad, that smoking is hazardous to one's health. Anyone who bought Old Gold cigarettes when their ads used to brag, 'Not a cough in a carload', was being deliberately myopic.

If nothing else, 'I'd walk a mile for a Camel' was a catchy slogan. But when the same brand bragged, 'More doctors smoke Camels than any other cigarette,' they were really saying, here's the emotional excuse you need to light up, so you don't have to listen to people who say you shouldn't. L&M Cigarettes went the same route with, 'Just what the doctor ordered'.

Then there was the incongruity of the Marlboro Man, on horseback, riding through the fresh air of Big Sky country, poisoning his own lungs. In fact, as it turned out, one of the models who posed as the Marlboro Man did die of lung cancer. And yet the campaign worked brilliantly and sold zillions of cigarettes.

Another dazzling campaign was Joe Camel.

Playing off a 'Joe Cool' image since 1988, the cartoon character was widely believed to have contributed to the rise in teenage smoking. Although the company have consistently denied that the colourful Joe Camel was aimed 'specifically' at children – the key word there seems to be 'specifically' – it would be hard to argue that this wasn't blatant emotional manipulation of young would-be smokers. Joe Camel equals cool. Anyway, the Clinton administration thought so when they deliberately targeted Joe Camel in their 1997 war on tobacco advertising, leading Camel reluctantly to agree to retire the cartoon image.

Rivalling Camel's emotional approach, although more subtly, is Silk Cut. That brand has spent years developing an association between their name and the image of a ripped piece of cloth. The reason must be because, the more colourful the cloth in the ads, the less prominent the health warning in print just under it.

By contrast, a purely intellectual approach requires us to accept as rational whatever the argument. Whether the logic is sound or faulty, it's up to us to make that judgement. That's what the cosmetics industry does.

For example, 'The proof is in, even the best can get better.' That's the way Estée Lauder tried to sell Fruition Extra, a multi-action complex skin care cream. The copy promises a 49% increase in smoothness plus a 58% increase in softness and suppleness, all within an hour. It also promises that, with regular use, lines and wrinkles visibly decrease.

If we believe that such a product can work, and have never tried this particular one, and if we accept those percentages as being accurate – even though the ad doesn't state how they got those percentages or, in fact, what they really mean – then rationally we might decide to buy the product. At least, that's what Estée Lauder hope.

It's no secret that emotion frequently overrides intellect. And advertising is unmerciful in its ability to exploit this.

Most of us know that buying Cindy Crawford's book of beauty secrets will not make us look like Cindy Crawford. Or that buying Warren Buffet's book on how to make a billion on Wall Street will not turn us into Buffet billionaires. Or that, in spite of what Candice Bergen insinuates, subscribing to Sprint will not make us better parents just because, once we have our account and PIN number, we will always be able to call home from anywhere in the world and check on the kids.

There is no way that wearing an Armani suit will automatically make us as physically appealing as the model in the ad. Although Armani spend a lot of money every year getting us to think it might. Nor is there any way that buying a set of Tiger Woods signature golf clubs will give us Tiger Woods' talent. Except that Titleist/Cobra paid him $20 million to convince us otherwise.

Emotionally, we want to believe all these things are possible.

What the young gunslingers realized in the 1960s was how to sell to our expectations. They learned to convince us that their product – any product – would do exactly what we wanted it to. And the moment that it did – which it invariably would because we wanted it to – we were hooked. Over the years, they've sharpened their skills, figuring out how best to angle those emotional hooks, and how to sink them in so deeply that nothing short of surgery will remove them.

Which is exactly what Pepsi had in mind in 1963 when they launched a nuclear war on Coke.

The gigantic amounts of money thrown into the 'cola wars' reflect both the brutality of the combat and the size of the spoils on offer to the winner. Pillaging even as little as one market share point can represent, literally, tens of millions of dollars.

Uniquely, and much to the chagrin of the smaller players, it is a two-cola conflict. As a result, whenever Coke and Pepsi go at it, both benefit at the expense of all the other colas in the category that have been left out of the war.

Not long ago, Richard Branson bragged that his Virgin Cola would one day surpass Pepsi in British sales. If he could pull that off, he'd deserve a Nobel Prize for Entrepreneurship. But it won't happen. Neither Pepsi nor Coke could ever find it in their hearts – or pocketbooks – to let him anywhere near the playing field. Their war chests are bigger than his. Their guns are mightier and carry a louder boom. What's more, mathematics is unconditionally stacked against him.

Studies show that the two or three top brands in just about every product category get about 80% of the business and that, no matter what the also-rans do, nothing happens. Second-division products almost never break through. Although there have been rare exceptions. Every now and then a sky rocket goes off and a product shoots up to the top. But what usually follows fast up is just-as-fast down. So it doesn't really matter how big the fourth or fifth place guys talk. In spite of their advertising, marketing and whatever kinds of gimmicks they come up with, it almost never changes anything. Once an also-ran finds a niche, it stays there.

Historically, the old-established also-rans, Royal Crown Cola and Dr. Pepper, would love to be included every time Coke and Pepsi rumble, and they've spent bundles trying to get invited. But Coke and Pepsi have spent even more, effectively shutting them out. For Branson, it's one thing to admire the Duchy of Grand Fenwick's invasion of the United States, it's another to confuse a Peter Sellers film with reality.

Not that Pepsi, the long-suffering number two, has always been a major player. Once upon a time, 50 years ago, Coke owned the category almost outright, outselling Pepsi in most markets eight–nine–ten times to one. It wasn't even much of a contest, until Pepsi came along and said, let's offer more than Coke does. So they bottled it bigger but kept the price the same. The resulting ad campaign was called 'Twice As Much For A Nickel Too'. Their ad agency even wrote a little jingle using that line and, nicely enough, invented the world's first singing commercial.

People sparked to it and brought Pepsi up to a marketing level that it had never achieved before. But along with increased sales came a very negative piece of baggage, in that Pepsi got tagged a 'kitchen cola'. It was the brand you bought at a bargain basement discount. It made Pepsi drinkers look like cheapskates. Legend has it that, to get twice as much for a nickel too, and not suffer the after-effect, people served Pepsi to their guests only after first pouring it into a Coke bottle.

It was a problem that Pepsi struggled with for many years. And they might never have found a response had it not been for the exuberance of some young gunslingers at Batten, Barton, Durstine & Osborn who put their heads together and decided to establish a new identity for Pepsi by creating an entire social group the company could call their own.

'Come alive' became the cry of 'The Pepsi Generation', which fitted the era perfectly because coming alive and being a distinct generation were what youth were doing in 1963.

'For the very first time,' recalls Phil Dusenberry, who was there then and is now head of BBDO, 'a product exalted the user rather than sanctified itself. For the very first time, a product wasn't being heralded as the chief reason you used it. They were asking us to use it because we wanted to be like the people who drank it.'

Emotion would forever triumph over intellect. It was the birth of lifestyle advertising.

'No one had thought about using lifestyle before. Television was still really in its infancy. There was still the attitude among advertisers and agencies alike, that the best way to sell products was with an in-your-face approach. You know, talking heads. You'd get a stand-up presenter who pitched the product like a door to door salesman, the way they did it on radio. Out of that, evolved the demonstration ad. People realized, hey we're on television, so we can actually show how our product works.'

The best depiction of demonstration advertising was the Timex campaign starring a then well-known newscaster named John Cameron Swayze. Live on camera, with all his journalistic credibility, he'd explain how these watches were built so sturdily they could survive even the most rigorous torture test. Then, right there, he'd submit a watch to some horrible fate. A pitching machine would toss it against a brick wall. A jack-hammer would try to smash it open. Or he'd strap it to the blades of an outboard motor, submerge it in water and set the motor spinning. At the end of the demonstration, he'd hold the watch up to the camera and proudly announce to the world, 'Timex takes a licking but keeps on ticking.'

'That was pretty dramatic for the time,' Dusenberry continues. 'By comparison, lifestyle advertising seemed too soft sell. It was also too revolutionary an idea. No one believed that you could sell a product by selling the people who used the product. Occasionally, you saw lifestyle ads in a magazine because in print you couldn't demonstrate the product. But no one had ever dared use it on television. When we did, it was unique. And that's one of the reasons it caught on.'

Because the advertising campaign had successfully created a difference in the two products – after all, they are essentially the same – the sales gap began to close.

'We drew a line in the sand. Pepsi was saying, if you're a young thinking person who wants to live life to the fullest, then Pepsi is for you. Pepsi is hip and Coke is not. On the other side of that line in the sand, Coke was saying we're the heartland drink, we're the drink you've been drinking all these years, we're America's cola. We made people believe that Pepsi was vibrant, contemporary, with it, the leading edge, and that Coke was old fashioned, fuddy duddy, the trailing edge.'

In the parlance of the trade, it all comes down to neckties.

That's a general product category, so named because a necktie has no genuine function. It doesn't keep a shirt closed. It doesn't keep anyone's trousers up. It doesn't even protect buttons from getting stained with gravy. The only thing it does is make a fashion statement about the person wearing it. A necktie product is, therefore, one that we consume in public that makes a statement about us.

Beers, for instance.

Again, we're asked to believe the products are different, when it's really their advertising that's different. Michelob says sophisticated. Budweiser says macho. Bud Light says friendly. Miller Lite says fun. Foster's says working class. Guinness says rustic. Coors says environmentally sound. It's much the same for watches and automobiles. If all you want is a watch that tells you what time it is, you can buy one for under a fiver. So why do some people spend 10 grand on a watch? If the only thing a car is supposed to do is get you from A to B and back again safely, then cars would simply have four seats, four wheels, a roof, seat belts and nothing else. In fact, at the lower end of the market, that's about all cars do have. So why do some cars cost more than a three-bedroomed house on half an acre? The answer to both questions is that watches and cars have been turned into fashion accessories, intended to make a statement about the person owning them.

The opposite category – non-necktie – is a product that's not usually seen when used. No matter which brand of toilet paper we buy, unless we start telling people what it is, few will ever notice. Nor do we buy cereal, soap or deodorant to make a statement about ourselves. Those purchase decisions are based on other criteria – price, availability, comfort, colour – just about anything but statement.

Where necktie products are concerned, two rules generally apply. The more expensive the statement, the higher the price we have to pay. And, the more the necktie says about us in a positive way, the more likely we are to pay the price.

By constantly reinforcing the hip, with-it image, Pepsi cut into Coke's lead. Because Pepsi were so successful, all sorts of other companies – airlines, insurance, fast food, electronics, cars – started coming up with commercials that celebrated warm and fuzzy snippets of life. After a while, even Coke went that route.

Which is why, by the mid-1980s, Pepsi decided to shed the lifestyle persona. So BBDO came up with a campaign based on the choice of a new generation. They hooked up with Michael Jackson and made commercials relying heavily on humour that were, again, dramatically different for the category.

What happened next was beyond the wildest dreams of anyone at Pepsi.

Notes Dusenberry, 'We captured young people in a way that we had never done before. We racked up some really big numbers. That threw Coke into a panic. So they decided to come out with a product that was sweeter, a little closer to the sweetness of Pepsi, and to package it as New Coke.'

It was one of the most outrageous mistakes in corporate history, an error of judgement to rival Edsel.

Before putting it on the market, Coke did taste tests and, to give the dogs their due, the product tested very well. But they tested it blind. In other words, the Coke *aficionados* didn't know what they were drinking. It was Brand X. All they knew was that they liked it.

Therein, Dusenberry contends, lay Coke's fundamental error. 'By testing blind, they took away the Coke brand that people admired, loved and were loyal to. It's a perfect example of how important branding can be. It isn't just what's in the can. It's what's on the label. If they had told people it was Coke, they probably would have gotten a totally different reaction from their consumers. The people who were loyal to Coke would almost certainly have screamed, wait a minute, you're changing my brand, you're changing my Coca-Cola. But no one said it so no one knew what they were drinking.

Coke didn't take the test in the right direction and as a result, it blew up in their face.'

Pepsi had scored a broadside hit of mega proportions.

'I have to believe that it was probably the greatest marketing *faux pas* in history. There is no greater marketing bone-head play that I can think of. And we forced it on them. When Coke saw the reaction to Michael Jackson and the new advertising that we were doing, not only in terms of sales but in terms of how people were perceiving Pepsi, it threw the fear of God into them.'

Needless to say, they capitulated quickly. To Coca-Cola's credit, they came back as fast as they could with Coke Classic. They took their losses, and today they play up their differences from Pepsi by proclaiming that Coke is 'The real thing'.

Still, the war goes on, fought in the trenches every day. 'It's a daily grind. All the more so now, because if you look at the numbers in what we call markets of choice – convenience stores, supermarkets, delicatessens, mom-and-pop stores, any store where you have a choice between Coke and Pepsi – in these markets, Pepsi and Coke are neck and neck. Now, turn the clock back 50 years ago when Coke was kicking the shit out of Pepsi. I'd say that's an amazing turn of events.'

Interestingly enough, when the magazine *Consumer Reports* blind-tested die-hard Coke and Pepsi drinkers, they discovered that both groups failed three out of four times to identify their favourite drink when put next to a cheap store brand.

Which explains why Coke and Pepsi together spend in excess of $300 million a year to build an image that is aimed at keeping us emotionally involved.

After proving their point by putting Avis in their place, Hertz shifted their advertising philosophy. The then chairman told Jim Durfee, 'You're giving people reasons they should use Hertz. I don't want them to have reasons. I just want them to like us.'

A new weapon for the arsenal – the product as friend – turned into a grown-up version of the button Burnett had pushed when he invented Tony the Tiger and the Pillsbury Dough Boy. It combined the 'If you like our cartoon, you'll like our product' school of philosophy with 'number two versus number one' to evolve into the highly exploitive strategy known as positioning.

'Is this manipulation?' Phil Dusenberry concedes, 'In one way or another all advertising is manipulation. But all we're doing is manipulating people either away from the competition to our brand, or into using our brand more often.'

He insists that there has never been a single piece of advertising written yet that can make everyone see everything in just one way. And that, in the end, the best any agency can hope for is to get as many people as possible to see it their way, given the dollars they've got to spend and the capabilities at their disposal. The business has got so complex and competitive that it isn't even enough any more to come up with a great slogan that will turn people's heads. 'No, today everything has to be rooted in some positioning, finding some part of people's lives that you want to dominate.'

When BBDO were invited to pitch for the Visa credit card account, the competition was Mastercard. But the research guys at BBDO discovered that Visa was honoured in five times as many places as American Express and, based on that, Dusenberry decided to ignore Mastercard.

'We dismissed them outright. We decided to pretend that they didn't exist. That was our positioning. We told people that Visa was, "Everywhere you want to be . . ." then reminded them, "And they don't take American Express." The strength of the campaign was positioning. It wasn't just a slogan or a catchy piece of work. It had a positioning strategy that still lives on.'

The idea is that we all like winners and believe that, by associating ourselves with a winner, we become one too. It makes us feel better to know that we've voted for the candidate who got elected. It links us to success.

Getting us to make that link with a product is a huge step towards winning a brand-loyal consumer. It's the reason some people go to McDonald's and others go to Burger King.

It's the reason BMW became 'The ultimate driving machine'. (You're going to feel awful driving something else.)

And, Budweiser became 'The King of Beers'. (Commoners drink commoner beer.)

And, Miller Lite fought back by bragging, 'Everything you always wanted in a beer, and less.' (How wrong you were to want more.)

And, 7-Up went against both Pepsi and Coke with 'The Uncola'. (Un must be in so, if you drink anything else, you must be out.)

And, Cadillac called itself 'The penalty for leadership'. (Even if you're in an ultimate driving machine, you're still not the leader you thought you were.)

And, the Chiquita Banana Company, whose ad campaign had, for years, centred on a catchy jingle, positioned itself as the market leader by asking, 'How strong is the Chiquita name? How many banana commercials can you sing?' (You'd better learn the words because you don't want people to think you eat the wrong bananas.)

And, Chivas Regal Scotch went for number one by associating price with quality in their ad headline: 'Isn't that a lot for a bottle of Scotch? Yes.' (If you don't want anyone to know how cheap you are, you'd better pay more.)

And, Heineken went after all the other premium beers by claiming to be more exhilarating: 'Refreshes the parts other beers cannot reach.' (If your beer has failed, so have you.)

And, Quaker Oats pushed hot cereal by asking, 'Does it make sense to jump out of a warm bed and into a cold cereal?' (You probably never thought of it that way. Bye bye, corn-flakes.)

And, Crosse & Blackwell bounced their reputation off Campbell's by referring to itself as 'The Other Soup'. (Don't ever fall for Campbell's again.)

And, stockbrokers Goldenberg-Pollen positioned themselves against the market leaders by pitching personal attention: 'Try walking into Merrill Lynch and asking for Mr. Lynch.' (Oh well, at least you now can sing the Chiquita Banana commercial!)

CHAPTER FOUR

Willing Accomplices

I have always believed that writing advertisements is the second most profitable form of writing. The first, of course, is ransom notes.

Phil Dusenberry, BBDO

There is a complex series of arguments that goes: advertising is everywhere because we want to be advertised to. That we accept advertising into our lives because it is, essentially, ego-gratifying. That we like being told how unique we are, even if we are being asked to express that uniqueness by becoming part of a group, say someone who wears Calvin Klein jeans. That we have accepted advertising as a code through which values have been assigned to objects because we need to believe that, by purchasing some object, we will acquire those assigned values. That advertising is no longer just a way of saying, if you have bunions here's the solution, it has become a ministry – it shows, it demonstrates, it instructs; it came, it saw, it conquered – and that much of its power stems from the fact that it is not usually acknowledged to be so all powerful.

'Advertising is of the very essence of democracy,' stated Bruce Barton in 1955, then chairman of the agency he co-founded, BBDO. 'An election goes on every minute of the business day across the counters of hundreds of thousands of stores and shops where the customers state their preferences and determine which manufacturer and which product shall be the leader today, and which shall lead tomorrow.'

Thought of in those terms, some ad men assert that it is unfair to criticize advertising. After all, it generates pleasure so what's wrong with that? But then, the secret of great propaganda is that it's never seen as propaganda.

'It is the job of advertising,' one London-based copywriter claims, 'to make lots of people uneasily unhappy with their lot and, at the same time, to make them believe that the only route to true happiness is by purchasing my client's product. Is that propaganda? Is that manipulation? When it works, I suspect it is.'

Consciously or not, we compare ourselves to the ads we see, accepting the discomfort they have created – because without discomfort there would be no need for salvation – then buying deliverance in the guise of their product.

Dr Jean Kilbourne, an educator who has written extensively about advertising, says the proof of its power comes from the many people she meets who are fast to claim an exemption from the influence of advertising. According to her, people are always insisting that they don't pay attention to ads, that they never watch them, that they tune them out, that they have no effect whatsoever. 'I hear this most often,' she notes, 'from young men wearing Budweiser caps.'

Estimates vary, but a safe one suggests that we are exposed to as many as 1600 commercial messages, in one form or another, every day. In some cases, it could be a lot more. But even if it's only half as many, that's still 50 an hour for 16 hours – nearly one per minute.

Besides television and radio, there are ads in magazines and newspapers, through the mail, on billboards, in train stations, in trains, at airports, in planes, in supermarkets, in department stores, in museums, at concerts, at sporting events, and even in the Post Office. There are promotions in doctors' offices and ads in schools.

There are also, now, commercials inside commercials. It's called multi-layering or, to get really fancy, 'an integrated communications mix'.

A tactic to dispatch similar messages from diverse sources, the coupon attached to the video you buy is paid for by the confectionary company, who have also paid to have a commercial spliced on to the front of the film, offering a discount on one box of candy next time you're in the cinema and/or a discount on the next video that you buy that has another one of their commercials spliced onto the front, together with another discount coupon. Then, if they've really done it right, every film they've stuck their coupons on also features some actor happily munching away on their candy, a cardboard representation of which confronts you at the corner shop's sweet counter.

In short, there is no escaping advertising.

Half a century ago, there was commercial-free television. Today, thanks to MTV, QVC, the Shopping Channel and others like them, there are entire stations entirely devoted to commercials. Because some of these stations wind up on subscription television, we are not merely confronted with non-stop ads, some of us actually pay to see them.

A 1995 study, conducted worldwide and reported in *Ad Age International*, showed that 72% of the consumers they questioned believe that companies exaggerate the benefits of their products, and 70% believe that advertising brainwashes children. The same survey said that only 38% of the consumers tested believe that advertising tells the truth.

The contention logically follows, if advertising lies to us and we know it, the reason we accept it must be because we want to be lied to. Leslie Savan, who writes on advertising for the *Village Voice* and is one of the best journalists writing about it today, defines two kinds of lies. 'All advertising tells lies.

That's their job. But there are little lies and there are big lies. A little lie is, this beer tastes great. A big lie is, this beer makes you great.'

The little lie, she says, is implicitly at the heart of most ads. But it's the big lie that permeates the advertising business. When she confronts people in the advertising business with the little lie, many of them laughingly excuse it as poetic licence. But when she confronts those same people with the big lie, she says, the laughter stops and they become defensive.

'They answer, we're not saying that this beer will make you overcome baldness. We're not saying it will get you a wife. We're just showing a fun, entertaining scene that makes you feel good and if some of that feel good rubs off onto the product, that's what we want to happen. They insist, it's not a lie. We're in the entertainment business. We just want those good feelings to be associated with our client.'

The danger there, she believes, is in their attempt to sell us a whole world. 'You buy a product which you hope will solve whatever anxiety is coursing through you at the time, which may have nothing at all to do with what the product purports to sell in the literal sense. For instance, when you wear a logo, YSL, Polo, you're buying an idea, a feeling, an instant connection to where it's happening, to a sense of excitement, to the idea that you're part of the engine that drives the shiny, glamorous world. It becomes a solution to isolation, loneliness, or impotence. It's not about the actual product we buy. That's almost the least of it. It's about achieving pleasure, happiness, resolution, the end of some anxiety. It's about buying into a world that advertising presents, where corporations are basically good guys who care about us as individuals. Through advertising, they are saying, we can connect you to a glamorous, powerful world.'

But, the argument comes back, different people interpret glamour and power differently. And not everybody believes in Madison Avenue's definitions of those words. Or, for that matter, Madison Avenue's view of the world.

Savan's answer is, 'Of course, there are people who are suspicious of advertising. They're the ones who are also usually resistant to establishment, mainstream culture. So you reach them with flattery. You tell them they're rebels, too individualistic to go for the other kind of advertising, and that you – whether you're Nike or Sprite or MTV or whoever – understand how they're special, that you agree they shouldn't go where everybody else goes. That's when you say, be unique and join us. It's almost transparent except that it works.'

Especially for young people.

She points to a moment in Monty Python's *The Life of Brian* when the messiah shouts to the crowd, 'Don't follow me. Don't follow anyone. Think for yourselves. You are all individuals.' And the crowd shouts back, in unison, 'We are all individuals.'

'That's advertising in a nutshell,' she says. 'Join us and become unique. Individuality sells.'

As the perfect example she points to MTV. In their ads, aimed at attracting a very well-defined market, they have some earthy 20 year old saying, whatever I eat, my friends eat; whatever I buy, my friends buy; whatever I listen to, my friends listen to. The idea is that, if an advertiser is looking for the rebel market, here they are watching MTV. The message is, the product MTV is selling is a flock of sheep who pride themselves on thinking that they're lone wolves.

'It's very hard and very rare to be immune to it,' she says. 'It's like being immune to pollution. Advertising has to affect you somehow. You may not know how and it may be difficult to measure, unless you're one of those people who has no resistance and has to go live in a bubble. But the rest of us are affected by it and in many cases it becomes us. Advertising sells us a world that doesn't exist, so we try to recreate that world or at least some image of it.'

Most recently, Sprite elevated rebel advertising to a new art form. Their nearest competitor, 7-Up, had positioned themselves against Coke and Pepsi by calling their produce 'The Uncola'. So Sprite – owned, incidentally, by Coca-Cola – took on 7-Up with a campaign to position itself as the rebel drink.

Aiming straight at the heart of the MTV-ers, they put a bunch of street kids on camera playing basketball, rapping on about how the establishment had done everything it could to get them to drink establishment drinks. They let you know, in no uncertain terms, that they're fed up with product shots, drink shots, mega superstars, jingles, 'and the kind of people I have never ever met in real life'.

The tagline is: 'Image is nothing. Thirst is everything. Obey your thirst. Sprite.'

An image cries out, reject image.

Lewis Carroll would be proud.

It is not without some justification that advertisers respond to criticism by claiming that they don't just create this world out of thin air. That they've found out through research what people want to see, or what people need to see. That advertising merely reflects society, it did not invent it.

However, Savan isn't convinced that's the way it is. She feels that advertising takes from the real world, polishes, distorts, links it up with a product, and only then feeds it back to us.

'The one question most people ask me when I talk to college students is, does advertising reflect who we are or does it shape who we are? Well, I think that's a false dichotomy. Advertisers say they only reflect who we are, which is one way they evade accusations of manipulation. And yet that's true. But they also shape who we are because by the time it goes through the machine and comes back to us, it's been designed to make us to want to look more like those images they show us.'

Reinforcing those images, she says, is the technological

might now available to the advertising industry. And it is the repetitive power of advertising that contributes to the danger.

'Most advertisers figure their ads don't even start to become effective until most viewers have seen them something like six times. Repetition is one of the keys to advertising. So yes, those ads are indeed shaping us. They're not just holding a mirror up to us, saying this is who you are. They're showing us people who look better than we do, who are happier and who, somehow, have their happiness and their good looks associated with a product, whatever it is. That is not what we originally fed into their machine. Is it manipulation? Well, as long as we make the connection between those people and the product, and we decide for ourselves that the product can turn us into those people, then we won't feel it's manipulative because the connection has come from us. Our eyes have been on the wrong ball, however, if we think that the manipulative power of advertising lies in its ability to make us go out and buy a particular product. If that's what we equate with manipulation, then it's that much easier for advertising to truly influence us in broader ways. Such as believing that products really can bring us romance and success. It's our illusion of immunity to it that makes advertising really powerful.'

One way ads induce that illusion of immunity is by making us laugh.

It had long been the dictum that humour doesn't sell, that people buy product benefit, not jokes. But the blurring of those lines between advertising and entertainment guaranteed a place for jokes. These days, it is widely accepted that if you can make someone laugh they will like you. The problem is, not everyone can make people laugh. Furthermore, humour is cultural. What throws Croatians into hysterics may well, and is probably likely to, leave Liverpudlians dumbfounded. When a Japanese soap commercial featured a young boy in a public bath breaking wind, Tokyo laughed. The reaction in Kansas, doubtless, would have been very different.

Howard Gossage understood what humour could do for a product when Fina, the Belgian petroleum company, asked him in the 1960s to make them famous in America.

As San Francisco's bad-boy of the advertising industry – and part-time monocle wearer – he opted to position Fina as the friendliest petrol station in town a with a humorous invitation to 'please like us'.

Under the tiny title 'Our Motto' he wrote in huge type, 'If you're driving down the road and you see a Fina station and it's on your side so you don't have to make a U-turn through traffic and there aren't six cars waiting and you need gas or something please stop in.'

Below that, in small print again, Gossage admitted, 'We know it isn't very pushy as mottoes go, but it's realistic and Fina doesn't expect you to do anything that isn't realistic or convenient.'

He followed that with a campaign explaining how, if a product wants to stay on top, it's got to have a little something new from time to time. So Fina were offering 'the additive of the future', a way to make the insides of everyone's tyres a little prettier – pink air.

'Pink sounds like as good a color as any,' the ad explained, 'and besides, it's short and catchy.'

The campaign took off and Fina racked up the lowest percentage of advertising cost against gross sales of any gasoline company.

Next, Gossage convinced them to start painting various parts of the station pink, including, of course, the air hose. That was followed by pink forecourts. Then he offered Fina's customers the chance to win 15 yards of pink asphalt. It was a legitimate contest and some months later, instead of announcing one winner, Fina gave away three prizes, 'because anything worth doing is worth overdoing'.

The same man who once suggested that the object of

advertising should be not to communicate with consumers but to terrorize the competition's copywriters had managed both with characteristic lunacy and humour.

Another approach to humour, this time classic bumbling, was what Barclaycard Visa had in mind when they hired Rowan Atkinson, now internationally eminent as Mr Bean, to play secret agent Latham.

Through 17 episodes, Atkinson – as the antithesis of James Bond, in that he always managed to get it wrong – was thrown into some foreign outback and pitted against the sinister forces of everyday life, such as trying to negotiate the price of a taxi. In each situation, it was Latham's trustworthy companion Bough who saved the day, *deus ex Barclaycard*. He produced it in the nick of time, reminding Latham and the audience that when you've got Barclaycard – featuring purchase insurance, cash advances and emergency assistance – there's never any need to worry. Humour gave Barclaycard a likeable personality, established its global credentials and, in the public's mind, distanced it from other credit cards, especially Mastercard.

In much the same vein, Persil washing-up liquid used humour to distance itself from the competition. But this meant taking on the advertising might of Procter and Gamble, who had positioned their Fairy Liquid as the market leader.

The two companies had been fierce, head-to-head competitors since the very early 1950s. A great deal of the power P&G have always wielded comes from their premier position in many product categories. But they spend to stay there and are the largest advertisers in the world. Their marketing philosophy is largely wrapped around the conclusions of the survey that showed that the top two or three brands in each category get 80% of the business. So P&G historically have always aimed to be in the top two brands in every category. In various places around the world they are known as Tide, Bold, Ivory, Cheer, Ariel, Bonux, Mr Clean, Fairy, Lenor,

Pampers, Camay, Max Factor, Head&Shoulders, Cover Girl, Hugo Boss, Rejoice, Crest, Nyquil, Vicks, Pepto Bismol, Scope, Crisco, Duncan Hines, Pringles and Folgers. And in those rare instances when they've launched a product that hasn't achieved a top two position, they're not shy about backing away.

They also brand similar things to protect themselves from predators coming into the market. In other words, they become their own competition to muddy the waters for everyone else. Which is the reason, for example, they make several brands of laundry powder – hence Tide, Bold, Ariel and Daz.

Unilever and their American subsidiary, Lever Brothers, work almost exactly the same way. Heavy advertising. Aim for the top two places. Where necessary become your own competition – hence Omo, Skip and Persil.

In addition to those three brands, they are Flora, I Can't Believe It's Not Butter, Batchelors, Iglo, Lipton, Birds Eye, Comfort, Lux, Dove, Lifebuoy, Domestos, Sun, Elizabeth Arden, Calvin Klein Cosmetics, Elizabeth Taylor Cosmetics, Karl Lagerfeld Fragrances, Chloe, Brut, Impulse, Fabergé, Ponds, Pears, Close-Up, Signal and Pepsodent.

Like P&G, Lever also understand the value of a brand, and when they decided to go after Fairy Liquid they committed one of their major assets to the fight, and added humour.

They already had a washing-up liquid called Sunlight. But they believed that another one, with the brand name Persil attached to it, could put a dent into Fairy's market share. So they launched Persil Dish Washing Liquid in 1990. However, 'free-riding' their name like that is a tactic not without serious risk. Persil had a premier position in Britain as a soap powder. If it failed as a washing-up liquid, the cost would be to soap powder sales. Lever were betting that their soap powder clients who were also using Fairy Liquid would switch to a Persil brand.

What they needed to do was come up with a commercial

that didn't look anything like P&G's spots – an actress show-ing tables filled with dirty dishes to demonstrate how Fairy Liquid washed more dishes than any other brand. So they hired actor Robbie Coltrane who, while visiting Grannie in the wilds of Scotland, decides to wash her dishes. The link between Persil soap powder and Persil washing-up liquid comes when he tells Grannie that it's going to rain, and together they run outside to take the now clean dishes off the washing line.

It worked because it was funny. It helped Persil find a niche because it worked.

Absolut Vodka also found that humour worked, in this case to position them in an overcrowded market.

In 1980, Absolut was just another alcoholic beverage in a field saturated with alcoholic beverages. Adding to the prob-lem, it was Swedish, a near-guarantee that it would stay un-noticed because, to most people, vodka meant Russian. Eleven years later, Absolut was the leading imported vodka in the United States.

The turnaround – despite research which warned that the bottle was the wrong shape, that the label was too complicated and that the only Swedish brands anyone outside Stockholm could name were Volvo, Saab and Bjorn Borg – came thanks to a sophisticated and humorous play on the brand's name. British graphic artist Geoff Hayes, who'd just gone to New York to be the art director at the agency TBWA, drew the bottle, put a halo over it and wrote at the bottom, 'Absolut Perfection'.

From there, they mimicked the pop artist's painting of the Campbell's soup can with 'Absolut Warhol'. They stripped a bottle naked of its label for 'Absolut Centerfold'. They designed a California swimming pool shaped like the bottle with the label on the bottom for 'Absolut L.A.'. They even made fun of Packard and Key by filling a glass with ice cubes, faintly embedding the words Absolut Vodka into them, and headlining it 'Absolut Subliminal'.

Proof of the campaign's brilliance came in a spoof ad from the Canadian-based advertising watchdog, Adbusters. To get across the message that advertising contributes to alcoholism, drunk driving and sexual abuse, they headlined their campaign 'Absolut Nonsense'.

The French have always shown a predilection towards humour in advertising, one of the best examples being a TV spot for Super Glue. In it, they applied their epoxy to the soles of the announcer's shoes, turned him upside-down, and stuck him to the ceiling, plainly demonstrating that the product worked. The punchline came from the very worried announcer, echoing what was on the minds of everyone seeing the spot for the first time, 'Now what?'

Whether humour is a button or a merely a device to push buttons, is difficult to say. Whichever, it is just as difficult to say if humour always works.

Jim Durfee isn't sure. 'That's been an argument and a debate forever. In my experience, if you strike the right chord it's going to work no matter how you do it, with the hard sell, with humour, with wit, with sex. Anything can sell at any given time as long as it's striking the right chord. It's like the old thing that nobody reads long copy. Baloney. People read what interests them. One line can be too long if it's not right. So all of these things work at some level some times. But there's no magic formula. Although I wish there was. I suppose that mixing product merit and entertainment value is about as close as you can come to a magic formula. So if humour entertains, and if you can reach in there and make that visceral connection, it's going to last a lot longer than any intellectual contact.'

He points again to Bill Bernbach and VW. 'Bernbach believed advertising was emotion and art. He could have sold Volkswagen as an economy car that only cost two cents a mile and got 100 miles on a gallon of gas. It probably would have sold cars, but not as many as it did. What he did was to make the car acceptable with humour. He was even almost self-deprecating about the automobile in their advertising. But through humour, he got people to like them.'

Gossage always felt that, through humour, he could create an identity, which he believed was on a higher plane than image. 'Identity is like the sun, it radiates energy from a solid mass. Image, on the other hand, is like a balloon, all surface, and spends far too much of its time avoiding pin pricks.'

For the sake of identity, he painted bread trucks to look like French loaves; sponsored a contest for Rainier Ale that offered a free trip to the Seattle World's fair – except free meant you had to walk there, although he provided five people who'd walk with you; ran a contest for Qantas, 'Be the first one on your block to win a kangaroo'; ran a campaign, complete with give-away buttons, to repeal the 19th amendment to the Constitution – which had given women the right to vote – simply because no woman had ever been seen drinking Rainier Ale; sold Paul Masson wines with the headline, 'Wine collecting takes up less space than antique cars, is quieter than hi-fi and tastes better than stamps'; and, again for Rainier Ale, invented the Beethoven sweatshirt.

He wrote copy for Eagle Shirts to imitate Ernest Hemingway – 'The stripes of Kilimanjaro, or, for whom the pipe bowls'; co-authored the ultimate book on paper aeroplanes and then sponsored what must be the all-time biggest paper aeroplane contest the world has ever seen; claimed to have discovered Marshall McLuhan and probably did; and had a very unassuming philosophy when it came to advertising – 'Ask the client what his biggest problem is, then write an ad asking the readers to help solve it.'

When he died at the age of 52 in 1969, most of the lengthy obituaries that ran around the world quoted him, correctly, as often saying, 'Advertising is no business for a grown man.' All of them, also, referred to him as an irrepressible wit.

When humour works, we laugh. When it isn't funny, we shrug and forget it. But then there is a third possibility, which illustrates additional dangers of humour in advertising. It's when the ad is funny but the message has been sacrificed at the expense of the joke.

Gossage had early on befriended one of America's great comic writers, Stan Freberg, and convinced him to dabble in advertising. Having spent years scripting radio shows and turning hit songs into parodies, Freberg created ads that made fun of advertising. He had gypsy tea leaf readers going out on strike to sell tea; had actor Jesse White pitching take-out Chinese food to an elevator filled with Chinese people; and wrote a radio spot for the National Association of Radio Broadcasters that drained Lake Michigan, filled it with hot chocolate, and had a B-52 bomber add the whipped cream and an ICBM missile put the maraschino cherry on top. The punch line was, 'Let them try that on television.'

For the same spot, he wrote a jingle that rhymed 'radio' with 'toast and marmaladio', rivalling the jingle he wrote for his first radio commercial – done at the behest of Howard Gossage for a frozen food company – which went, 'Pictsweet, Pictsweet, something something something something . . . lah dah dah dah dah dah dah, you and me . . .'

In 1997, *Advertising Age* named a Freberg TV spot, done two decades before for Sunsweet Prunes, as one of the 50 best ever. It opens with a man saying, 'I warn you in advance, I'm not going to like your prunes.' His reason is because prunes have pits and wrinkles. Then he's offered Sunsweet Prunes, only to discover they've been pitted. He likes them, but still complains about the wrinkles. The punchline is the promise, 'Today the pits, tomorrow the wrinkles.'

Deciding that his own advertising agency should be called 'Parsley, Sage, Rosemary and Osborn, a division of Thyme, Inc.', Freberg surpassed even himself when he was hired by Pacific Southwest Airlines (PSA) to do their ad campaign, forever remembered in the annals of advertising as 'White Knuckle Flyer'.

He was aiming at people who hate to fly and are forever worried that planes crash. To pacify them, he got the airline to hand out security blankets – literally, tiny blankets with the PSA logo – to any passenger worrying that flying might get them killed.

It was hilarious.

And the airline died laughing.

'Somewhere between gag writing and all the fun,' comments Jerry Della Femina, who was called by PSA in a panic to undo what Freberg had done because they didn't think they were going to survive him, 'someone had to sell something. The kiss of death in advertising is when you make the mistake of falling in love with your own words.'

PSA had succumbed to humour and, unfunnily, went out of business.

That humour coerces us into a likeable relationship with a product seems obvious.

That sex sells is indisputable.

But sex differs from humour because, by definition, it is gender linked. Men will, for instance, take notice of a woman's body in an ad faster than a woman will notice a man's body. This is not to say that women don't respond to sex, either as a vehicle or as a button, but, because female sexuality is considered more complex than male sexuality, it is usually an adjunct. Use a naked woman in an ad for men and the message is, get the product, get the woman. Use a naked man in an ad and you're not necessarily saying anything about sex at all. You might be saying strength, security, health and/or partnership. When sex is used to sell a product to a woman, the message is just as often likely to be, get the product, get the romance.

Ogilvy said that the guiding rule should be relevance. For

beauty products, naked bodies are obviously relevant. For off-shore hydraulic drill bits, naked bodies are patently less so. The grey area is just about everything in between.

Some years ago, the Dim underwear company in France produced one of the most erotic commercials ever. A bunch of great-looking young women danced onto a set to a very bouncy tune and – with lots of smiles and giggles and inno-cent teasing – stripped down to their Dims. It ran first in cinemas, then on television. Because it was fun and not sexually threatening – in other words, there was no bumping and grinding – the French took it in their stride. It obviously appealed to men. But it also had a certain appeal to women and was the vanguard in a wave of unisex underwear, which culminated with companies like Calvin Klein designing men's-style jockey shorts for women.

To sell the power of outdoor advertising, the French hoard-ing company Avenir put up huge posters of a young woman in a green bikini with the headline, 'On 2 September I'm tak-ing off the top.' On the date in question, that poster was replaced by one in which she was wearing only the bottoms. Now the headline read, 'On 4 September I'm taking off the bottoms.' Two days later the much-awaited third poster arrived, this one showing her nude from the back, with the headline, 'Avenir, posters that keep their promises.' It worked in France, would probably worry people in England, would never happen in America and would constitute a capital offence in much of the Third World.

Not long ago a certain bottled drink was shooting a com-mercial with a gorgeous model in the middle of the desert. On the surface, the spot was supposed to say, here's a way to quench your thirst in extreme heat. Beneath the surface was the idea of a woman, vulnerable, who will somehow be con-quered by this drink. And just so that the message didn't run too far below the surface, the model was directed in no uncer-tain terms to hold the bottle and drink from it exactly as if she was performing oral sex.

If nothing else, sex does tend to get the public's attention.

Molson's, Canada's largest brewery, found itself on the front pages for a commercial no one had seen, when the press learned that a 30-second television spot for Molson's Dry beer featured an overtly homosexual theme.

A man in a bar buys a beer for a woman. Just then, another woman enters and the two women share a passionate kiss. The man's reaction is to order another beer, this time for himself.

An earlier version of the commercial was rejected by the Ontario Liquor Board who, by law, vet these things. Alcoholic beverages cannot be seen to be a catalyst to a pick-up, so the board said no. The spot was re-edited. Apparently, the kiss was never a problem. At least not for the Liquor Board. All sorts of conservative, family values groups did however voice their objections. Molson's promise to test the spot with focus groups before putting it on the air simply kept the story in the papers, feeding the public's curiosity. Toronto's gay community announced that it was refreshing to see advertising pushing back the boundaries a little. But breweries have been targeting the gay market for years, and some of them regularly run candidly homosexual ads in the gay press. What Molson's did was different. They purposely used lesbian imagery because it worked on two levels. It said to the gay market, we recognize you. And, at the same time, it appealed to the brewer's mainstream market by playing to male heterosexual fantasies.

One of the most lasting examples of how sex sells came out of the 1960s, when a copywriter named Shirley Polykoff, working at Foote, Cone, Belding in New York, set out to sell Clairol.

It was a hair-colouring product that wasn't doing terribly well, Polykoff remembers. 'Redheads used to be the thing in those days. I guess this was about 1964. But men have always had a fascination for blondes. The problem in those days with hair colouring was that most of them weren't too great.'

By her own admission, she herself had mousy brown hair and, like many women, wanted to lighten the colour of it. There were already all sorts of ways of doing that, including using lemon. But there was also a social stigma attached to dyeing hair. Bleach blonde meant bawdy. What she realized when she took on the campaign was that, in order to get Clairol accepted, she'd need to reassure women that no one would know.

So she went out and found a bunch of beautiful young models, lightened their hair and used the headline, 'Does she or doesn't she? Only her hairdresser knows for sure.'

On one level, it appeared as if the ad was asking whether or not the woman colours her hair. On another more subtle level, the ad was wondering if the woman was sexually active. The tagline said outright that her hair colouring was so good, only someone who intimately knows her hair can tell for certain. The tagline suggested that her hairdresser is the only other person who knows her true sexual history.

At first, several major magazines refused to take the ad, claiming that, by putting a question mark in the headline, it was too obviously a reference to the young models' sexual appetite. To placate them, Polykoff re-shot the picture, putting a young child in there with the women, making it seem less sexual. But *Life* magazine still found the ad suggestive, this in an era that seems now remarkably innocent. Polykoff suggested that the *Life* editors should show the ad to all the secretaries in the office and ask them if they thought there was a double meaning in the headline. *Life* fell for it, never realizing what Polykoff knew, that no young woman would ever – at least, not in that era – admit to seeing the double meaning.

Since then, Diet Rite Cola tried to make fun of sex by showing a great-looking woman in a bikini with the headline, 'Men have one-track minds', and under it a can of their soda with the headline, 'Women have taste.'

In 1979 Calvin Klein put a 15-year-old Brooke Shields into a pair of skintight jeans and had her say, 'You know what comes between me and my Calvins? Nothing!' The innuendo being, obviously, that here was a teenage girl with no underwear. The campaign itself made news, giving Klein that much more exposure for his jeans.

Next, he used a male model in a fairly explicit underwear ad. That was followed by a campaign using the waif-like Kate Moss. In one ad she posed nude with a dog. In another, she was topless with a black eye, suggesting that she'd just been involved in some sort of sexual violence.

Both times, sex double-bounced the campaigns. They became news stories in their own right and the subjects of editorials. In order to illustrate those stories and those editorials, newspapers and magazines reprinted the ads.

When Klein tried it yet again in 1995, this time using spreads of extremely young and sexually ambiguous models, he wound up being accused by critics of promoting child pornography. The American Family Association demanded to know the models' ages and subsequently petitioned Attorney General Janet Reno to investigate whether or not Klein had violated any laws. No charges were filed but he definitely got a lot of attention.

Less controversial, but no less effective, was the modern variation on Clairol's cerebral approach from Impulse Body Spray.

Their T spot centered on a nude male artist's model getting turned on by a beautiful young art student when she walks by wearing the scent. 'Men just can't help acting on Impulse,' the announcer says.

And, just so that everyone gets the idea, a feather floats upwards and a clock's minute hand abruptly moves one notch higher.

CHAPTER FIVE

Smart Sell

There is no such thing as soft sell and hard sell. There is only smart sell and stupid sell.

Charles Browder, then president of BBDO

That so few people openly admit to being influenced by advertising seems to suit the advertising industry just fine. No one in the business may say as much, but they know that, in this case, ignorance is profit. After all, much like one of the tenets of propaganda, the less we know about any force trying to influence us, the less capable we are of defending ourselves from it.

At first glance, anyway, advertising appears to have taken more than just one lesson out of the political propaganda textbook.

Name calling is a typical propaganda technique. The idea is to create a negative reaction towards a person or a group solely through the use of symbols projected onto him or them – as in placards decrying 'Commie fascist pig'. Name calling is a typical advertising technique. The idea is to create a positive reaction towards a person or a group solely through the use of symbols projected onto him or them – as in sweatshirts emblazoned 'Yves Saint Laurent.'

Transfer is another. In propaganda, it's all about politicians wrapping themselves in the flag, transferring everything that a flag symbolizes onto them. In advertising, it's all about wrapping perfume bottles and menswear in the flag, transferring everything that a flag symbolizes onto Ralph Lauren and Tommy Hilfiger.

Politicians are fond of using the 'plain folks' gag as part of their spiel, talking about how it was back home when he or she was growing up poor. How does that differ from soft-focus images in a magazine of a long-ago childhood kitchen with a box of Kellogg's Cornflakes sitting on the table?

The opposite of plain folks is anything-but-plain folks, an approach usually known as snob appeal. In political propaganda it was once about gathering support for the creation of a master race. In advertising it's a bottle of Piper-Heidsieck champagne, with its bright red label and the words, 'Red is not the colour of innocence'.

Join-the-bandwagon is widely used in politics to entice voters to cast their vote not for the best candidate but for the winning candidate. It's exactly like 'If you're not a millionaire yet, perhaps you're not clicking the right buttons' – Dow Jones News/Retrieval.

Arguably, the most powerful political rallying cry is fear. Ban guns, the National Rifle Association warns, and only bad guys will have guns. In essence, it is the same as, 'If you had started using Night Repair in 1982, your skin wouldn't look 15 years older today' – Estée Lauder. Does it matter if you call the NRA's message advertising and Estée Lauder's propaganda? Certainly not any more than it matters whether or not either message is true. Both sell.

Yet there are also distinct differences between political propaganda and advertising and it is in those differences where advertising proves more powerful.

Thanks mostly to the minute scrutiny of the media, politicians are recurrently seen as haughty, contemptuous and, in many cases, completely untrustworthy. Thanks mostly to the huge pool of creative talent that has come into the ad business since the 1960s, the Pillsbury Dough Boy, the actress with the washing-up liquid and the supermarket manager in the television commercial who squeezes the toilet paper have sort of become our friends.

Politicians make us angry.

Commercials make us laugh.

Political messages get clouded with our perception of the baggage they bring to the encounter.

Commercial messages have neat little jingles that we can hum inside our own head.

Consequently, many of us tar all political candidates and all their messages – regardless of doctrine – with the same cynical brush, disdainful of their claims and often completely dismissive of their promises. At the same time, because commercials seem harmless enough, we allow them to float past us and, almost stealthlike, penetrate our defences.

Consider the notion that the weakness of political propaganda and the strength of advertising come down to one-man-one-vote.

Politically, it seems that every election year commentators remark on an observable trend towards voter apathy. It is true that a shockingly small percentage of any democracy's entire population actually elects its leader. Since World War II most American Presidents have been put into office by fewer than 20% of the entire population. In Britain's parliamentary system and France's hybrid presidential system – where, in both cases, more than two parties are active – the percentages are even smaller. Understandably, many people believe they have been disenfranchised from the process and that, in the end, their vote doesn't really matter.

Commercially, each vote definitely counts. That's reflected by what gets tossed into our shopping basket. What's more, the election doesn't take place every four or five years, it's happening all the time, every day.

If Kodak's electoral campaign is successful, we will buy Ektachrome instead of Agfa. If Chicken of the Sea wins our vote, we will buy their canned tuna and not Safeway's. By the same token, if Nike loses our trust, confidence, friendship or favour, we can make our objections heard – and gain instant gratification in the process – by purchasing Adidas.

Seeing advertising, then, as a form of political propaganda – call it smart sell and think of it as the culmination of all those years learning which buttons to push and how to push them – might be one way to build defences against it.

Years ago, there was a cute little film based on the story of a soda bottle falling out of an aeroplane and into the midst of a primitive jungle tribe in darkest Africa. The tribespeople didn't know about planes and didn't know about soda, so when this thing came down from the heavens they began worshipping it as a sign from the Gods.

Smart sell tries to manage the same trick.

'Like any other kind of hypnoid suggestion,' believed psychologist Erich Fromm, 'it [the ad making the smart sell pitch] tries to impress its objects [us] emotionally and then make them [us, again] submit intellectually.'

Put another way, smart sell doesn't waste time appealing to reason but, instead, goes straight for the emotional jugular. It is, if you will, much like a Sunday morning church sermon, comforting the indisposed, rattling the complaisant and never giving anyone in the congregation enough time to think, hey this is really nothing more than someone's discarded cola bottle.

The essence of smart sell is the claim.

The key to demystifying smart sell is in dissecting that claim.

Whether it be on radio or television, in newspapers or magazines, on billboards or popped through the front door as junk mail, it is the claim that tells us why the product is unique, how we cannot live without it, how the simple purchase of it will make us taller, hairier, thinner, sexier, able to dance like Fred Astaire and capable of singing like Pavarotti.

The claim is the serum the advertiser is trying to inject into our bloodstream in order to alter our perception of life. Everything else is the hypodermic needle.

Like serums, there are those that actually work and those that merely pretend to. Some are outright lies. Some tell the downright truth. Most, however, lie somewhere in the middle, like something out of *Alice in Wonderland*, making words mean whatever they want the words to mean.

Although there are as many categories of claims as there are pundits, critics, commentators, analysts and faultfinders of advertising, they generally fall into six basic categories.

First is the 'Qualified' claim.

A broad-brush statement, it appears to say something very positive, but hidden inside it is some sneaky little, otherwise harmless-looking qualifier that keeps the claim from being an outright lie.

Qualifiers such as: 'helps', which doesn't mean the product actually accomplishes what we're supposed to think it does; 'can be', which doesn't mean it is; 'better than', which doesn't mean best of all; 'best you can buy', which doesn't mean the product actually works; 'as much as', which doesn't mean more than; and 'fights', which doesn't mean wins. And claims such as:

—'So clean it's virtually spotless' – Cascade Gel Dishwashing Detergent. Virtually? How about totally?

—'We guarantee the next 50 years will be just as original' – Hewlett Packard. As original as what?

—'Five delicious varieties of pizza. All around five grams of fat' – Healthy Choice. Around five grams of fat? Does that mean six? seven? nine? And what about the small print at the bottom of the ad that goes on to qualify the word 'around' by pointing out it only counts if you take 'one average serving.'

—'Increases skin moisture by 200%' – Vaseline Intensive Care. Isn't that called sweat?

Second is the 'Loaded Dice' claim.

This is one in which a product is compared with something else, presumably a competitor, customarily unnamed and invariably unfairly. For instance:

—'Doctor-preferred sleep ingredient' – Sominex. Does this mean it puts more doctors to sleep than anything else, including sex?

—'Crest Toothpastes prevent more cavities each day than any other brand' – Crest. How on earth can anyone measure that? Are they saying it's the largest-selling brand and therefore the most used? But largest-selling brand doesn't mean it's the most used and, anyway, best-selling toothpaste isn't the same as best toothpaste.

—'Gives clothes the most fluffy softness' – Downy Softener. The most fluffy? Compared with what?

—'You can always count on Aunt Jemima pancakes to cook up light, fluffy and delicious' – Aunt Jemima Brands. Which means, the others don't. But, fluffy again? Pass the Downy.

Claim three is 'Uniqueness'.

This ploy hovers around the claim, 'We're Better Because We're Different.' The idea is that we will automatically agree with the assumption that different means better and not think too hard about how the same claim – often phrased as a variation on the line, 'There's nothing else like it' – applies to Beethoven's Fifth Symphony as easily as it does to rap music.

Another way this claim is made is by giving some added ingredient a fancy technical name, suggesting that any other product not featuring this added ingredient is inferior. Left unsaid is that the named additive is trade marked and therefore exclusive to that brand. A good example is Goodyear's 'Polyglass'. Competitors might have a similar kind of fibre-glass belt built into their tyres, and those tyres might even be better than Goodyear's, but Goodyear own the word so no one else can make the claim that their tyres contain Polyglass. All Goodyear has to do is get us to respond to the need for Polyglass in our tires and there's nowhere else to go but to the Goodyear store. Of course, the claim itself has nothing to do with which tyre is actually better. That's left to us to take for granted.

'We're Better Because We're Different' claims include:

—'All Chevron gasolines have the exclusive Techron additive.' Tony the Tiger in drag?

—'Not all great wine cellars are underground' – Delta Airlines. Yeah, but when was the last time your wine cellar lost your luggage?

—'The jewels of Cartier Ltd are mounted and set by British craftsmen on their premises.' Same goes for Lymeswold cheese.

Claim four is 'So What?', so named because certain facts are juxtaposed in a way that is supposed to impress us but that can, given one quick yank, quickly unravel. The Coach leather goods people ran an ad not long ago which showed an attractive young woman and one of their bags. The tagline was, 'Thomas Edison's great granddaughter, Lizabeth Sloane, with her Coach Manor Bag.' Wow, what could be better than that? The Wizard of Menlo Park and his granddaughter and her purse and . . . huh?

You can get the same reaction out of ads that boast long-standing traditions, such as, 'Patek Philippe, watchmakers to ladies since 1839'. The watches happen to be good but the fact that the company began in 1839 doesn't guarantee that, any more than seeing something like 'Union Pacific – The Railroad that brought you the California Gold Rush in 1849' is any reason to give up flying. That said, as long as they can put the claim in some form that keeps us from saying so what?, they've got a chance to sell us something. For instance:

—'When you read a newspaper on Air France, it's not your neighbour's.' Gee, what about those of us who worry more about getting somewhere safely and on time?

—'Women know' – Tampax. Thank goodness there aren't any men working for that company.

—'Sometimes touchable hair needs more than just a touch of conditioner' – Finesse Deep Fortifying Conditioner. Huh? What about shampoo? Haircuts? Baseball hats? Clairol?

—'For a perfect fit all day. Jockey – Genuine Underwear for Women.' Of course, it helps if she doesn't wear his size.

—'Man? Woman? Does it matter?' – Ultra Dry Deodorant. First unisex jockey shorts, now unisex deodorant.

Closely related to 'So What?' is claim five, known as 'Say that again?'

This is one in which, unless you read it or hear it a second time, you're likely to accept at face value whatever the advertiser says. Instead of being based on juxtaposition, it hangs almost entirely on vagaries well put together (some-times called sophistry) – sentences that sound wonderful but don't actually mean anything. For instance:

—'If oestrogen is the answer, why are there so many questions?' – Lilly Pharmaceuticals. Are they suggesting that if oestrogen isn't the answer, there would be fewer questions?

—'No wonder the English have kept cool for 192 years' – Gordon's Gin. Anybody ever notice the weather in Birmingham?

—'Life is best played without a script' – Guerlain Perfumes. Would they say the same thing about a shopping list?

—'For the office at home, here is the solution: No office' – Apple Computers. Buy one quick because tomorrow there might be no Apple.

—'This is the hairspray to love if you hate hairsprays' – Pantene Pro-V. As if there's something wrong with going through life hating hairsprays.

—'Dear Head. Couldn't agree with you more. Regards, Heart.' – Volvo. Does the claim lose anything if you change Volvo to vulva?

Finally there is number six, the 'Flattery' claim.

'You can follow the flattery,' advises Leslie Savan, 'by asking, who's being praised for qualities they probably don't possess?' Do that, and the ad's power disintegrates. An obvious example, she cites, is a Canada Dry TV spot that featured a white teenager playing basketball with a slick, inner-city black teenager. The flattery? It's not the black kid who's being accepted into a hip, cool world. It's the white-kids-can-jump theme. How did he get there? Obviously by drinking Canada Dry. You figure it out!

Following the flattery takes you to:

—'Keeping machines in the air taught us how to stick them on the ground. Saab, beyond the conventional.' Believe this and you too can be as sexy as a jet fighter pilot simply by paying for the car named after the fighter plane.

—'To the vows we make' – Tiffany & Co. Believe this and the vows become love, honour, obey and pamper.

—'That little voice that's been telling you to diversify overseas just started hollering' – Janus Funds. Believe this and you'll let everyone else build hotels on the purple properties while you set off to own the world.

Following the flattery also leads you to:

—'Nothin' says lovin' like somethin' from the oven' – Pillsbury. Bake to show your kids you care.

—'Breakfast of champions' – Wheaties. Eat this every morning and you don't have to bother breaking the four-minute mile.

—'Victorious. That's how you feel behind the wheel' – GMC Yukon. Wheaties are cheaper.

—'To go off-road, you've gotta have backbone' – Suzuki. Is the opposite being a coward and driving a Rolls?

—'We spend $3.5 billion a year to ensure our vision of the future matches yours' – Fujitsu. Does that include global warming, famine in Africa and the end of the rain forests?

*

Smart sell lives.

But, to all intents and purposes, the modern age of 'advertising as manipulator' reached its pinnacle late on Sunday afternoon, 22 January 1984, in Tampa, Florida, during the second quarter of Super Bowl XVIII, with the Los Angeles Raiders leading the Washington Redskins in what would eventually prove to be the most lopsided game in the American football championship's history. The Raiders won 38–9.

Unbeknownst to the 72,920 fans in the stadium – who, when that particular time-out was called on the field, were ordering hot dogs or buying beer or just taking a stretch in the winter sunshine – a technician sitting in one of the huge air-conditioned caravans parked outside Tampa Stadium, pushed a button to roll a commercial.

The result was the ultimate technique.

And, almost ironically, it hung largely on an abstraction of propaganda.

The numbers 1984 came onto the screen. Then a long shot of huge buildings appeared, connected by a tunnel, through which very tiny and very dim figures were marching. As they got closer, they looked like prisoners, with shaved heads, ill-fitting uniforms and heavy-soled boots. Suddenly, a quick cut showed a beautiful blonde woman in red shorts and a white shirt, running through the tunnel. Just as suddenly, she had gone. The prisoners were there again, then came another shot of her, this time being chased by storm troopers in helmets. Then it was back to the prisoners sitting dehumanized in front of a huge TV screen, being lectured to by an enormous electronic image of Big Brother.

Almost hypnotized, they listened to him talk about celebrating the first glorious anniversary of the information purification repentance. They listened to him describing his world as, 'One people with one will, one resolve, one cause.' They listened to him warning, 'Our enemies shall talk themselves to death and we will bury them with their own confusion. We shall prevail . . .'

That's when the blonde woman reappeared.

Suddenly, she hurled a sledgehammer at the giant TV screen, shattering it in a massive explosion.

Now, against the faces of the stunned prisoners, these words came onto the screen: 'On January 24th, Apple Computers will introduce Macintosh and you will see why 1984 won't be like "1984".'

Created by Lee Clow at the Chiat/Day Agency in Los Angeles, and directed by Ridley Scott – whose highly polished style was so evident in films such as *Blade Runner* and *Alien* – the commercial was shot in England, featured British skin-heads as the prisoners, lasted 60 seconds and was shown only once. It cost around $800,000 to make and about $1 million to put on television. In those days, that was a lot of money. Which is why it came close to never being seen.

It was a critical time for Apple. They were going up against IBM and David hadn't beaten Goliath since the Bible. Because corporate boards sometimes look at things from a stock-holder's point of view, Steve Jobs and Stephen Wozniak suddenly got nervous about spending so much money on a commercial that was going to air only one time and wouldn't even show the product.

They decided to pull out.

But the commercial was finished and Clow had already bought the airtime.

Jobs is said to have offered to Wozniak, 'I'll pay for half of it out of my checking account if you'll pay for the other half.' So Clow made the call to see if he could get them out of it. But when they learned that the best they could get for the airtime, at such a late date was 50 cents in the dollar, Jobs and Wozniak gave in and said, run it.

'We knew we were doing something kind of cool and daring while we were making it,' Clow says. 'But we didn't know it would end up being as neat as it ended up being.'

In fact, it is generally regarded by people in the business as the best commercial ever made.

'We did a story board that was fairly close to what we shot,' Clow goes on. 'Scott took it to the next level in terms of creating Orwellian people and the lines they were marching in and the TV monitors and the big screen. Actually, Ridley almost took us down another path. He had this idea that they all lived in Quonset huts and walked through mud, and it sounded to us a little too much like something out of Nazi Germany, and that wasn't the right thing to do. But we agreed that the futuristic people are all mind controlled and that Big Brother telling them what to do is the metaphor for Big Blue, you know, IBM, controlling you with their computers versus your having the ability to control your own future with an Apple computer.'

Because it was so different, and so good, and shown during the Super Bowl, which guaranteed a colossal audience, Apple got a huge double-bounce.

'We got tons of mileage because the news talked about it as having upstaged the game and for the next week they ran it over and over again on shows just to talk about it. Of course, part of this had to do with the fact that Apple was, and is, a fascinating company. The media was fascinated with what Apple was doing and with the commercial.'

Some people say it worked because it was directed by Ridley Scott, or because Chiat/Day spent a fortune to make it, or because it upstaged the Super Bowl and got turned into a news story. But Clow believes those were just the tactics.

'It worked because it was such a special moment in time. It's rare in this business that we get a chance to introduce a product nobody else makes that could change the world. Of course, it helped that we came up with a commercial that did not look anything like a computer commercial. And it was lucky timing that we could tap into 1984 and that Orwellian notion. But it worked because all the stars were lined up, everything was right at the same time, which is almost impossible to do. Having a product as unusual and amazing as Macintosh, having a client like Steve Jobs who wanted us to do something that didn't look like business machine or computer advertising, having a date that correlated with the perfect metaphor, having a media vehicle like the Super Bowl where three-quarters of the country are watching, having the business world all with their eyes on this interesting company which was competing with IBM, so many things were all there for us. All those factors came into play at the same time.'

The commercial did everything it was supposed to do and arguably, because all of the various forces came together at precisely the right instant, did it better than any other advertisement – at least on film or tape – has ever done. It went as far as any ad could go.

It also brought the business back full circle. From advertising that pushed buttons because it didn't look like a commercial – Kodak's 'Turn Around Little Girl' – to advertising that pushed buttons because it was a work of art.

From that point forward, advertising's power was defined.

From that point forward, it became increasingly obvious that button pushing had reached a pinnacle.

The next step, if there was to be one, would depend not on anyone's creativity – not on Madison Avenue's ability to recognize buttons or on its skill in pushing them – but on technology.

On new research.

On new marketing tools.

On what would come tomorrow.

In 1984, everything lined up for Apple, almost by accident. But the game has now become so big – and is getting bigger all the time – that accidents are no long a bankable option.

In 1984, the time when the manipulation equation could begin to be completed by anything but lucky stars seemed a long way off.

Today, it is tomorrow.

CHAPTER SIX

More Than Simple Research

Advertising is not a soloist. It is a member of an ensemble of all those activities that can be classified under the general head of marketing, and it must do its part in harmony with them.

Leo Burnett

Advertising moves people toward goods.

But it is marketing that moves goods toward people.

Both a managerial concept and a corporate discipline, marketing is a company's ability to satisfy the requirements of its customers, to put its goods or services within reach of customers and, eventually, to procure sales. In this case, success can be judged in real numbers – turnover and profit.

If internationally recognized brands such as McDonald's, Kellogg's and Sony are universally accepted, it is because they have understood the markets in which they operate and have conditioned us, as their customers, into paying for their products.

If internationally recognized failures such as Edsel, New Coke and Sir Clive Sinclair's C5 electric car have become synonymous with fiasco, it is because they failed to identify a need for the product. Or they failed to satisfy that need. Or they simply failed to convince us that the product was something we wanted to spend our money on.

Where once there were two approaches guiding marketing research – an analysis of markets and consumers, and a bundle of borrowed theories from various related sciences, notably psychology and sociology – today's research has been refined and, in turn, melded into a more common tactic.

The business equivalent of military intelligence in a war with global markets at stake, demands on research are driving it further than being just a means of identifying opportunities, sussing out the power of the competition, and quantifying our desires and buying habits. Research is now being asked to formulate a tactic that will hold sway over the design, distribution, advertising and sale of a product.

Consider the idea that, if any art form can be seen as a vision of the future, and if technology is the means through which any art form produces that vision, then the future must often wait for technology before visions of it can be painted.

One argument might go: Until Johannes Gutenberg invented movable type, there could be no such thing as the novel. Without novels, there would almost certainly be no such thing as cinema. Without cinema, there might never have been enough mass imagination about space travel to vault man onto the moon.

Another certainly goes: Until computers sat on every desk and modems sat inside every computer and digital replaced analog, manipulation as an art form would have remained frozen in time.

That the world has changed radically since 1984 is an understatement. That with it has come the possibility of discovering radical solutions to formerly unsolvable problems is manifestly apparent in all sorts of new sciences that are being developed to determine more accurately what-where-why-when-how we buy, who is buying and, just as importantly, who is not buying.

Fuelled by corporate demand, 'consumer sciences' is being nurtured by academia, where university marketing departments and advertising departments and schools of mass communications have grown up to underpin major, well-funded disciplines, a long way from what they were in the in-depth days – minor courses taught in the back rooms of Business Studies departments.

From campuses to commerce, psychologists, number crunchers, pollsters, trend analysts, feedback response examiners and interviewers – by phone, by mail, by face-to-face intercepts on the street – have taken the $12 million industry of Dichter's day and turned it into a $4 billion business in the United States and Europe.

Ominously, somewhere there is someone looking into every nook and cranny of our lives.

Roper Starch Worldwide compiles a consumer lifestyles, attitudes and marketplace behaviour database, and includes a specific study of trends exhibited by today's youth. Equifax National Decision Systems combines consumer demand with demographic data divided into postal codes. Claritas targets consumer segments using 62 demographically and behaviourally diverse categories to define every neighbourhood in the United States. BDRC does a survey of British hotel guests and also monitors customer vulnerability in various financial markets.

A consulting firm called PeopleTalk specializes in video-taping people's cupboards to see what they buy and what they actually use. Another sneaks tiny cameras inside frozen-food compartments in supermarkets to chart the eye movements of shoppers in the hopes of determining better placement for high-margin items. Beaufort Research surveys Welsh speakers. A company called Percept specializes in providing strategic information to church leaders in a survey they call 'The Hearts and Minds of America's People'. Langer Associates specialize in qualitative studies, through focus groups and telephone interviews, to produce their report on lifestyle trends. Trans Union produces lifestyle segmentation studies based on individual credit behaviour. PMSI studies the British healthcare market. Donnelley Marketing maintains a consumer file on over 90 million households and can segment that information in a myriad of ways, including by hobby, disposable income, magazine subscribers, book interests, occupation and whether or not someone in that household orders things by mail.

Leisure Trends charts what consumers do when they're not working. Management Horizons does surveys on shopping attitudes, which include such areas as fashion and crime at malls. Produce Studies Group Ltd collects data on agricultural distribution and machinery. The Mendelsohn Media Research Company produces a survey of households with incomes in excess of $100,000 a year. GfK Marketing Services has conducted retail studies on the British car care market. Teenaged Research tracks brand use, purchase behaviour and media preferences of 12–19 year olds. The Zandl Group goes a little further, looking exclusively at 8–24 year olds. Yankelovich Partners publish studies with segment-specific reports on African Americans, Hispanics, Asian Americans, senior citizens and teenagers. They also cover Europe, Canada, Japan and Australia.

If the in-depth research of the 1950s was roller-skates, and if today's research is the Concorde, then tomorrow's will be the Starship Enterprise.

These days, we all live in glass houses.

The seeds of tomorrow's research were sown in the roller-skate days. As scientists evolved theories to move away from their 'in-depth' origins, they sermonized that advertising was just one of many tools, albeit an important tool, in a complex marketing mix and, if great marketing was ever going to happen, it would not be because of great button-pushing but rather as a direct consequence of great number-crunching.

For the Young Turk copywriters and graphic artists who'd grown up with television – and who would, in turn, inspire an entire generation of artists to create Pop – marketing was all about button-pushing, and that was a strictly visceral thing. It wasn't anything accountants could understand. Only artists could summon up those juices.

It was left to the agency executives – those older guys on their way out – to convince their clients that it was more like a combination of both. And to give those older guys their due, advertising research was then, is now and has always been just that.

At least, Jerry Della Femina, these days an older guy, says so. 'I was always heavy on research. At the same time, I am visceral. But I would never tell someone that they should spend their money just because I had a gut feeling. Anyway, I don't call it research, I prefer to call it pre-search. If you do it right, you can learn a great deal about what it is that makes something work. If everyone has a button, then what you do is try to find that universal thing that will press everyone's button at the same time.'

The process begins with a whole slew of ideas. 'I've never believed that there is only one answer. I have never said to a client, this is it, take it or leave it. If you start with several concepts that you think should be on target and do your pre-search, show them to focus groups, then you can see what works and how effective it is. Focus groups are very important. They've been my education. I've learned more from focus groups than anything else.'

A focus group is 30 or 40 or 50 people you don't know, guinea pigs, crammed into a screening room, perhaps sedated with some wine and cheese, then shown videos – they don't even have to know what the product is – and asked to fill out a questionnaire. After they've gone home, the agency folk sit around for the rest of the night trying to figure out what their responses mean. It's a standard rite in product testing, especially popular with ads, movies and TV shows. In the old days, if the focus group gave you a thumbs down, the product might have been axed. These days, it's not about yes or no, it's about did we touch the buttons we were aiming for and, if not, what do we have to do to touch them by tomorrow night when we bring in another 30 or 40 or 50 guinea pigs?

'We aren't caught up in research today they way everyone used to be,' Della Femina goes on. 'We no longer consider it the Gospel. Clients are starting to think and listen. That wasn't true before, but it is today because clients are more knowledgeable and more sophisticated today. Everyone is. We take advantage of research rather than use it as a weapon. Think of it like a disaster check. Even if the focus group tells you that they don't especially like the commercials, you can run them anyway as long as the focus group hasn't said they hate the commercials to the point that they're going to burn down the corporate headquarters.'

Case in point. Della Femina's focus groups were asked to test the concept of Permalens, an extended-wear contact lens. He'd written a line that promised users could keep the lenses in their eyes for 14 days before taking them out to clean them. But, in the first four focus groups, the response came back that the people in the group wouldn't buy the product.

'They kept telling us that they didn't want to keep the lenses in their eyes 14 days. They said, what if I keep them in my eyes for 16 days, am I going to go blind? And what happens if I take them out in three days? So, after the fourth focus group, I changed the copy. Instead of saying you can keep them in your eyes for 14 days, I wrote, you can keep them in your eyes for up to two weeks. Now, I happen to think that two weeks is 14 days, but the people in the fifth focus group decided they liked that better. They said, that's a great product and sure we'll buy it. Fourteen days scared people. Up to two weeks reassured them. That made the difference.'

Today, with so much money at stake in the fate of every product brought to market, the gathering of research – or pre-search, if you will – has become a worldwide, multi-billion dollar industry. In turn, the interpretation of what those researchers discover has become a bubbling cauldron for the manipulators.

Take, for instance, the games that can be played with quantitative analysis.

Relying on statistics and percentages, research results can be made to say anything anyone wants. Case in point: 'Eighty per cent of the women we spoke to said that Brand X had changed their lives.' To the unsuspecting, an 80% acceptance rating might be impressive. But who were those women and where did they come from? Is that 80,000 out of 100,000 or just four out of five? And what would you think about the statistic if you found out that all of the women surveyed happen to work in Brand X's factory? What would that statistic be if you spoke to women who worked in Brand Y's head office? Does 'changed their lives' necessarily mean for the better? What did the other 20% say? How were the questions posed? If the possible answers were 'Changed my life', 'Contributed to my death', and 'No opinion', what would the percentages be if you asked, would you buy the product more than once?

Statistics here become the story of the man on a beach staring at a woman in a bikini. What he sees is important. What remains hidden is fundamental.

That qualitative analysis is much the same was perfectly illustrated in a 1960s' spoof report on eggs. After detailed study, researchers concluded that eggs were an unsaleable product. Not only did they all look alike, but because they couldn't stand up on their own – and all too easily rolled away – they required special packaging. That increased unit costs and also made stacking eggs on shelves cumbersome. Then there was the unfortunate matter of the shell. The worst of both worlds, eggshells were too difficult to open but too easy to break.

Thirty years later, the same report would have included the additional caveat that eggs were high in all the wrong kinds of cholesterol, which made them unhealthy. Except that, 30 years later, all those problems had been solved with products like Egg-O, which eliminated the shells and the cholesterol and, by virtue of being a powder in a box, also stacked well on shelves.

It's one thing to mislead consumers with statistics. That's sometimes called marketing. It's another when manufacturers misinterpret their own research. That's frequently called the road to bankruptcy. So, realizing the fallibilities that come hand-in-hand with statistics, new approaches have been born out of necessity. One of them is psychographics, a series of disciplines structured to help companies discover more precisely who their clients are, who their clients aren't, how to keep the ones who are, and how to get the ones who aren't.

Its power is real.

Its goal is manipulative.

And we are the targets.

We are also, it turns out, accomplices in our own seduction. Every time we hand out any information about ourselves – which we do all the time – we are feeding databases with more details. To get a credit card, we have to reveal where we live, how much we earn, where we bank. But that's only the beginning. Every time we buy something with that credit card we leave a breadcrumb on the trail of our consumer habits. When we subscribe to record clubs or magazines, or when we send in a coupon to enter a draw to win a prize, we are giving people information about our lifestyle which is being saved, analysed and disseminated. The conclusions that companies make from the data they study affect the mail offers we receive, the telemarketing calls we get, the type of stores that open in our neighbourhood and what products go on their shelves.

Based on no more than our postal code, even an apprentice psychographic researcher can establish a great deal about us. It's called 'cluster analysis'. The idea is that, for the most part, people who live in the same neighbourhood have the same economic profile; that neighbourhoods can be sorted into groups by median income, family types, educational background, profession and age, among other categories. Full postal codes – or Zip Plus4 in the United States – pinpoint our location down to around six addresses on the same block. Such precision has been a boon for the cluster analysts, who use whatever information they can find to pigeonhole us in a batch of geo-demographically similar people.

But our postal code is the least of it. The amount of information they are able to compile and store about each of us is astonishing. And, again, the bulk of that information comes from us.

In the UK, supermarket chains Safeway, Sainsbury's and Tesco have all launched customer loyalty programmes. They are equally common in North America. It's a lead they've taken from the airline business, where frequent-flyer programmes have been a major marketing tool since the early 1980s.

When we apply for a card, we give the supermarket our name, address and phone number. In some cases they ask about family size and previous shopping habits. At the checkout, our loyalty card gets swiped, and in exchange for what we buy, we receive points that can then be converted into goods. It works out to about a 1% discount. It's better than nothing, but are they paying us for our loyalty or for the information we are otherwise supplying to them?

Armed with information about us, including a detailed list of all our shopping purchases – known as 'basket level' data – the supermarket's researchers can make certain assumptions. Because we never buy meat, fish or bread at the supermarket, they assume we deal with a butcher, a fishmonger and a baker. Because we never buy breakfast cereal, the conjecture is that we don't have children at home. We buy more pasta than might be expected for someone living alone but not as much as a family with two children, which leads to the conclusion that we have a partner. Because we buy two different brands of toothpaste, and one of them is a smokers' toothpaste, it seems logical to suppose that someone smokes cigarettes.

Little by little, as we feed information into the system, the supermarket develops a profile of us. It then doesn't take long before the research people conclude that they have a better chance of selling fresh tomato sauce to us, because they know about our pasta buying, than fresh salmon steaks, because they know that we buy fish somewhere else, or not at all. So they put together a direct mail shot, targeted especially at us, with a coupon enclosed offering two tagliatellis for the price of one if we buy a large-sized jar of their own-brand sauce. The coupon offering a 10% discount on our next purchase at the fish counter is sent to someone else.

With only a little more effort, profiling can take them even deeper into our lives. For instance, by categorizing the types of foods we do purchase, they can direct us towards some of the specific products we don't usually buy. For example, if we've shown the supermarket that we buy health-consciously, and over a period of time they see that we are buying fewer and fewer eggs, we become a prime target for a coupon offering a discount on Egg-O. If they've noticed we used to drink their own-brand cola but have recently switched to Pepsi, out goes an offer to induce us back to the store brand. Then, by combining what we purchase with where we live, they might deduce that we'd be receptive to discount theatre tickets, so they put together a marketing joint venture with a theatre promoter, selling us as a client to him.

At the same time, by matching our profile with others in our cluster, not only do they have an accurate record of what brands sell best in which clusters, they also know how far their customers travel to shop there. A researcher sitting in front of a computer screen pushes a button and up pops a series of colour-coded maps. It tells him which stores are moving which products, that our store could sell more smokers' toothpaste than Cheerios – stock levels are adjusted accordingly – and that we, in fact, did use our coupon to buy pasta sauce. The next coupon on its way to us is a special offer linking Parmesan cheese with their own-brand Chianti.

At Total Research in Princeton, New Jersey – one of the new breed of consumer investigators – they admit that they can't yet find out as much about us as they'd like to, although they do tend to find out more about us than many of us know about ourselves.

The original idea behind the system they developed called EquiTrend came to John Morton in the mid-1970s. He'd been working for a market research firm in Connecticut, doing studies for several dominant brands that he describes as 'boring and predictable'. What struck him was that so many products worried only about their rightful place in their own market category and never considered that they needed to become more highly regarded than non-competing dominant brands. In other words, Morton believed that a company such as Kodak saw Fuji, Konica and Agfa as the competition, but needed to think about their relationship in consumers' minds to other dominant brands, such as Heinz, Disney and Coca-Cola.

Trying to convince people that Coke was more like Nike than Pepsi, and that IBM was more like the *Wall Street Journal* than Apple, was a radical idea that took some selling. But by 1988, now teamed up with Total Research, he ran a small pilot programme to test the concept. Within two years, he'd refined it to the point where several major brands – Mercedes-Benz, AT&T, Johnson and Johnson, and Volvo – were signing on with Total Research to see where they actually stood in relationship to each other. From there, Morton began to assess the relationship between brands and consumers. Out of that, he and Total Research were able to develop EquiTrend into the principal research source of brand equity segmentation.

His contention is, we are what we buy. 'We each express who we are through the brands we use. They are like a fashion accessory. They become our identity.'

Rather than ask us why we buy something, EquiTrend records our evaluations of hundreds of different things – airlines, running shoes, media outlets, fashion, coffee, insurance, hotels, investment services, vitamins, soft drinks, appliances, restaurants, stores, petrol, even celebrities. The results are fed into computers that synthesize the information to determine the nature of the judgements they are making.

Because most of us make judgements that are subjective and irrational – and often subconscious – our motives for any particular purchase may be so obscure that even we can't accurately verbalize them. So it's down to EquiTrend to delve into our 'decision model'. As Morton explains, 'We have people rate 300–400 properties that are scientifically selected. We present them with long lists – say it includes, Arnold Schwarzenegger, Kodak Film, Cream of Wheat cereal, the *New Yorker* magazine, Reeboks, the *National Inquirer* newspaper and CNN – which they are then asked to rate on a sliding scale. From that, we hope to find an underlying theme. We hope to find what makes this person different from other people. We're looking to establish what kinds of things this person likes and doesn't like and then project what he will, or will not, like from that.'

Each item is judged on quality – because they've found quality judgements to be predictive of behaviour – using a rating system of 0–10, where 10 is outstanding and extraordinary quality, the middle 5 represents quite acceptable quality, and 0 is poor, unacceptable quality. The numbers in between become degrees of those ratings. There is also the possibility of saying no opinion of the brand at all. The results are then used to type people, through a process that is technically called 'factor analysis', into one of seven main categories that Total Research uses to classify American consumers.

Start with 'Conformists'.

These are people who, no matter what product they are asked about, will prefer the dominant, mainstream, well-accepted brand. If it's film, they'll judge Kodak to be much better than any other. If it's a telephone service, they'll opt for AT&T. If it's a celebrity, they'll prefer big, conventional stars such as Harrison Ford, Kevin Kostner, Demi Moore and Julia Roberts. These are people who are keeping up with the Joneses, who believe brand is more important than price and that dominant brands mean reliability. They think of themselves as hardworking members of the middle class, eat Campbell's soup, wear Levi's jeans, love Bill Cosby and Frank Sinatra, and read *Time*, *Sports Illustrated*, *People* and *Reader's Digest*. Their television comes from the main networks and their favourite programmes included 'Cheers' and 'Jeopardy'. Demographically, 61% are 20–39 years old and 57% have some university education.

By characterizing people this way, their future purchase decisions can become predictable.

'And yet,' John Morton insists, 'if you sit down with Conformists and ask them what motivates their behavior, they'll give you all kinds of answers. The thing about selecting the dominant brand in any given category may not even come up. Most of the time it doesn't come up. They're not aware of it themselves. They have a reason why they buy Kodak film. They'll tell you that the pictures are sharper. That you can get a good deal on it. They'll tell you that Gillette blades shave better, and that AT&T's service is better. They'll give you rational explanations for their behavior. But what they're really doing is simply wanting to follow the masses more than anything else.'

The next category is 'Intellects'.

Here are people who believe that the highest quality is always found in the most sophisticated, upmarket, technically advanced brands. They like international and exclusive products. In that way they are the opposite of Conformists. They don't want to buy something that everyone else owns. They want to be different. Although they tend to imitate other Intellects. For instance, they prefer foreign automobiles to domestic automobiles – making them prime clients for Lexus and Volvo – and drive those cars on Michelin tyres. They listen to music on Sony stereos, cook with a Cuisinart food processor, read the *Wall Street Journal* and watch the Discovery Channel.

Higher prices don't scare them off because they equate price with underlying quality. They avoid discount stores and in-store brands. Although 71% of them are the primary food shoppers for their family, they seldom use discount coupons. They admire Luciano Pavarotti, Ralph Nader, Meryl Streep and Gloria Steinem, own an expensive home computer, which they regularly update with the latest software releases, are likely to read *Architectural Digest*, *Gourmet* magazine and the *New Yorker*, will buy from a catalogue but almost never from a telephone sales pitch. Sixty per cent of the people in this category are female, most are in the 30–49 age bracket, and one-third have postgraduate degrees.

It turns out that around 80–90% of all marketing and other business executives fall into this category. These are people who often brag that they make business decisions based on their understanding of the world. However, this category represents only about 14% of the population. So, when an executive assumes the world is like him and then bases a business decision on his own experience in that world, he could be heading down a dangerous path.

Next come 'Popularity Seekers'.

Here's youthful trendiness. The newer the better. Their

main interest is in impressing their peer group and associating brand names with themselves in a way that will, they hope, make them more well liked. In that sense, they are a less mature group than the Intellects. And, in general, they're anti-establishment. They'll go for products with labels like Ralph Lauren, not for the reason the Intellects do – which is because Lauren is expensive – but because Lauren is seen to be stylish and a famous label. These are people who drive BMWs and fancy utility vehicles, drink Coke, wear Nike, and watch MTV and sports on cable.

Because just over half are 15 to 29 years old, there is an element of immaturity. It means that, if a brand can promise to make the user more attractive or more popular, the better it is judged by this group. That's why they also buy off-road bikes and video games, frequent theme parks, subscribe to on-line computer services, watch MTV, and repeat jokes they've heard on 'Saturday Night Live'. They like 'The Simpsons', 'Roseanne', Prince and M. C. Hammer.

Category four is 'Relief Seekers'.

Associating brand quality with a product's ability to uncomplicate their lives, these are people who see life as problematical and worry about a lot of things. Consequently, it's very hard for many of the brands in the survey to get a good grade with them.

'We named them Relief Seekers,' Morton says, 'because they are very positive only about certain kinds of products, such as those that create relief. They like headache remedies. They like health and beauty aids. They like anything that makes them feel better. These are people who are also very much into technology, who like to escape into the world of the computer. They like glamour-oriented and fantasy-oriented positioning. These are people who would happily whip out their credit card to buy a ticket to someplace half way around the world so that they could get away from life. Anything that's mundane or represents drudgery, like kitchen gloves or soap powder, no, they really dislike things like that.'

Argumentative and opinionated, and especially vocal about rip-offs, they frequently talk about brands in terms of whatever problems they've had with them. They buy where it is easy, which means the best department stores, preferring to pay a higher price than shop around. These are people who are receptive to the home shopping networks, drive a Honda Accord, read *Playboy* and *Cosmopolitan* magazines, carry Mastercard, and use a Nokia cellular phone.

Then there are 'Pragmatists'.

Probably the most rational of consumers, they're suspicious of anything that has a lot of brand imagery associated with it. For the most part, their priority is value for money, so in categories where there are a number of national brands, and given that the brands are basically the same, they will usually choose the least expensive. They wear Lee Jeans instead of Levi's. They buy BIC disposal razors instead of Gillette. They shop around for the best deal, then use coupons to save even more money. These are people who watch all those 'funny home video' programmes, enjoy 'Unsolved Mysteries', rent Clint Eastwood and Arnold Schwarzenegger videos, and read magazines like *Parents*, *Women's Day*, and *Family Circle*. Not surprisingly, just over half are married with children.

Naturally sceptical of many things, but especially of advertising, it's not easy to influence this group with advertising. In fact, they're the toughest of the seven to sway. That means it's also very hard to engender loyalty in them. If somebody else offers a better deal, they're gone.

By contrast, Morton says, the easiest to influence would be the Popularity Seekers. 'Come up with a catchy ad on MTV and you're pretty well set with them. In fact, just look at what's on MTV these days. People recognize that this segment exists and a lot of reputable major brands have their own special advertising that they run on MTV which makes them look a lot more irreverent and a lot more stylish than the advertising that they run elsewhere.'

The sixth group are known as the 'Sentimentals'.

Morton believes that if Total Research had been doing EquiTrend back in the 1950s or the 1960s, and took the top 20 brands from that era, those brands would be the same ones these people still prefer. They are price sensitive, which makes them loyal customers for the big discounters, tend to avoid brands that emphasize the latest technology, disfavour foreign-made products, and are not impressed with youthful style. They drink Lipton tea, buy Avon products, watch 'Wheel of Fortune' and 'Oprah', frequent McDonald's, listen to Barry Manilow and read *Good Housekeeping*. They are 62% female and are 66% over the age of 50.

'Sentimentals go for brands that other people may well consider passé or over the hill. They're very slow to adopt to new brands. They tend to be older people. I see this as the Julio Iglesias set. They are behind the times. But for brands that have passed their heyday, these people are very important because these people form the basis for whatever franchise they have left.'

The final group are known as 'Actives'.

Transactionally oriented, they want to know who's standing behind something. They don't like anonymous products and services, or anything, for that matter, about which they know very little. They want brands that are seen to 'go that extra mile' for the customer. They judge products by who stands behind the brand and how well they stand behind it. They also want to be able to speak to a representative of the company. They're looking for reputation and service from the brands they buy. They appreciate warranties and guarantees and are generally suspicious of advertising. These are people who admired Margaret Thatcher and voted for Ronald Reagan, George Bush and Dan Quayle. They get their news from the main networks and think Clint Eastwood is their kind of movie star.

They fly on American Airlines, drive Toyota 4-Runners, carry a Visa card and read *National Geographic, Ladies Home Journal, House and Garden* and *Better Homes and Gardens.* They are overwhelmingly female – about 70% – half of them are at least 50 years old, and 72% do not have children still living at home.

'Once subjects are classified into a group,' Morton continues, 'we assign a weight to each of the seven quality models, so that we can look at someone as, say, 70% Intellect, 20% Relief Seeker, 5% Active and very minorly associated with the other groups. That gives us a very accurate prediction at the individual level of how to influence somebody.'

Being able to see consumers this way, he insists, gives a company a huge advantage that it wouldn't otherwise be able to command with run-of-the-mill geo-demographics. And he cites, as an example, the company's home town of Princeton, New Jersey.

Seat of a major Ivy League university, there is no denying the school's influence. Geo-demographic surveys – which base common likes and dislikes on area, as determined by a postal code or a telephone exchange – generally assume that the entirety of Princeton is an Intellect environment. They identify the university as the dominant theme in Princeton and group common traits around that. Morton agrees there might be some truth in it, but insists there is as much, if not more, error in it because only about 45% of Princeton's population would fall into his Intellect category.

'Geo-demographics tries to tell you the traits of people by generalizing about other people in that neighbourhood. But it's a gross over-generalization. They can literally put anybody in any country into one of their segments.'

Seven years after first doing EquiTrend in the States, Total Research decided to try it in Great Britain. They polled more than 1000 people on 173 brands readily available in the UK. In several cases, British taste matched American taste, giving high ratings to Kodak, Mercedes-Benz, Levi's and Fisher Price.

Where the surveys differed greatly was in the categories Total Research assigned. Instead of seven, they used six.

'Rationals' are mostly 50–59 years old, educated beyond school age, basically male, with no children, and living in the Greater London area. They give high marks to Ericsson, Scottish Widows and Mercury, and don't like McDonald's or Mars. They read broadsheet newspapers and take both the *Sunday Times* and the *Independent on Sunday*.

'Self-gratifiers' are *Mirror* readers, generally female, under 40 and with one child. They liked McDonald's, Amstrad and Snickers, and give a thumbs down to Miele, Pirelli and Citroën.

'Functionals' are less well educated than Rationals and a few years older. They're practical and unemotional, buy Dunlop tyres, drink Heineken beer and bank at Lloyds. They read the *Financial Times* and the *Sunday Telegraph*, dislike designer labels and frequent Pizza Hut.

'Conventionals' are mostly well-educated females over 50 who shop at Safeway, insure themselves with Prudential, take the *Mail* or the *Express* and still, despite the give-away fiasco, have faith in Hoover.

'Status Seekers' are mostly men under 40 with children. This is the BMW, Sky Sports, tabloid and Reebok crowd. They fill up at an Esso pump and avoid both the Midland Bank and Homebase.

Finally there's 'Fast Trackers', the group with the biggest age spread – 20–60. They're customers for Christian Dior, Calvin Klein, *Elle*, *Esquire*, the *Guardian*, the *Mail on Sunday* and *Vogue* but not for Daz or Avon products.

The way EquiTrend sums up Britain, Marks & Spencer is the highest-rated store – it came in fifth, one spot ahead of Disney World Florida – with Legoland in 14th place, one spot higher than Sainsbury's supermarkets. Rover was 22nd – well behind Mercedes, which was first, and BMW, which was second – but still ahead of Ford, which was 47th and Vauxhall, which was 49th. Tesco supermarkets were 40th, Asda 52nd and Safeway 72nd. British Telecom came in 71st.

Significantly, not one of the big high street banks managed to make it into the top 100.

Morton says that, once a brand knows how it profiles against a segment, they can see what's working and what's not working. Knowing the group to which the brand appeals becomes a road map leading to the proper buttons to push.

'Groups are formed on how they respond to brands and properties. It means they're very homogeneous in terms of what will influence them, what will turn them on, what will turn them off. In fact, if you know you want to target a particular group, you have plenty of examples of what works for that group in terms of real life brands. And plenty of examples of what doesn't work with them, too. So you know what to do to target them. People implicitly define brand quality and those definitions have a strong effect on brand preference. Understanding that, companies can begin to increase sales, increase profit and even increase their stock market valuation. In general, each improvement in quality perception of one point on the 11-point scale coincides with about a 30% increase in unit sales.'

Therefore, if a manufacturer can change our perception of their brand to the point where it achieves an increased EquiTrend rating, they will have successfully manipulated more of us to buy the product. Because they've been shown their target, they can now manage that more easily with their advertising.

Understanding who buys what and why, says Morton, means that advertisers can reach a big proportion of any category by advertising to them in the media that fit their category. 'You know the media they like and the message that's going to turn them on. You also have numerous role models of things that are very effective. Volvo, for example, have positioned themselves dead centre on Intellects. So while Buick have totally missed the boat as far as Intellects are concerned, all they really have to do is what Volvo is doing. They can see how Volvo is appealing to people in the same group.'

There are certain messages that are effective with each of the groups. With Intellects they have to be subtle and they have to be tasteful. Advertisers wishing to reach them can't blatantly announce that their product is the upscale, snob brand. In fact, that is precisely the sort of message that turns Intellects off. Because they're looking for high levels of sophistication, they're also looking for subtle statements confirming that this is for people who are well educated and well to do.

It's a message that, at times, might also be aimed at Popularity Seekers. But that's not surprising because some messages will work across multiple groups and, in this case, Popularity Seekers are also looking for exclusive products. Where they differ from the Intellects is that they latch onto a product that will make a good impression on their peer group. Currently, brands such as Tommy Hilfiger are big with the Popularity Seekers.

Clearly Hilfiger understood that when he launched his brand in 1984. He bought $3 million worth of posters to declare, 'The 4 Great American Designers for Men Are: R—L—, P— E—, C— K—, T— H—.'

Putting himself in the same category with Ralph Lauren, Perry Ellis and Calvin Klein, he followed that with even more posters, this time proclaiming, 'First Bill. Then Perry, Then Calvin, Now Tommy.'

Having told the white middle classes that he was a designer whose clothes they could wear to make the same statement they might have been making with the other three, Hilfiger went one step further, where none of the other three had dared go. He took aim at the black street kids and said to them, I'm not just for white Popularity Seekers, I'm also a way for you to make a statement. He did that by understanding how those black kids wanted baggier garments, so he redesigned part of his line for them – staying with his red, white and blue sporting themes – and by 1994 had become the designer of choice for inner-city kids. His so-called 'street popularity' having been corroborated by singer Snoop Doggy Dogg who showed up one night on 'Saturday Night Live' in a Hilfiger rugby shirt.

Although Morton is not willing to concede that EquiTrend gives an advertiser the ability to manipulate the market, he does maintain that it offers information an advertiser would not be able to find anywhere else in market research.

'It enables an advertiser to accurately classify people by subconscious and irrational influences. The things we learn about them are things they would not willingly admit to. Not because they wouldn't want to but because they don't know what or why. But once we establish what their judgment model is, and we can then model it very accurately, we know how to influence that person. Manipulate? No. I wouldn't say that. But I guess I would say that it is a little like Big Brother, after all.'

CHAPTER SEVEN

Digging Even Deeper

There is only one valid definition of business purpose – to create a customer.

Peter Drucker, management expert

Once upon a time, anyone who thought about bringing a new product to market merely had to follow a comfortable, tried-and-true formula – observe the need for the product, plot a strategy to satisfy that need, set out design requirements, analyse how the product fits into a marketing mix, construct a prototype, test-market it and, if everything is satisfactory to that point, commercialize it.

But those seven steps aren't enough any more. The world has changed and an estimated 60–90% of all new products are guaranteed to fail.

A study conducted at the University of Pennsylvania's Wharton School of Business estimated that nearly one-third of those business failures were down to inadequate research and development. Just under one quarter were because the product idea was bad to start with. Then came wrongly anticipating costs, strategic marketing mistakes, bad timing and too much competition.

Now, leaving as little to chance as possible, a complex marketing strategy of 'matching activities' has evolved – that is, a tactic that revolves around the design of specific products to meet specific needs of specific customers with button-pushers already built in so that it is the product itself that begins the process of seducing us to buy.

In other words, businesses are demanding that researchers fashion psychological hooks that can be hidden inside lures, then baited, then dangled deep into our psyche. Cleverly managed, the result is manipulation in ways that Messrs Dichter and Vicary only dreamed of.

Colour is used in exactly this way.

Because we react to different colours in different ways, manufacturers, advertisers and retailers who understand how to use colours to suit their own purpose can regularly manipulate us.

Culturally, colours have meanings. A red heart means love, a red flag means danger, a yellow light means caution, a blue mood means sadness and green has become synonymous with ecology. In the West, we assign the qualities of purity, chastity and cleanliness to white, and relinquish magic, demons and death to black. In other cultures, white is the official colour of mourning.

But colours can also have hidden meanings, things we instinctively feel.

'Color influences us in a variety of ways,' says Donald Kaufman, one of America's foremost authorities on how colour influences our daily lives. He is also one of a growing legion of experts for hire by people who want colour to do more than simply look pleasant. 'If we are placed in a controlled light space, say a room that is red, and then all of a sudden that room is switched to blue, instantaneously our body temperature will lower. So the colour that surrounds us has a direct physical impact on us.'

It also has, he insists, a direct psychological impact on us. 'There is a universal desire for warm colours because of our universal desire for warmth. These are the colours at the red and yellow end of the spectrum. They evoke the fire by which we roasted our first meat. Red is the quintessential colour of warmth. It also evokes blood and is the colour associated with the most elemental forces of life. Apparently, it was also the first colour to be given a name, after black and white.'

Red is the most effective colour for attracting attention, which is one reason red is the most popular colour for cars, sweaters and packaging. It brings with it a universal elemental appeal. Perhaps even more important is that our eyes focus on red more sharply than any other colour. Red letters, when put against the background of another colour, appear to have crisper edges than any other colour. This is why red is widely used to sell toys to children. In fact, red is almost always the dominant colour in toy packaging. The only time another colour is used is when the fourth or fifth toy in a category needs to do something radical to break out and get noticed, so the box is blue or yellow or green.

'Our eyes focus differently on different hues,' Kaufman goes on. 'When we focus on red, we become far-sighted for blue and when we focus on blue, we're near-sighted for red. We see by contrast. Warmer colours appear to advance and cooler colours appear to recede.'

Just as reds and yellows are associated with lightness, blues are associated with darkness and shadows and, depending on how dark they are, can actually make us feel depressed.

Putting two colours together causes them to vibrate, which creates impressions of the way light performs in nature. That feeling of luminosity refers us directly back to our origins. Our natural tendency is to want to see light as a complete full spectrum, which is similar to the way we experience natural light. When fluorescent lights were originally introduced, green phosphors were the cheapest and easiest to produce. But the effect was a cold light that distorted other colours. These days, fluorescent bulbs are built to imitate natural light by using tri-phosphors made up of red, yellow and blue. People who work under that light are more productive because we perform better under a full spectrum.

We also buy more under that sort of lighting. It makes products look better and, because it is more akin to sunlight, our body responds better to it. That's why, for instance, fast food restaurants are especially conscious of their lighting and rely heavily on orange, red and pink. Those colours excite, make us eat more quickly and therefore vacate the table sooner for the next customer. In fancier restaurants, where orange, red and pink might not fit in with a more sophistic-ated decor, richer shades such as burgundy can have a similar effect. The one colour that hardly ever appears in restaurants is blue, not just because the effect is to relax us – which means we will tend to linger longer – but because very few foods look good when surrounded by blue.

The basis of research like this is the notion that we buy something because we think we want it or need it, but beneath our conscious thoughts there's a current of emotion running silently inside us that can be generated by the product.

And while several techniques have been developed in recent years to probe these currents of emotions, one that has produced ominously accurate results is known as NLP – neuro-linguistic programming.

Loosely defined as the study of the structure of human experience, NLP incorporates several different disciplines to establish how we create our own experience, how each of us has come to think and feel about certain things, and how we use those experiences to form our individual view of the world.

Devised in California in 1972 by John Grinder, a university professor in linguistics, and Richard Bandler, then a graduate student in psychology, it was an attempt to explore the relationship between neurology, linguistics and observable patterns of behaviour. They wanted to analyse the structure of successful experiences in order to make it understandable to others. They believed they could use success to teach personal improvement and greater enjoyment of life, to make excellence an ascertainable skill, to find out how talented people are able to do what they do and to pass some learnable abilities along to people not otherwise born with that talent.

Following on from their initial research, others took NLP in two distinct directions. The first continues to look at ways of uncovering patterns of excellence. The second uses successful models to establish effective ways of thinking and communicating. Since then, both directions have become tributaries for all sorts of distortions, such as self-help courses – how to learn the power of positive thinking, how to get better dates, how to succeed in life without really trying – and general, run-of-the-mill psychological voodoo. But when you head back upstream, back to its roots, there are things about NLP that some people are calling a commercial wonder drug.

In its purest form, NLP teaches that we make sense of the world by using our five 'representational systems' – sight, sound, touch, smell and taste – then recalling those impressions to re-create experiences that in turn re-create emotion.

For example, remember the first time you ever rode on a roller-coaster. With very little effort, you should be able to re-create to some extent that same bottom-of-the-stomach excitement that comes from being hurled downwards. Or, think about your favourite food and, in many cases, you can easily cause yourself to salivate.

Our senses perceive stimuli which we take in, code and store as memory to represent experience. Collectively, those memories form our internal world. By understanding how we create that world, NLP says we can learn how to make it the way we want it to be. In other words, if we understand the formation of our environment, our behaviour, our capabilities, our beliefs, our values, our identity and our spiritual being, we can then go back to those influences, reform them and change how we function in our external world.

In order to replay these things in our mind, we need to go beyond the five senses – called modalities – and deal with the building blocks of each sense, called submodalities. Colour and depth perception are submodalities of the visual system. Sweet and sour are submodalities of the taste system. Loud and soft are submodalities of the auditory system.

It is through the coding of our memory with submodalities that we can tell the difference between an experience that happened yesterday and an experience that happened 20 years ago. Logically, then, if we change the structure of an experience by changing the submodalities, we will change its meaning. When the meaning changes, our internal response changes.

A typical example is to think of an irritating experience. If you see it from the inside – if you allow yourself to be associated with it – you will re-experience a sense of irritation. People who hold on to bad experiences, storing them in their memory as an 'associated' picture, find returning to them uncomfortable. That's why they never learn from bad experiences. However, by dissociating oneself from an irritating experience, the irritation is confined to the picture in your head. By seeing it from the outside – by stepping back and separating yourself from it – the irritation will not be re-created.

We do not experience life in the abstract, and experiences do not come with meaning attached. That's why submodalities are such a valuable clue to how our memories affect us. But when we express these things we often speak in code. There is a 'surface structure' to speech, which hides the 'deep structure' where the real meaning lies.

An oversimplified illustration is when someone uses that popular response, 'I hear what you're saying.' On the surface it means, 'I have taken into account what you're telling me.' But deep down it might mean something totally different. It could mean, 'I don't need anyone's advice because I'm capable of thinking for myself.' Or it could mean, 'I will never forgive my second-grade school teacher for being nice to some of the kids in class and not me because she was always telling me what to do.'

Understanding the code can unlock deep meaning.

Superimposing this on products sells us stuff we might not consciously have ever considered buying.

Companies that focus their marketing efforts around their advertising spend whatever they can to tell us what the product is and what it will do for us. They're betting that, once informed, we will make a judgement to buy. How rational our judgement is becomes another matter. Although we tell ourselves that we buy things we like, most of the time we buy on emotion. We then justify on fact, reassuring ourselves because it is comforting to do that.

What's more, most of the time we're not buying goods or services, we're buying solutions that we hope will suit us.

A few years ago there was an ad for power tools that made the point brilliantly. A fellow wanted to hang something on a wall. In order to do that he needed to drill a hole in the wall. In order to do that he needed a drill. So he went to a store and bought whatever brand drill it was. As he was walking out with his new drill, the voice-over went something like, at Such-and-Such Company we understand you're not buying a drill bit, you're buying a hole.

But what if we buy something, not because we want it or need it, but because someone has built something into the product that pushes a button inside us that somehow makes us feel an emotional attachment to that product. That's how NLP is being used.

Researchers convinced that rational appeal strategies waste time and money – they see products conceived in a designer's mind then haphazardly tossed over to the other side of the room where the marketing department tries to position them for maximum appeal – are finding ways of emotionally coding products so that they trigger a positive response deep inside our subconscious.

The password is 'imprint'.

Konrad Lorenz was an Austrian zoologist who won the Nobel Prize for Physiology in 1973. The father of 'ethology' – the study of animal behaviour – he demonstrated that brains could be imprinted with information that would control behaviour, in some cases for life.

He studied dogs, cats and wolves, but his most famous work was with baby geese. Understanding that first experiences create imprinted behaviour patterns, he defied biology by imprinting himself on goslings' brains, making them believe that he was their mother. They reacted to him accordingly. The application of his work on human behaviour has led to similar results.

An easy way to understand imprinting is to consider a phobia. Take something fairly common, such as a fear of snakes.

In the *souk* at Marrakesh, Morocco – the sprawling market that takes up most of the heart of the city – you find several snake charmers sitting in front of woven baskets, where for a few *dirhams* they will wrap a huge serpent around your neck long enough for your friend to take a snapshot. Most of the time, however, Western tourists stare into those baskets agog. Somewhere in their brains it is imprinted that snakes are dangerous and we are all, in some ways, fascinated by danger. It's understandable then that they might be reluctant to accept the snake in their arms when the charmer tries to hand it over. Their excuse is usually, ugh, it's so slimy! That too is imprinted.

Except it's not true.

Snakes are not slimy at all. Whether or not they're actually dangerous depends on the species. Some are. Most aren't. But these imprints on our brain – NLP defines them as initial learning experiences charged with emotion – cause us to react in a certain way. Even when someone tries to argue, in a calm and rational manner, 'It's not slimy and it's not dangerous,' they won't easily effect a behaviour change.

If you accept the concept that behaviour creates experience, which is then translated by thoughts into memories, and that memories combine to become imprints, then in order to understand behaviour you've got to understand the imprint.

It also holds that the strength of the emotional stance is directly related to the power of the coding. So when an emotional stance is very strong – as it can be with many phobias, often to the detriment of the lifestyle of the person owning the fear – no amount of reasoning or logic will undo it.

To change things permanently you need to undo the coding.

At the same time, if you can successfully decode an imprint, you've identified an emotion that can then be triggered by a purpose-built button. A common example of how this is done all the time is baked bread.

Supermarkets cottoned on to this trick years ago. The odour of freshly baked bread is wafted through the air-conditioning system, provoking an expected reaction. We salivate, our brain tells us we're hungry and bread sales increase.

In very large supermarkets, the bread department is purposely placed towards the rear, and the smell of freshly baked bread is used as a decoy to bring customers through the store. In smaller supermarkets and bakeries, the bread counter is at the front of the shop and the smell is broadcast towards the pavement to bring people in.

There's only one thing slightly suspicious about it. Although larger stores are now baking throughout the day as demand warrants, bakers usually work at night and bread is usually baked in the very early morning hours. So how do they get that smell carrying through the store at 4 in the afternoon? It's force fed into the air-conditioning system straight out of an aerosol can.

Now, most people recognize the baking bread trick as pure Pavlovian manipulation. But real estate agents also use this ruse, and it has nothing to do with selling an extra loaf of seeded rye. They advise property sellers to have bread baking in the oven whenever a potential buyer shows up because they reckon it makes the place feel lived in and comfortable.

Not quite.

Making the place feel lived in and comfortable is a result of what's really happening, which is that the smell of baking bread is tapping an imprint. It is evoking memories of a gentler time, such as a warm and cosy childhood when mother baked and life seemed innocent and safe.

One insurance company, realizing how NLP could be used to their advantage, have instructed their agents to show up at clients' houses actually carrying a loaf of fresh baked bread. They've been told to say, I was just driving by the bakery and thought I'd bring this for you.

The smell of the bread pushes a button.

The agent receives a better reception because he's got directly in touch with a positive imprint.

Paul Losee describes himself as something of a pioneer. Now pushing 50, running a company in the Salt Lake City area called M+, he was one of the first researchers to produce successful commercial applications for NLP.

Because his background is technology based, what fascinated him when he first started studying and working with NLP, was the collection of so much data which he could then put through software algorithms that he'd developed to analyse words, to place them in categories and, from there, to sort out the hidden emotions that were being expressed.

'I've taken a very technological approach to a soft science,' he says.

But the more he's got into it – having done work for Chrysler, Procter & Gamble, 3M, Kodak, Kellogg, Disney and Canada Trust – the more he's come to understand the power of the genie he's letting out of the bottle.

'NLP is a tool in my research to figure out what drives behavior when someone is thinking about making a purchase. I've developed methods which allow me, systematically, to get deeper and deeper into the true reasons why people buy whatever it is they're buying.'

The process begins with a series of intense meetings with his client, to analyse what the client is looking for and to learn as much as he can about the particular industry.

Next, he puts together a focus group. The ideal size is about 15 people and the best overall results seem to come from at least four different groups. He looks for cross-sections of people, depending on whatever demographics his client is trying to target. If the client is just looking for a broad cultural level of understanding then it doesn't matter too much where he conducts his tests. If the client is looking for regional differences, then he goes to several different places to collect the data.

At the beginning of a session, Losee breaks the group into subgroups of two or three people. Everything the participants say and do over the next couple of hours is recorded, to be transcribed later.

'Traditional research doesn't supply all the answers. People are apt to tell you what they think you want to hear. They'll try to sound intelligent. They will give a rational answer but not necessarily the real answer. If you want the truth, you've got to decode their mind. You've got to understand the modalities, the submodalities, and the emotions surrounding the product experience.'

Getting people to respond properly, to unlock those earliest experiences, is one of the skills that researchers such as Losee have had to develop. He's found, for instance, that the opening question in a focus group is the one that sets the mood for the rest of the session.

If he says, 'Give your name and tell us about your computer system,' that becomes the cue for everyone to start jockeying for position and trying to come up with more appropriate answers than the person before them. Instead, he might ask, 'If your computer system had a name, what would it be and why?' That tends to eliminate peer group intimidation and begins to elicit information that can be decoded, giving clues to someone's true feelings about their computer system.

To give him a better idea about product benefit, the group plays word association games. He goes through a list of 20 words, all of them somehow referring to the subject of interest, and everyone in the group is asked to fill in the blank. For example, 'A computer allows me to . . .' With those responses, he can plot the positive or negative direction plus the emotional intensity of each word. The resulting graph provides valuable clues about which buttons advertisers should try to push.

Believing that when a focus group is fun the participants will more easily reveal their inner self, Losee hands out crayons and asks the group to draw pictures. They are also given clay, string, glue, scissors and coloured paper so that they can build models. In both cases, they must then describe their creation to a session partner.

'When people play, their defences are down and they tell the truth. There's no pressure, no group listening to critique their descriptions.'

Another game is called selling.

Instead of asking them to describe how they think a product should be sold, he asks them to try their hands at selling it. He allows them to choose one product from a choice of several. Usually the sample product is there, along with a selection of competing products. And it doesn't matter what they choose because their insights into the competition are just as useful when it comes to discerning product benefit. So he says to them, pick one and in five minutes figure out how to peddle this to a stranger who will walk in that door.

Five minutes later, he leaves the room, one of his staff shows up and the spiel begins.

In playing this game, the group's decision on key selling points and the approach they use reveals more than Losee says he could get in two hours of questioning. By leaving the room, he's removed himself from the session as the authority figure, reinforcing to the group the idea that they can say whatever they want.

In one case, a large insurance company asked Losee to put together a group that would help them understand what was happening when their salesmen went out into the field.

'I found that when we first learn about the concept of insurance, and this can be under the age of six, we have very mixed associations. On the positive side, insurance has something to do with a relative or a friend of our parents because that's who was selling it. The members of the focus group were able to give me the situation when they first learned about insurance and a lot of the time it was sitting around the kitchen table, papers were spread out and the relative or family friend or whoever was welcome. But there were also negative things. There is the concept of death. Oddly enough, there was also smell. People remembered the strong odour of cigarettes or cologne.'

Through Losee's use of NLP, the company concluded that they needed to give their salesmen a new identity. They stopped referring to themselves as agents. He found that the word was connotative of something undesirable, too closely associated with secret agent and IRS agent. Salesman was also a negative term. Now they talk about being professionals, and career agents, taking away the huckster image and giving themselves an aura of permanence. It's a subtle way of saying, I'll be here for you when you need me. They have also been warned never to go on calls smelling of strong cologne or cigarettes. And, whenever possible, to conduct their meetings in the kitchen so as to get in touch with that early childhood experience.

Needless to say, the people they're pitching have no idea that any of this is deliberate. But they respond because they get a good feeling. And the company have reported big jumps in the conversion rate of contacts to clients.

'When the people leave the focus group at the end of the session,' Losee says, 'they think, hey that was fun. They think, someone actually paid me to do that. I didn't have to sound intelligent. I didn't have to answer any dumb questions. I just went in there and played. They don't know the client or the product, although they can get a pretty good idea about the product because the group is centered around the experience with a certain type of product or service. But they don't generally care. They get 50 bucks or 75 bucks and they go home. They have no clue that they've just unzipped their brain and left it on the floor.'

Marketing theorists continue to come up with shorthand to define what it is they think companies should be doing. One in vogue is 'The 5Ps': product, position, price, packaging, promotion. Pay attention to these, the theorists claim, and all will be right with the world.

Losee is highly suspicious and his response is 'The Unfair Advantage Wheel'.

It is a wheel with three spokes, product, product benefit and the emotional hook. His contention is that, if all three spokes are working together, a product will literally fly off the shelves. But, if one spoke is missing, it will suffer a flat-tyre effect and sales will grind to a halt.

Ideally the product should be low cost and high volume. That's good for profit. It's also a must if you're selling to the mass market.

Product benefit means that it actually has to solve a problem. And its ability to do that must be clearly apparent. Losee believes that, if a company have to spend time and money training us, as consumers, to see the benefits of their product, we won't buy. We'll go somewhere else where the benefit is evident.

As for the emotional hook, they need us to get a special feeling about their product – to override our rational side with emotions – to say, I like it, I want it. We may not know why we want it and frankly, as far as the manufacturer is concerned, it's unimportant. The point is, we're more likely to buy it if we feel an attachment to it.

Losee continues, 'We all know that supermarkets put the high-margin items within easier reach on the shelf than the low-margin items. But that doesn't explain why you might choose pineapples instead of peaches. It may not be significant to most people, but it's very important to the guy who makes pineapples. If I can tell him why, then he can better position his product, make it stand out from other products, by getting in touch with your emotions. It doesn't matter if you're talking about computer keyboards, cereal or running shoes. It's sometimes hard for companies to understand this stuff. But when they get it right, the results are astounding.'

The Iomega Corporation, makers of the computer-hardware bestseller Zip Drive, clearly got it right.

When the product came onto the market in the early 1980s, there was some initial growth, but it flattened out quickly as the Zip Drive got stuck into its own niche market. It stayed there for 10 years and, no matter what the company did with the product's positioning, sales remained constant.

Then, in 1993, new management came in and called in Losee to find out if, in fact, they were giving customers what they really wanted.

Losee set up several focus groups and was, admittedly, surprised when he realized what they were telling him. 'I always considered computers to be tools and figured that most people thought of them that way too. I also understood how, at a certain age, people turn off to computers and technology. I've always believed that if a computer company understood how someone's brain was imprinted, they could make the experience with the computer match something that the person is already familiar with so he doesn't have to think he's got to relearn something. And that's a real problem because, for the most part, people can't relearn. They just flat out have a hard time changing what's already there. What I didn't expect to find out was that tools was the category of the rational benefit but toys was the emotional hook. We call them tools but deep down they're really toys.'

So now he started looking at toys.

'I found that most American children, and admittedly this is a cultural thing, had a toy box in which we put our toys. We would take our toys out and line them up against the wall and when we had them out we were the king of our kingdom. We presided over those toys. They were our subjects. But when our mother came in and made us put those toys away, it caused us all kinds of trauma because she stripped us of our power. Remember how she would say, "Time to put your stuff away." The word "stuff" was also important. So I took this research to Iomega and said, first of all, we're not making disk drives, we're making toys. And second, we've got to figure out a way to make sure that these toys never get put away.'

Iomega responded by redesigning the Zip Drive. They made it brightly coloured – deliberately using colours to excite – then they put little buttons on it and gave it nice curved soft shapes.

In short, they made it look more like a toy.

They then addressed the problem of never having to put a toy away.

Their answer was a plastic window on the top of the drive

so we can see our toy spinning around inside, doing its thing.

Next, following Losee's advice to use the word 'stuff' in their advertising, they created a feel-good factor with the advertising line, 'It's just your stuff.'

'Psychologically, it gave people the feeling that their toys were always out and that they were always in charge of their stuff.'

That was the spark that ignited Iomega. The Zip Drive's brightly coloured buttons touched our psychological buttons. People saw it and said, I want one of those. Demand created a backlog, which in turn brought about high-volume manufacturing. Product costs quickly halved, and the competition was left far behind. Within two years of the initial NLP focus group, Iomega Corp became the fastest-growing stock on the NASDAQ exchange.

'Consumer behavior is like an iceberg,' Losee says, 'you know, where you can only see 10% of it. The rest, that 90% of what's really going on, is below the surface. The elegance is in figuring out how to make the product conform to what's already in the customer's head. That's the whole thing. You don't try to change the buyer. All you do is make the product easily fit in with the customer's own experience. This isn't manipulation of buyers' habits, it's manipulation of the product to match those pre-established habits.'

CHAPTER EIGHT

Naming Names

In real life, unlike in Shakespeare, the sweetness of the rose depends upon the name it bears. Things are not only what they are. They are, in very important respects, what they seem to be.

Hubert Humphrey

A name is a verbal tattoo. It doesn't rub off. And years later – when you've outgrown the letters H-A-T-E stamped across your knuckles, or all that remains of Chuck is that tiny butterfly on the inside of your hip with his monogram next to it – everybody still notices. It's the panic every parent feels when trying to come up with a handle for a newborn. Even if we play it safe and name the baby after someone we love, a relative or a close friend, the haunting thought for ever lingers – what if the child grows up to hate it?

Naming a product is just as much a burden. All the more so because a great name can influence a sale, a bad one can stop a sale and everything in between is a crap shoot.

As a rule of thumb, a product's name should be easy to say, easy to spell and, most importantly, easy to remember. In the most general terms, names tend to fall into four categories.

Fanciful names, the ones that are totally made up for a specific product, are usually the best, which is why we remember Sony, Kodak, and Exxon. Now consider Jägermeister. A thick, medicinal-tasting 70° proof firewater concoction, it may be a cheap way for college kids to get high, but it has a long way to go before becoming a household word.

Arbitrary names are real words used to describe a product that has no direct relationship with the word – Eagle Star, Godiva, Ivory, Midas. The rock-solid image of a company called Perpetual is obvious. What chance then for a company called Ephemeral?

The third category comprises suggestive names, real words used to imply something about product quality – Rely, Sure, DieHard, Accent, Mr Clean, Dry Look, Close-Up, Dustbuster, Intensive Care. This might explain why a breakfast cereal whose name bragged Screaming Yellow Zonkers probably never stood a chance.

Finally, and arguably the weakest of the four, are those descriptive names, which are supposed to tell you about the product itself – Animal Crackers, *People* magazine, Hamburger Helper, Lean Cuisine, Face Shaver, Chef's Blend, Kool cigarettes, Instant Breakfast, I Can't Believe It's Not Butter. By definition, the product name invites contention – yes, I can believe it isn't butter – and, more importantly, limits possibilities. British Midland Airways sounds as if it should fly only between Birmingham and Manchester. Eastern Airlines suffered the same kind of limitation, leaving the public to think that if they wanted to go further afield than the Eastern seaboard of the USA, they needed another carrier. In fact, Eastern did fly to California, just as British Midland does fly from London to several European cities. It was for that very reason that BOAC – British Overseas Airways Corporation – dropped the O and the C to become British Airways.

Even the best name is no name at all if you can't use it. Which means it must also be protectable by law. You can't call yourself American Airlines if you intend to fly planes, because they beat you to it, but you can call yourself American Air if you happen to sell oxygen. You can't sell cars called Cadillac unless you're General Motors, but you can sell dog food called Cadillac because the courts have ruled that no one in their right mind would think GM had gone into the dog food business.

Every now and then, as happened not long ago in Britain, someone named Duncan decides to go into the doughnut business. Even though his name may actually be Duncan and even though his 'doughnuts' aren't the same as the more famous Dunkin's 'donuts', the big kids close in on the Duncan-come-lately and shut him down. Although, once upon a time, in Syracuse, New York, there was an old Hungarian chap named Hilton who opened a small hotel. Innocently, he named it after himself. Some years later, Conrad and Nicky showed up hoping to explain the facts of life to this fellow, but they went away empty handed. While *père* and *fils* had every right to call their hotels the New York Hilton, the London Hilton and the Paris Hilton, they apparently did not have the right to call theirs, simply, The Hilton, as the old man in Syracuse had registered it first.

Because there is so much at stake when a new product is launched and because most new products fail, a tiny group of professional linguists – Merlins in a quest for alchemy – invent names to enhance sales invisibly.

Notable among them is Ira Bachrach, an electrical engineer in an earlier life, who with three other fellows once founded a company called Calma which invented computer-aided design. The four of them sold the company to General Electric and still in their twenties – but now with bulging bank accounts – they all sailed off into the metaphorical sunset. However, for Bachrach, figuring out what to do for the rest of his life was a little more difficult than he'd expected it would be. He stayed retired for a while. Tried his hand at a few other jobs for a while. And retired again, for a while. At least until his wife finally insisted that having him around the house all day was driving her mad.

Off again on yet another search for some way to stay amused, he thought back to his year of graduate school at the University of Rochester where he'd begun to write a thesis on linguistics. That was something he really enjoyed but, except for teachers, there have never been a lot of people earning a living in the linguistics field. Then again, he realized, he didn't need to earn a living. So he started a linguistics company called Namelab.

He based his new business on units of meaning called morphemes. *The Oxford English Dictionary* defines that as, 'The smallest meaningful morphological unit of language, one that cannot be analysed into smaller forms.' Bachrach's definition is considerably shorter. 'They're semantic kernels of words.' For example, the *van* in *advantage* is a morpheme meaning top of or leading edge of. Prefixes and suffixes are usually morphemes, like *un-* in *unable* meaning not, and *-tion* in *concoction*, meaning the result of an action.

At university, he'd already developed a notational system for morphemes. Now he hoped he could use it in his business to create new language. He convinced IBM he could do it, so they gave him a contract to invent words that might one day become part of software language. But it quickly became apparent to Bachrach that the real market was in naming products and companies.

'The overwhelming majority of products,' he says, 'have typically been named by marketing folk, or the people who make the product or an ad agency somewhere. When I started Namelab in 1981 there was only us. There were some very large design companies who did name development as part of the design process, but the mechanical part of it, the design part, was 98% of their business, and mostly still is. There were no other specialist firms in the name businesses then.'

Today there are a handful, the result of a growing realization by manufacturers that limiting their downside risk means paying minute attention to every detail, especially names. What was happening before Namelab came along was pretty much what might have been expected. A bunch of very bright fellows sat around a conference table tossing ideas back and forth until one of them snapped his fingers and said, hey let's call it Kleenex.

Bachrach mixes his potions differently.

'It's a bit like being a psychologist, actually. We have to get the client to tell us exactly what it is he will be doing, exactly what the product can do. From that, we create a set of instructions in the form of narrow, linguistic commands. Take, as an example, a laptop computer. The messages we want to put in the name are small, integral object and computer. That's how we came to name Compaq.'

A fellow Bachrach knew in Houston, who'd been working for Texas Instruments, decided to go out on his own with a couple of engineers as his partners. They found space in the Gateway Office Center and, based on that, decided to call their start-up Gateway Technology. If nothing else, they reckoned, somebody might think they were big enough to own the building.

Their original idea was to make portable computers to compete with a company called Osbourne, named after the guy who'd started that company by inventing the first portable computer. Those were the days when portables weighed something like 30 pounds. Except Osbourne wasn't really the competition. IBM was the dominant company. And Gateway's real concern quickly became, would anyone buy an IBM compatible computer from anyone other than IBM?

'It seems laughable now,' Bachrach says, 'but in the context of those days it was a very serious consideration. Both RCA and GE had just folded in the computer business. They were out of it. The fellow I knew at Gateway believed that, since computers in those days were entirely bought by very conservative corporate types, they might not want to take the risk that a non-IBM computer might fail.'

So the guys at Gateway decided they needed to find a way to appear to be larger than their business actually was and as trustworthy as IBM. Their plan was to change their name.

'They came to me because they wanted a name that would be remembered when it was seen in the *Wall Street Journal*. But they were a very small company at the time and, when I said it was going to cost them $20,000, the two engineers thought it was nuts. In their frame of reference, instead of a name they could buy an oscilloscope for $20,000. In the end, it was my friend down there who paid us out of his own pocket.'

Bachrach worked his way through the morphemes – small, integral object that was also a computer – and came up with 'comp' to denote computer, then 'paq' to denote a small integral object. He also thought about 'pod' as a morpheme that means a small object. Which is to say, he might have named the company Compod. However, he insists that wasn't one of the choices. Compaq was better because of the 'q' on the end of it.

'With names, the easier you remember them, the more often you think you've seen them and, when it's a company name, the more you think you've seen it the larger it grows in your mind. That's why we turned the phonetic K at the end of Compaq to a Q. Because there's no natural word in English, and no proprietary name that any of us could find, ending in Q.'

So Gateway Technology of the Gateway Office Center in Houston, Texas, became Compaq – there is now another computer company named Gateway, no relation – and when people started reading about Compaq in the *Wall Street Journal*, they did in fact stop to look at this strange word ending in 'q'.

'When we read, we automatically turn the notations, the letters, into sounds. Don't forget, we learn to speak five years before we learn to read. In this case there was an extra step to turn the phonetical K into a Q, and that extra step, that stop and stumble, we believed, would make the word more memorable. In fact, we were right.'

Although, in the beginning, not everybody thought so.

Compaq's lawyer came up with a pretty sound argument against the name. He figured that, if the day ever came when they wanted to go into the desktop market, their name would be a hindrance. He argued, no one will ever buy a desktop computer from a company whose name says portable and small. Bachrach tried to make him understand that after a while the name Compaq would simply identify the source of the product and not the product itself. The name would be smoothed of its semantic meaning, like so many other product names, and come to stand for the company. The lawyer was sceptical. But Bachrach was convinced that the name would not prevent them from one day building larger computers.

Which is what they have since done.

Just because a word works in one language, with the world being as small as it is today the danger is that it will mean something totally different in another. There's a soft drink in Italy, for example, that English speakers always remember because it's called Pschitt. There's a toilet paper in Sweden called Krapp's. And there are two dishes in Britain – Faggots and Spotted Dick – neither of which would ever show up on menus in most of the United States.

The Japanese have shown a proclivity for naming products with English words. For inexplicable reasons, they've got beers called Beatnik, First Lady and Train Tunnel. Perhaps someone thought they were being exotic. Another possibility is that whoever came up with these names didn't totally understand English, as might have been the case with whoever decided to call a canned beer 'Drafty'. On the other hand, an ad agency's influence is unmistakable in the name and subsequent slogan of one Japanese soft drink: 'Escape the summer heat, get Nude.'

The Rolls-Royce people once seriously considered naming one of their cars Silver Mist, until they found out that in German *mist* means manure. With such a high-status product, they were right not to go ahead with the name. But if they did it because they worried that Germans wouldn't buy a car called *mist*, then they did it for the wrong reason. After all, it's fair to assume that the majority of Germans who already have a Rolls-Royce speak English so there wouldn't be confusion. It was the press who would have had a field day.

What tends to happen in these situations is that somebody comes up with a clever name that, by accident, turns out to mean, say, pork chop in Arabic. Suddenly, everybody in the company panics, convinced that the Arabs won't buy the product because they'll be horrified by the reference to pork. The truth of the matter is that when someone who, say, speaks Arabic sees a word that isn't part of his language, he knows it's an English word. He knows it's not pork chop in Arabic.

Bachrach even goes as far as to insist that accidental meaning almost never has any effect on how names function.

'We named a new generation of consumer medical devices using the Greek alphabet. The first letter we decided to use, for a whole variety of reasons, was kappa. And one day the company got a fax from somebody in Japan demanding to know why they were doing that because kappa in Japanese is a river monster who devours people's innards.'

Almost immediately, the company came back to Namelab to ask, how could you not know that? Bachrach answered that he had, of course, looked into the name and culturally, in Japanese, a kappa is a turtle. As luck would have it, however, the same way some mothers say to their kids, don't wander off in the dark or the bogey-man will get you, mothers in Japan apparently say don't go near the river or the kappa will get you.

'That's the kind of thing that goes on with names in one language when they're used in another place. When we see a word that's Hungarian, or Polish, whatever, we know it's not English. But rarely, almost never, is it an issue.'

Legend has it that it was once a very big issue in Mexico.

The story started back in the 1970s at a meeting of the Mexican–American Chamber of Commerce in San Antonio, Texas. For some reason, and no one really knows why, a stringer from the Associated Press showed up to cover it. He was supposedly dozing at the back of the room while a Mexican lawyer was giving a luncheon speech, at which he said, you guys in the States don't pay enough attention to us in Mexico as a market. The example he gave was of General Motors trying to sell a car there they called the Nova. He claimed that someone in Mexico who can't read would think that Nova meant *no va*, which translates as 'doesn't go'.

At that point, the AP stringer woke up and put the story on the wire that GM was a bunch of morons trying to sell cars to Mexicans which they won't buy because they're called 'doesn't go'.

It's a story that gets repeated all the time when people who name things gather. The only problem with it is, it isn't true.

Nova means star in Latin. In those days, the Roman Catholic liturgy throughout Mexico was in Latin. Something like 97% of all the people who might have bought that car in Mexico were Catholics who went to church every Sunday and would know the word for star.

Which is what it was supposed to mean in English, too.

The actual process, from first contact with Namelab to getting a name, usually takes five to six weeks. It begins with a call from a company – take as an example an automobile manufacturer – to say they've got a product for which they need a name. They send Namelab a detailed description of the product, where they intend to position it, how they want it to be perceived, the names of products that are in a similar position at the moment and how those competing products are perceived. From that, Bachrach and his staff of four – including two other linguists – look for directions to take that might make sense. Once they've got some sort of idea, Bachrach meets with the client to agree the set of messages that they want expressed in the name.

Based on the car manufacturer's understanding of the problems he's facing in bringing this new car to the market, his sense of how consumers will react and Bachrach's findings from his own analysis of the language of the category, they decide on that message. In this example, say it's 'luxury car with high engineering'. Once that's fixed, Bachrach heads off on a computer-guided expedition for morphemes.

'By our notational system, there are 6000–6200 of these in American English. By conventional notational systems, either the 40-character phonetic alphabet or the Roman alphabet, there are somewhere between 900–1400. The largest dictionary of these is Indo-European Word Roots, published by Johns Hopkins Press. But our system is more powerful. And I believe it is the most complete lexicon of morphemes in American English.'

The computer extracts every morpheme that bears in any way upon each of the messages he's using as a guideline. It's been programmed to work by denotation, by connotation, by simile, by idiom and by metaphor. It then combines each morpheme with all the others to make every word or short phrase that is possible in expressing that idea.

He's looking to create a new word. The term he uses is 'neologism'. This is not about tying words together, like Shake-n-Bake, this is about coming up with something that will identify the product as something apart from anything else in the world. And because most Western languages derive from the same linguistic source, Indo-European, it's possible to come up with neologisms that are meaningful regardless of the language involved and also in markets like Japan, where approximately 10% of Japanese stems from English.

Using morphemes as his base, and intensely analysing all the possibilities, he eventually comes up with a shortlist of neologisms, which he then subjects to a series of elaborate legal searches. He also does a thorough linguistic investigation to avoid, where possible, pork chop in Arabic, 'doesn't go' in Spanish and anything else that could, potentially, create a problem.

The revised shortlist goes to the client with a detailed report on each word. It is then down to the client to make the final decision.

For the car manufacturer, Bachrach used the Latin word *acuarae* – which means precisely, or with care in a mechanical sense – and the manufacturer quickly settled on Namelab's option, Acura.

Probably the greatest compliment the world can pay to any company is to steal its name. Some products were born with names that were so well thought out, they've become universally accepted to mean all of the competing products – Fiberglas, Band-Aid, Sanka, Hoover, Formica, Aspirin, Shredded Wheat, Xerox, Rollerblade and Thermos.

'Intellectual property lawyers will fall on their swords when you say that,' Bachrach notes, 'but it is the ultimate compliment. Every time somebody ignorantly uses the word Xerox to mean photocopy, somewhere the cash register that maintains the value of the Xerox Corporation's net worth goes ca-ching. By doing that, you are reinforcing the company as the pioneer or the expert in the field.'

The pre-eminent generic name has got to be Kleenex, which, despite a trademark, is now used widely to mean all paper tissues.

The product itself derives from processed cellulose acetate, an artificial textured cotton which was invented by Kimberly-Clark during World War I because there wasn't enough real textured cotton to make wound dressings. There were also nurses stationed in Europe during World War I and another thing they didn't have was any way of dealing with menstruation. At least not until those big puffs of fabric started coming in from Kimberly-Clark. The nurses quickly realized they could pack this stuff into a wad and use it as a sanitary napkin.

After the war, the market for cellulose acetate diminished greatly. The people running Kimberly-Clark were trying to figure out what else they could do with it, when somebody remembered how those nurses had been using it. So they worked out a process to take a huge sheet of it, fold it back and forth on top of itself and sew it into a pad. Being a bunch of men, they weren't going to name it anything that suggested menstruation. Instead they returned to the words 'textured' and 'cotton', reversed them, abbreviated them and came up with Kotex.

A few years later, somebody was wondering around the factory and noticed that the machine guys were using this stuff to wipe down their machines. It worked as good as any rag, but had the added benefit of never having to be washed. It could be thrown away. It took them another few years to figure it out, but eventually they decided they could sell this stuff for cleaning.

As long as they already had something called Kotex, when it came to a name for something that cleaned stuff the next step was only logical. The idea that someone might start blowing their nose with it never occurred to any of them at the time.

The fact that some very big names – Kleenex, Kotex, Xerox, Exxon – all use the letter 'x' is, according to Bachrach, just coincidence. 'No, there's nothing special about the letter x. There are thousands of brands that work really well that don't have "x"s in them.'

Yet, the double-x of Exxon is significant.

'Exxon is a meaningful name and was absolutely brilliant. It was made by a firm in New York and is one of the great innovative historically important brand names.'

A judge in New Jersey had broken up the huge Standard Oil conglomerate into a bunch of smaller companies. But when it was all sorted out there were two companies called Standard Oil. There was Standard Oil of California (Socal) and Standard Oil of New Jersey. Because they couldn't decide which one would be Esso – derived from the letters S and O, as in Standard Oil – it was agreed they would both change their names.

Standard Oil of California became Chevron.

Standard Oil of New Jersey became Humble – named after one of their subsidiaries – until somebody decided that the word humble wasn't a terrific association for a company thinking internationally. So they decided that they really needed to look for a world name.

They wanted to express engineering and energy. The *'on'* suffix derives from Greek and means energy in several languages – such as *neutron* and *electron,* and all those words ending in *'onics'.* The *'ex'* in this sense was intended to mean experimental, in order to suggest science or engineering.

The reason it became 'xx' was because they needed to create a word that was unique and not going to be found in any language around the world, so they wouldn't have trademark problems.

The story of Xerox is just as good.

In 1938 a patent lawyer from Seattle named Chester Carlson had invented a method of electrostatic printing, which transferred images using a charged selenium plate to attract toner, and then transferring the toner by changing the charge on the plate.

He took his invention first to Kodak, trying to get someone there to buy the process. But Kodak was, in those days, the leading manufacturer of wet copiers and they weren't interested. His next stop was a company called Haloid. They liked it but the war got in the way and it wasn't until 1959 that they brought the product to market. In the meantime, Carlson himself named it. Except, he made a tiny mistake.

Linguistically unsophisticated, he was trying to say 'dry', because in his view the importance was that it was dry copying. He used the Greek root *'xer'*, which does mean dry. But the Greek alphabet is notationally different from the Roman alphabet, which the rest of the Western world uses. So in all other languages the *'xer'* root, unless used in science, is more commonly *'ser'*. In other words, Carlson's invention should have been called Serox. The fact that it isn't puts the word he came up with, at least as perceived by linguists, in the category of absolutely fanciful and without any meaning.

That said, Xerox remains one of the most brilliant product names ever. For one thing, it's visual. The x on both ends is pleasing. It is also an easy word to design into a logo. Secondly, it comes pretty close to being phonetically transparent. That means, it is almost spelled the way it sounds. The uninitiated might spell it 'Zerox', but even with the first 'x' it's easy to pronounce. Thirdly, and perhaps most important of all, the word sounds good. In general, shorter is better. And while very few people other than linguists ever think about a name's sound, it is from the sound of the name that a company acquires some of its meaning.

'Language is speech,' Bachrach notes, 'which means that we have to convert words into sounds in order to understand them. There is something in the brain called the circulating register. When you read, you slide words across an area of the retina which converts them into electrical signals which eventually get to the brain. These signals are converted into sounds in the circulating register and that's language. That's how you know what the words mean.'

Because words are sounds, sound patterns become very

important. A name which is phonetically French inescapably evokes a French association, and if the company has something to do with food, the association might be of gourmet standards or of complex cooking. But there is another kind of phonetic affect, and this is when the sound of a word suggests a relationship with a product category. This has to do with the public's expectations and a company's ability to manipulate those expectations with a name.

Explains Bachrach, 'If you want to convince somebody that a product is a cosmetic, don't call it Acetylene. That word suggests chemicals rather than cosmetics. Making that mistake would mean that at the start of every sales pitch you'd have to explain and convince people that Acetylene is a cosmetic. It's an argument you would have to get into. Instead, by manipulating the expectations properly and, say, naming a product Renova, as we did for Johnson & Johnson, it's assumed to be a cosmetic because the word itself is phonetically structured at the centre of the language of cosmetics. That's what makes names such as Clinique and Neutrogena so good. Neither have to fight the expectation battle. And that battle can make or break a product because, in business, battles are fought with money.'

A great name cannot alone guarantee the success of any product, but a bad name can kill a great product. Case in point, the world's first caffeine-free cola.

It was launched with what was said to be, at the time, the largest ever advertising investment in a new product. And if you don't remember the name, that's okay, because no one else does either. This, after the 7-Up Company spent $100 million in a year and a half to promote it.

The drink came about as a result of their huge success with the term 'Uncola'. A tiny line of copy underneath the word – which had been invented to separate it from Coke and Pepsi – bragged that it did not contain caffeine, which parents liked because their kids could drink it without getting wired. So when 7-Up realized they were onto a good thing, they took every cent they had to make a caffeine-free cola. The question then became what to call it.

Presumably, a bunch of 7-Up guys put their heads together in a think-tank kind of meeting and decided, 'Hey let's call it Like-Coke.' Except they knew they couldn't do that because Coke would kill them. Instead, they decided, 'If we can't call it Like-Coke, why don't we call it something that suggests the same thing?'

So they named it Like.

Bachrach picks up the story. 'You can't believe how many problems there are with that name. The word like is part of the core working vocabulary of virtually everyone in the audience they were trying to reach, and it is almost impossible to identify a product in the language memory of a human being by using a word which is part of the core working vocabulary. For instance, you couldn't call a product "The". It simply won't work. Another thing is that, in the parlance of teenagers, who are per person the single largest consumers of colas, the word like was being used at that time to mean 'not really'. Think about that. There was a cola that had something missing, specifically caffeine, and the company making it was telling teenagers, who drank a third or half of all colas, this stuff is not really a cola. There was absolutely no way in the world they could have succeeded. It was a totally moronic name.'

Not only did the product fail, but that version of the 7-Up Company did too, largely because of Like, and was eventually sold – to Coca-Cola.

A better way of doing it was the way Namelab did when they were approached to come up with a name for a soft drink.

'There is a pattern of phonetic organization in the soft drinks category. There are major products like Coca-Cola and

Pepsi Cola at the dark and potent end, and products like Sprite and 7-Up at the light end. If you want to name something which is positioned like 7-Up, you want to find a name which fits at that end of the category. The input message in looking for the name of this new product was "contains fruit but not fruit flavoured". So we came up with the name Slice. The fruit image is obvious. But the name actually comes from the morpheme *'sli'*, which means partial. And I'm happy to say it worked. On the other hand, if we'd have named it "something-ola", we would have been phonetically misleading consumers' expectations. They'd be thinking it was a dark and hearty beverage, which we then would have had to prove wrong.'

Good names associated with good products 'free-ride,' clearly demonstrating how we can be led by the nose to fall for a product just because of its name.

After establishing the name of their toothpaste, Colgate free-rode the same name to toothbrushes and mouthwash. The association they're making is obvious – if you like and buy Colgate toothpaste, you'll like and buy Colgate toothbrushes and Colgate mouthwash. But the boundaries of a free-ride are usually well defined. Say that they wanted to extend the name to something as far afield as an abrasive sink cleaner. A fair question is, what does a toothpaste have to do with a sink cleaner? The answer is nothing at all. A free-ride here would not sell the abrasive powder and might, in fact, cast doubt on what the toothpaste did to your teeth. Which is why the Colgate Palmolive company didn't call it Colgate Abrasive Sink Cleaner, but instead invented the name Ajax.

Now consider Richard Branson's use of Virgin.

It started life as a record company with a jokey name, became a chain of music stores with a jokey name, then extended to an airline with a jokey name. The thinking was that the airline would benefit from the youthful audience of the music business. And in the beginning, Branson was right. But the airline has since grown up and extended its reach, with business-class service, executive lounges and frequent-flyer programmes, all products aimed beyond that initial teeny-bopper customer base.

What then of Virgin Direct Financial Services?

If they're targeting the rock music crowd, that's one thing. Except the rock music crowd spend money on records and are too young to consider retirement plans seriously. If they're targeting the airline's business-class passengers, that's fine too. Except front-of-the-plane frequent flyers are usually grown-ups who are in a position to place their money with grown-up financial service operations, not ones that sell rock music. Anyway, what's the association – the free-ride benefit – of an airline's name on a financial services business? Where he might have been smarter is in associating his own entre-preneurial prosperity with that business to create the image of a money-making success by calling it Branson.

Admittedly, the success of the airline has done for its jokey name what the success of Compaq's computers did for their made-up name – it's identified Virgin as the source of the product and not the product itself. Nevertheless, such a ploy is not without inherent risks. Take, for instance, the company in the States that leases old beat-up cars called Rent-a-Wreck. Amusing, yes. But what does the name say about the quality of the product? It would be like buying a coffin from a company called Death Traps or visiting a dentist whose name is I. M. Payne.

That said, jokes seem to work well in the food business – we laugh, we buy, we eat. The El Paso Chile Company searched for names that would jump out at us, be easily remembered and tell us too what we're buying. Hence, Hellfire & Damnation hot sauce, Sweet Texas Fire jalapeno honey mus-tard, and Snakebite Salsa. The same corporate philosophy per-meates much of the ice-cream business.

Back in the days when ice-cream was chocolate, vanilla, coffee and strawberry, it was the flavour that mattered. If you were lucky, you might find Dixie Cups featuring two flavours – chocolate and vanilla, side by side – in your local supermarket. The Good Humor people used to pedal around American neighbourhoods on bicycle-driven push-carts ringing bells to announce their presence. It was a favourite summer job of high school kids, especially if you could cycle up and down the street in front of a beach where high school girls hung out. Good Humor gave you a spiffy white uniform and a neat little cap and the combination of a sunburned fellow in a uniform and 'hey, for you it's free' ice-cream was more than some high school girls could handle. But Good Humor was pretty basic fare. The most adventurous they got was sometimes surrounding their vanilla ice-cream on a stick with burnt almonds.

The best anyone could really hope for in those days was to live in a place where there were a lot of Italians, because Italians made *gelati,* which usually meant tutti-frutti. Of course, if you could hie yourself to Italy, get right to the source, to villages like Forti di Marmi and Viareggio on the Mediterranean coast not far from Pisa, you could find all sorts of places that were famous for making *gelati* – places where they had annual contests and where, one year, the winning flavour was zucchini.

But ice-cream was still all about standard flavours with standard names until a bunch of small companies decided to get bigger by taking ice-cream out of supermarkets and making it high-street fast food, sold in outlets generally referred to as 'scoop shops'.

One of those first companies was Baskin-Robbins, started by two guys in California who put their own names on the front door, some odd flavours in their freezers and wacky names on their ice-cream. Pralines-n-Cream and Rocky Road, early attempts to be witty about a promise of benefit, are now considered old-fashioned, although they were once pretty radical compared with the Dixie Cup days. It was when Baskin-Robbins got into Yankee Doodle Strudel, Mango Tango, Swiss Almond Bliss, Mad About Chocolate and Check It Out Cherry, that people really started taking notice. Although they eventually said no to Grape Britain and Last Mango in Paris, they did say okay to Pink Bubblegum and Stars and Stripes. And the public said okay too, this place is fun so let's try their ice-cream because that must be fun as well.

Hot on their heels came Häagen-Dazs – a totally made-up name devised to appeal to an American market as something exotically European – and Ben and Jerry's, named after Messrs Cohen and Greenfield, in that order.

Ben and Jerry's bestseller is Chocolate Chip Cookie Dough, rather grotesquely referred to on the street these days as 'Nicole' because that's the flavour Nicole Brown Simpson bought the night she was murdered. Also on the list is Cherry Garcia (after the late leader of the Grateful Dead), Phish Food, Chunky Monkey, Rainforest Crunch and Wavy Gravy. In addition, at times they have sold Dastardly Mash, Fred and Ginger, Tennessee Mud, That's Life Apple Pie and 10th Anniversary Waltz – Nutcracker Suite.

Häagen-Dazs, on the other hand, have moved away from oddly named ice-cream to position themselves against the other two as the ice-cream of the indulgence set. In their advertising, they use pictures of a beautiful couple, mostly naked, eating ice-cream. The ad has nothing whatsoever to do with the fun of ice-cream, and everything to do with indulging oneself – in this case, the French word *gourmandize* is perfect – and the lifestyle of people who are willing to pay premium prices for Chocolate Midnight Cookies.

Then again, names like Chocolate Midnight Cookies reinforce the image of midnight wallowing with the promise of all sorts of product benefit.

CHAPTER NINE

Going Retail

Who's kidding whom? What's the difference between Giant and Jumbo? Quart and full quart? Two-ounce and big two-ounce? What does Extra Long mean? What's a tall 24-inches?
Marya Mannes

On Thursday mornings, from the large square just below the post office down both sides of the narrow streets to the covered esplanade in front of City Hall, then along both sides of the street that leads to the ramparts, which open onto the crowded port where large white boats sit huddled next to each other like cars too close in a shopping mall carpark, the weekly *marché* in Antibes, France, is what supermarkets were for centuries before anyone ever heard of Messrs Safeway, Sainsbury, Publix, A, P, Marks or Spencer.

It is an accumulation of old wooden tables, set up at dawn, then covered with tomatoes and flowers and fish and fennel and cheese and women's underwear and sweatshirts that say Syracuse Football. It is men and women, some very old and some not so old, standing behind their wares, calling out to the passers-by, *'citrons . . . voici, l'ail . . . ici, les rougets du matin . . . oui mesdames . . . les chausseurs . . .'*

Lemons . . . here's garlic . . . here's red mullet caught this morning . . . yes ladies . . . shoes . . .'

There is the noise of the sellers, and there are the crowds pushing and shoving past the tables, and there is the smell of fresh cut flowers. An old man behind the cheese counter hands out a sample of *brie*. A woman just across the narrow aisle is warning some tourists, 'If you touch my nectarines you have to buy them.'

It all smells good and sounds good and with all that produce piled high on those tables and all the colours that complete the picture, without thinking, you find yourself caught up in this ritual, believing that you are buying the best of the *marché*, at the best price, from the best street hawker.

This is manipulation by fun.

The notable difference between the street peddlers of the Riviera and today's supermarkets, besides the noise, is that Messrs Safeway, Sainsbury, Publix, A, P, Marks or Spencer have substituted fun with deadly serious.

A supermarket is a near-perfect example of how a retail store can be turned into a minefield.

On an average visit, which lasts around 30 minutes, we are exposed to 17,000–20,000 products. Every one of them has been packaged, advertised and displayed with only one thought in mind – getting us to put it on our trolley. More often than we ever intend to, we oblige.

Setting aside the 'product as friend' school of advertising, we get emotionally involved with products because they cost a lot and we want to be sure we're buying the right thing. Often that entails products with which we are unfamiliar, or not in a category that we frequently buy. The risks can be economic – the higher the price the more we need to reassure ourselves, especially if it's above our means; social – if owning something will ostracize us from family and friends we can be expected to take time to investigate the purchase; and personal – it helps to know what we're letting ourselves in for when we shop for sports cars, bungee jumping lessons, yachts and exotic travel. Performance can also be considered a risk, such as when we shop for a home computer, a dentist or a school.

More limited decision-making takes place when we purchase something only occasionally, say soap powder. Unless we have a regular brand, we may spend some time looking into the benefits of several brands, but not a lot.

Then there is programmed behaviour, which we use for our more routine purchases. There is very little involvement in a purchase of cola. The shopping list says Coke or Pepsi and, because that's what we always buy, when we get to the supermarket, unless something comes along to change our mind, that's what we're going to buy.

The final category is arguably the most interesting, and that's the one that requires no conscious planning because it is the impulse purchase. Here's where we clearly put our common sense on hold.

A staggering 60% of what we buy in a supermarket is unplanned.

It's the old joke about the woman who asks her husband if, on his way back from work, he could stop at a store to pick up a box of Tampax. Realizing that he's not going to have any sex for a few days, he walks out of the store with one box of Tampax, one boat, some fishing gear, a trailer for the car and a tent.

Retail researchers have discovered that in stores where customers are served the 60% impulse buy figure drops dramatically. This is equally true in supermarkets and in department stores. To avoid that, sales staff are purposely thinned out. It's not only a way of keeping costs down – which is the usual excuse – but fewer people serving stimulates impulse buying. Now factor in the idea that the longer we ponder a purchase – whether it is soap powder in a supermarket or a new car – the more tension plays a role in the decision. The more time we are given to think about a purchase, the more time we have to talk ourselves out of it.

It goes without saying that shopping can be stressful, which is why many of us make the easiest choice. Recognizing that Vicary was right when he said we tend to walk through stores in a quasi-daze, the more expensive, higher-margin items are purposely placed in the most obvious spots, tempting us to take the path of least resistance and buy the first or second thing we see.

Any store that can get us to do that is guaranteed to make more money. Because making more money is the nature of the exercise, as little as possible is left to chance. And study after study constantly refines the deliberate application of manipulative techniques. It's why products are purposely categorized by families: fruit and vegetables, fresh – which is milk, cheese, yogurt – frozen foods, household cleaning materials, cereals, etc. It's why the opening aisles in most modern supermarkets are where we find fruit and vegetables and the last aisle is where we find drinks. If it was the other way around, drinks would fill up our trolley too quickly and not leave room for anything else.

Other families are then spread throughout the store, making it impossible for us to go through a reasonably complete shopping list without making an entire circuit of the place. The meat counter, fish counter and bakery are usually placed at the rear – milk is also usually sold from the back of the store – so that even a quick stop for one or two vital items draws us through the rest of the supermarket.

Like-families are normally kept close together. For instance, the cereal aisle is next to the aisle with other breakfast foods. The supermarket is counting on us, when we buy cornflakes, to remember we also need hot chocolate, tea, coffee, orange juice, eggs and milk. It's the same reason the sweet biscuits aisle is next to the savoury snacks aisle. As long as our mind is on Jaffa Cakes and Penguins, they know we're open to the idea of pretzels, salted nuts and crisps.

Shelf placement is the next step and here there are three considerations: margin, which is how much profit the supermarket is making on the item; turnover, which is how fast the item is moving; and who's paying what to be where.

The items with the biggest margins – or slightly smaller margins but which move faster and therefore represent a higher turnover – are put on the best shelves. Those are the ones at eye level, usually the fourth or fifth up from the bottom. Second-category profit/turnover items are put above that, on the next higher shelf. Third-category profit/turnover items are put on the shelf under the first category, fourth goes under the third, and so on down to the floor. Shelves are always stacked vertically with like-items because lengthy studies have revealed that when we're standing in front of shelving our eyes move vertically, first going up from eye level, then down. Sugar, for example, which is a necessity and at the same time a low-margin item, is relegated to the bottom shelf. We need to buy it and the supermarket knows that we will bend down for it.

The only exception to the profit/turnover up and down rule is when a company comes along and, literally, bribes the supermarket to give their product better placement. In fiercely competitive areas – detergents, for example – placement can be vital to the success of a product. Globally, Procter & Gamble spend $3 billion a year on advertising and marketing. Unilever, Europe's biggest advertiser, spend around $2 billion. For smaller brands, competing against that kind of might can be a near-impossible task. And yet other soap powders wind up on the eye-level shelves. They may not be the most popular brand, or even a good brand, but they get placement because someone has paid the supermarket to make it the easiest brand to buy.

Another 'rule of shelves' is that they must be kept full. This also applies to the fruit and vegetable bins. Everything must always be piled high – a throwback to the street markets – because mass sells. No one wants the last container of milk or that final green pepper. Both will sit there for the entire day. But a pallet full of fresh milk and a huge stack of green peppers become a temptation.

Finally, items specifically aimed at children are put on lower shelves – at child's eye level – not only so they'll see them, but also so they'll be able to reach them. Supermarkets know how tough it can be to get something out of a child's hand once he or she is intent on having it.

Because the biscuit market is a kids' market and biscuit companies know exactly who they're aiming for, they do whatever they can to tempt that child into demanding that parents buy their product. Promotional tie-ins, back-of-the-box games and give-aways are the usual methods. Cereal companies use the same dodge, which is not surprising when you realize that they are sometimes one and the same. The biscuit market is worth £875 million a year, so finding a way to get another 1% of the share is worth £8.75 million. Nabisco control around 38% of the market, and spend around £69 million a year to maintain and then better that position.

Their Chip's Ahoy cookie is the bestselling chocolate chip cookie in America. As long as Nabisco can't improve on being number one, they go for better percentages. For instance, they've repackaged Chip's Ahoy into bags that are small enough to fit into a school kid's lunch box, and had them conveniently placed so that kids can grab them off the shelves. Nabisco now sell one extra package of Chip's Ahoy for every seven they used to.

The kids' market is one of the major growth areas in all food categories, from fish fingers to 'Turkey Dinosaurs'. There is even Barbie Pasta. Heinz make it because they learned that pasta is the second-favourite dish for girls – French fries are first – and they felt that the tie-in with a $2 billion brand like Barbie would exploit 'girl-oriented pasta'. It gets placed in the section with other kids' pastas – just like sweets, biscuits and bubblebath, always at kids' eye level – tempting children so blatantly that many parents with children in tow now purposely avoid certain aisles.

Because supermarkets know that we know, they've started putting biscuits, sweets and even cartoon character bubblebath in unexpected places. And just in case the kids have somehow escaped, sweets are purposely dangled in full view at the checkout.

It's a given that what kids see and like they usually ask for. It's also a given that many parents are simply too embarrassed to say no while other people – the checkout person and customers in the queue – are listening. The child who wants something badly enough to scream for it, has learned during the first few episodes whether or not this type of blackmail works. Where the parent gives in to the screaming child, this reinforces the screaming technique. Retailers understand this and do whatever they can to manipulate the child into manipulating the parent.

At this point, all sorts of other elements come into the equation.

Where baskets or trolleys are not easily available, we buy less. The opposite is also true. Where they are easily available, we buy more. But baskets limit us to buying what we can carry. So, little by little, they're disappearing and trolleys are getting bigger. Trolleys are also starting to carry ads. Point-of-purchase advertising – signs that seem to be everywhere in a supermarket trying to draw our attention to a particular product – is huge business. We're a captive audience openly susceptible to buying things that we see in front of us. So point-of-purchase advertising is scattered around the store. A new trend is for trolleys to carry discount coupon dispensers.

Then there is the physical plant – the store itself.

Overhead lighting has been chosen to be bright and clear

but soft. Too harsh makes the meat and fish look bad. Special coloured lighting is also being installed in cold cabinets to make the produce appear fresher and more appetizing. And, where possible, traffic is directed to keep us moving at a generally slow and easy pace and in the same direction.

Some stores are particularly manipulative this way. Take for example Marks & Spencers' main branch at London's Marble Arch. Although the food halls there have polished floors – typical of supermarkets because they're easier to keep clean – the aisles are broken up, slowing us down, by being slightly angled or by having cross-aisles forming intersections. More subtly, throughout the rest of the store where they sell clothes and household goods, polished walkways wander through carpeted areas. The walkways direct traffic from one side of the store to the other, weaving a path through the various selling areas. But in order to look more closely at an item, we have to step off the walkway and onto carpet, which immediately slows us down. They keep us moving through the store, but don't let us move too quickly when we get close to the goods.

Back in supermarkets, the air-conditioning system is set slightly higher than most of us would put it at home because a store that is cool – not chilly but cool – keeps customers awake.

It's the old Las Vegas trick.

When gambling became a 24-hour-a-day business, the casinos discovered that neither the punters nor the employees were too swift at 3 a.m. They found that, by turning up the air-conditioning, people yawned less and gambled more. Then, to keep the punters and the employees wide awake, they started pumping oxygen into the rooms. Supermarkets haven't yet had to re-oxygenate to keep us buying, but they do keep the temperature down. Also, as in Las Vegas, clocks are not a good idea. You can't find one on a casino wall for love or money. Same thing at really smart supermarkets. Seeing the time is a reminder that we have to be somewhere else. It gets us out of stores, not into them.

Women who wear glasses are more likely than men to leave them at home when they go shopping.

Someone did a survey and that's what they found.

It is, perhaps, a minor vanity, but it's one that can cost those women a little more money. Because the bigger, brighter package has been purposely designed to be more easily found.

Packaging is more than just a container. It is a last-minute sales pitch. Bigger and brighter also plays off the myth that larger boxes always work out cheaper – that buying the 3 kilo variety is less expensive than buying three 1 kilo sizes. It's not a given any more because manufacturers know that we know, so they've been jiggling prices to squeeze a few more pennies out of the margin.

In many places, supermarkets are required by law to label items with the cost per unit – price per 100 grams or price per ounce – which tells us right away which package costs more. So, in this sense, the shopper is better armed. But women shoppers who leave their glasses at home don't bother checking, and studies show that men – with or without their glasses – don't check unit costs either. Anyway, to keep us from looking too closely at the price, manufacturers have fought back with brighter colours and more creative packaging on the more expensive boxes, and made those sizes easier to find by buying better shelf position for them.

Touch is a useful tool in retailing. For obvious reasons, it is perhaps the least-used sense in advertising. Although we buy fewer than one-quarter of the items we touch, making certain types of goods available for tactile inspection still draws attention to them. That's why supermarkets set up displays at the ends of aisles offering bags of exotic rice, or a world of spices, or all sorts of different types of bread piled into woven baskets. An invitation to touch is an invitation to buy.

In case we hesitate, there is often someone standing near the table to offer us a taste. Every supermarket knows that 'self-gratifying' point-of-purchase displays – a sample of cheese, a sample of sausage, a sip of a new drink – provoke an impulse buy and can raise that 60% figure to as high as 90%.

Smell and taste are naturally intertwined – we smell what we taste – and both can evoke strong memories. The reason smell is used more is because it's easier to re-create and also less expensive to give away. Using smells to trigger sales is the reason the popcorn stand at the local Odeon is placed right in the middle of the lobby. It's the same with department store perfume counters, where armies of young women enthusiastically accost everyone entering and leaving with sample bottles at the ready. It is also the reason glossy fashion magazines have scented inserts bound between pages and 'scratch and sniff' pads have been used to sell everything from sausage meat to gin.

The problem with memories evoked by smell and taste is that they can vary wildly. The odour of freshly cut grass might evoke images of summers past to some people, but not necessarily to someone who suffers from hay fever. Hot dogs grilling on a barbecue might mean one thing to a Boy Scout, something totally different to a vegetarian.

The next sense is sound, as in the way music plays an integral role in modern retailing. Music creates ambience and when the ambience is properly constructed we wind up spending more. In hip fashion stores, the music is loud because the clientele are young and that speaks to them – great music is translated to mean great clothes. In supermarkets, music is paced purposely on the slow side so that it slows us down. The slower we walk the longer we stay in the store, and the longer we're in the store – spending more time in front of products on shelves – the more likely we are to make yet another impulse buy. The tunes being played are also, usually, vaguely recognizable so that we are relaxed into humming, but not relaxed enough that it interferes with our buying.

Recently, a study at Leicester University and reported in the magazine *Nature*, concluded that music might even be more influential than previously thought. Four French wines and four German wines, equally matched in price, were put on a supermarket's shelves in the drinks' aisle with equal visibility. For the first half of the experiment, accordion music was played in the background. For the second half, German music was played. Customers who purchased wine were asked a series of questions about their choice and more than 80% responded that the store's music had no influence whatsoever on their choice. Yet the accordion music was playing as the French wines outsold the German wines by slightly more than 3–1 and the German music was playing when the German wines outsold the French wines by almost 3–1.

A product's individual personality helps us to identify it and, more deliberately, to distort our judgements about it.

Enter here the thoroughly illogical concept of brand loyalty.

Manufacturers hire advertising agencies to invent a personality for their product so that we will feel some sort of relationship with it and, because of that relationship, stay loyal to it. This, in spite of the frequent mountain of evidence to prove that the product we're loyal to is technically the exact same stuff, albeit in a different package, as the competing brand. Logically, we know that competitors imitate ingredients and claims of quality. Emotionally, however, we stick with our friends.

Does Ariel actually get whites whiter? Rationally, the answer is probably no. But emotionally, the answer must be yes. If Ariel is our regular brand, it will win because that's the brand we want to win. It's reassuring. Of course, Ariel is the brand someone else never buys because his or her regular brand is Persil and, as far as they're concerned, it's Persil that washes whites whiter.

Now consider toothpaste.

Without getting technical and cataloguing chemical proportions, all toothpaste is the same. Manufacturers advertise in such a way as to convince us this isn't the case – some brag about fluoride, some brag about extra foaming agents which make the paste bubble quicker in our mouth, others still brag about using baking soda instead of peppermint – but toothpaste is toothpaste is toothpaste and, except for a few minor variations, it doesn't actually matter what name is on the tube. They all accomplish the same task, which is nothing more than to make our mouth taste better.

As far as doing what all toothpaste promises to do, that is reducing cavities plus fighting tooth and gum decay, they share the same secret ingredient, which is four words on the back of every box: Brush after every meal.

Dentists universally agree that it is regular brushing that reduces tooth decay. What toothpaste manufacturers don't want us to know is that, if we brushed without any toothpaste as often as we do with any toothpaste, the results would be the same. In fact, there is now an electric toothbrush manufacturer that advises purchasers not to use toothpaste. And while that's because they've discovered toothpaste jams the mechanism of the brush, they can say it with confidence knowing that the more we brush the less chance we have of getting cavities. So it really doesn't matter what toothpaste we put on the brush, or if we simply brush with tap water. The reason we buy Crest or Ipana or Colgate or Arm & Hammer is because the brand has become familiar to us. We have established some sort of emotional relationship with it, like a friend.

While we are all, at least to some extent, receptive to new ideas – more so if we've been led to believe that the new idea will prove beneficial to us – we are all, naturally, less receptive to being told that we're wrong. Therefore, 'This brand is better than your regular brand' is going to be met with resistance. Not surprisingly, a totally different response might be prompted with, 'This brand will do more to make you a wonderful person than your regular brand.'

Mix into this the fallacy of 'linear credibility'. If you've established a relationship with Paul Newman's Salad Dressing, presumably you will also like – and therefore buy – his range of spaghetti sauce and microwave popcorn. It doesn't matter if they're made by different manufacturers and have nothing to do with each other. It's how you feel about Paul Newman himself that becomes the overriding factor in whether or not you'll buy his brand instead of a similarly tasting, similarly priced brand.

Slightly more far-fetched, Harley-Davidson motorcycles have licensed a line of aftershave and deodorant. The message is, obviously, macho. Still, someone is asking us to transfer credibility from motorcycles to our underarms.

Easier to fathom is the assignment of a store's credibility to selected items.

Own labels, or store brands, are those products that have been commissioned by a store, usually a large chain, and marketed exclusively. It's A&P's Ann Page and M&S's St Michael. It's an entire range of products with logos that say Macy's, Bloomingdale's, Harrods, Selfridges, Galeries Lafayette, Exxon, Gulf, Shell and BP. If we like the company, we will supposedly like their raspberry jam, their coffee, their aprons and their beach towels.

It is widely assumed that own brands are made by leading manufacturers, that every can of Safeway pineapples, for example, is really made by Dole. That may or may not be true, depending on the store. But leading manufacturers are thrilled to become their own competition in that way because, if the choice is between Dole pineapples, Safeway pineapples and somebody else's pineapples, Dole reckon they've got the advantage two-to-one.

There is an additional belief that store brands bring with them established quality plus a discount off the price of the leading brand. That also may or may not be true, depending on the store.

Take breakfast cereals.

Most supermarket chains sell a full range of Kellogg's, Nabisco and Quaker cereals, and then in the same aisle put their own versions of Cheerios, Cornflakes and Shredded Wheat. The real thing is priced accordingly, which means that the generic version is less expensive. For many people, there's not much of a difference between Kellogg's Frosted Flakes or the generic version, so they buy on price.

Why then do other people always opt for the big name brand? Either because the major companies have positioned their product in our minds to be of the best quality; or, they've paid for position on the shelves to become the most visible; or, they've designed their package better – used hotter colours – to attract attention; or, their package designs suggest high quality; or, they worked out a movie tie-in; or, there's a prize inside the box; or, some celebrity has asked us to buy it; or, they've just made the amount they're selling look like more and suggest that it is therefore cheaper to buy bigger.

The breakfast cereal industry is worth $8 billion a year. Being able to increase sales by a measly 1% is worth $80 million.

So why then do we opt for the big name brand?

Because big name brands got that way by being big name manipulators.

Twenty years ago, the grocery business was dominated by the traditional supermarket. Today, convenience stores, mass merchandisers, discounters and warehouse clubs have substantially cut into the market share. It's understandable that diverse retailers would want a slice of this business because food is what we buy more frequently than anything else.

The popularity of warehouse clubs in North America, and their advent in Europe, should be enough to sound panic bells in the boardrooms of supermarket corporations. Twenty years ago there were only eight warehouse clubs in the United States. Today there are nearly 1000. In just the past 10 years, North American warehouse clubs – like Priceco, Costco and Mr. Sams – have cost supermarkets a reported 21 million customers and upwards of $40 billion.

True, it means we have to buy in bulk. A warehouse club is not where we go for a six-pack of Pepsi, two cans of tuna and one frozen turkey dinner. But families with room to store a pallet of Pepsi, 24 cans of tuna and a dozen frozen turkey dinners will, in the long run, save money.

Offering bulk quantities at bulk prices, the warehouse clubs cut down on expenses by being aircraft hanger big in low-rent areas. There is no storage area because the whole place is the storage area. There is very little advertising and no interior decorating. They sell electronic goods, clothes, toys and sporting equipment as part of the draw. They exclude certain products on purpose – fresh meat, for example, where butchers would be required and wastage would have to be factored into the price – in favour of certain high-mark-up items, like health and beauty products.

Outflanked by these warehouse clubs, traditional supermarkets are forced to eke out profits wherever they can. They try to compete by opening longer hours and by getting into goods that are non-traditional to supermarkets. Over the years they have resolutely pillaged products from other retail outlets, such as records, videos, prescription drugs and clothes.

In some cases, too, where supermarkets have decided that the game is lost, instead of trying to beat them, they've joined them by creating their own warehouse clubs. Others have set space aside in their stores as 'Super Deal' or 'Max Pack' sections, where they offer bulk and multipacked items.

The supermarket scene in Britain, until now largely dominated by Sainsbury's, Tesco, Safeway, Waitrose and Asda, will change radically over the next 10 years when warehouse clubs take hold. The American club Costco has already moved in, to the considerable annoyance of British retailers. Although Costco does not yet have the locations they need to make an impact, and the British haven't yet understood the advantages of warehouse clubs, it's only a matter of time. Which is why at least two of the major supermarket chains are studying ways of getting into the business – WalMart became its own competition with Sam's Club – rather than let the American clubs invade and devastate their market.

Two other recent innovations – home delivery and computerized supermarkets – have both been slow to happen. It's one thing to phone a company that home-delivers drinks – let them schlep the cartons of bottled water inside – it's another to order fresh produce that way.

It's the same problem with computerized shopping. Most family food shoppers are women. Most computer freaks are young men. They can understand a virtual supermarket but don't usually care for shopping. The women who need to go shopping wouldn't trust a computer to find the best prices and the best quality. What's more, those supermarkets that have dabbled in computer shopping – like Tesco – are finding that it's tougher to create impulse purchases on a computer screen than it is in the yogurt aisle. Virtual supermarkets will almost certainly happen one day, but not until the supermarkets' programmers figure out how to get the computer itself out from between the woman doing the shopping and her need to smell the freshness of the melons.

In the end, the real battleground is price.

Warehouse clubs and discounters set their prices by taking cost and adding a fixed percentage, say 5%. Here, traditional supermarkets not only have some room to manoeuvre, they also have several 'price weapons' they can bring into play.

Although price is related to costs, it is not entirely dependent on them. Manufacturers determine a price range based on the cheapest price they can put on the product and still make a profit, and the highest price they believe the consumer will pay. A pair of rubber flipflops might not cost more than a pound or two to manufacture and market. In mid-July, near a crowded beach, a store might price them at £5 because there's enough demand for them. Okay, call it a very hot, very crowded summer and put them at £7.50! By the end of September, the store owner might be pleased to get rid of his stock for less than half that. And yet DKNY on Bond Street in London, a long way from any crowded beach, was selling rubber flipflops with the company logo on them for £39 – a long way from beach prices, too – because DKNY is playing off customers who are willing to overpay simply to have the company logo on the instep.

What traditional supermarkets do – and, to varying degrees, this is true of other retailers as well – is lure us into the store with loss-leaders. By offering watermelons in the middle of summer at 5p a pound, the supermarket figures it'll easily make up the loss with all the other things we'll buy having been seduced into the store by the cheap watermelons.

Another trick is bundling. They offer six frozen hamburgers, six buns, two large bottles of Coke, two fresh onions, two fresh tomatoes, a jar of ketchup and a disposable mini barbecue all for one 'Summer Festival' price. As a bundle, it's cheaper than it would be buying each item separately. The store takes a smaller profit but moves more goods in one transaction.

Then there are coupons. Whether clipped from the newspaper, arriving through a direct mail promotion, or handed out in-store, we are very susceptible to buying that second box of whatever – especially if we never intended to buy it – just because we're getting 50% off on it. Everybody loves a bargain. Even when we might not be getting the bargain we think we're getting, if it feels like a bargain that's sometimes just as good.

The interesting thing about coupons is that when we get them outside the store – say through a direct mail campaign that the store has done in cooperation with a manufacturer because our name showed up on their loyalty card database – it draws us into the store. But fewer than 3% of all coupons printed actually get redeemed, and then we tend to redeem them for a second or third item of something we normally buy only one of.

Yet another well-thought-out ploy is the 'Price Promise'. You know, find the same thing at a lower price anywhere within a 50-mile radius and we'll refund the difference. Sounds great. It sedates us into thinking that we're getting the lowest possible price. But that might not necessarily be the case. More often than not, we're getting a competitive price. The retailer is simply counting on the fact that we will be too lazy – and probably too embarrassed – to come back with the news that we found the same thing 40 miles away for a few pennies less. On a high-priced item where the difference is 5–10–15% – say a big-screen colour TV and a video – that's one thing. But on a jar of pickles, not likely.

Refunds and rebates work much the same way. All we have to do is buy four instead of one, submit proof of the purchase and send it all in the mail and someone will magically refund us a set amount or send coupons for merchandise. Aimed at promoting trial use, it works to some extent because it counts on the fact that most people will either lose the proof of purchase, forget to mail it in or simply not bother.

Free stuff is always good, which is why petrol stations are forever offering free coffee mugs with a fill-up, and McDonald's hand out toys with kids' meals.

However, the oldest trick of all is odd-numbered pricing.

When something is tagged £1.99 we fool ourselves into thinking that it falls in the £1 range and is not what it really is,

£2. Proof of that becomes obvious when an item is priced £19.99. When asked how much it costs, we're more likely to say £19 than £20. Or at worst we explain, I got change from £20.

And change is another thing. Getting change makes us feel as if we're paying less for something. Playing up to that, smart retailers won't hand us back a 50p coin in change, instead they'll give us back five 10p pieces because that feels like more money than just one coin.

Where even-numbered prices become manipulative is in upscale goods. Because we've been conditioned to think that change equates to a bargain, when we buy something that is supposed to be expensive, the even-priced tag reassures us in our misbelief that price is always equated to quality.

The bane of all retail outlets is the checkout.

It is the final impression we get and, for that reason, can be the most lasting. Few shopping experiences can rival the bad taste of a long wait to get out.

Supermarkets and other retailers have come to understand that there are three kinds of waiting time. There is the real time we spend in the queue. There is the perceived time we wait. And there is the combination of the two.

To cut down real time, they open more checkouts. If they don't, they create a major problem for themselves because while we're standing there waiting we look around. If there are only six checkouts working and 30 that are closed, we start to imagine that the store doesn't care about its customers. When that sinks in, we start to look for somewhere else to shop.

In an effort to prevent us from doing that, they not only open more registers – which requires spending money on another employee – but they also work out ways to cut down on that second category, perceived time. In this case, it means investing money in getting us to buy more. So they give us stuff to look at.

They put sweets and other temptations there, magazines, gossip sheet tabloids, and in-store promotions.

Turner Broadcasting, the parent company of CNN, has been working on the development of the Checkout Channel, similar to the in-store television you see in post offices, selling insurance and credit cards. In this case, ads are linked to in-store promotions. A variation on that are the back-lit ads that are appearing in some checkout lanes, again to promote in-store bargains. Both, when fully operational, will hook up with computerized interactive shopping trolleys, some of which now have only poster advertising, but which will eventually print out made-to-order discount coupons. The idea is to direct us to whatever it is we think we want and that the supermarket intends to sell to us.

Some stores in Britain, notably Safeway, have begun experimenting with hand scanners. We swipe our loyalty card in a machine and a scanner is assigned to us, with relatively easy to follow directions. The promise is that, if we're honest enough to scan everything correctly, the store will trust us and we won't have to wait at a checkout counter. But that's only half the deal. Once we've put our loyalty card into the machine to get the scanner, they know who's in the store. If they were organized properly, by matching our loyalty card with the information they hold on us in their database – they know what we buy – they could create a point-of-purchase sale expressly for us, tempting us with specials that would be different from the specials offered to the next person. A properly programmed computer could print coupons on the spot.

Many people believe that the scanner is an invitation to a customer to cheat. In some cases, customers take that opportunity, 'forgetting' to scan in the second package of pasta on the chance that they'll almost certainly get away with it. Even if they're caught, the worst anyone will think is that it was a mistake and they'll have to pay for it. Of course, the next time they come in and ask for a scanner, the computer will remember and they will have to check out with a cashier anyway. What the chains that use the scanners aren't saying is that the occasional short-count by a dishonest customer is more than compensated for by the honest customer who makes the mistake of scanning an item twice.

Another thing they're not saying is that the scanner experiment is doomed, unless they can work out one very real problem. Because the scanner allows us to see the total of our purchases at any time, many of us are using it to shop to a limit, then stopping. For a scanner to do everything the supermarkets hope it will, they'll have to keep us from knowing how much we're spending until it's too late.

Finally, if the Japanese have their way, the time we stand in line at the checkout will disappear completely. They see the future as supermarkets with only one cashier, just in case someone has the silly idea of paying with cash. Instead of having employees staffing six checkouts and customers staring at the empty 30, the Japanese are developing a system similar in some ways to airport security machines. It will do everything a cashier can, without making us first take everything out of the trolley and then pack it all in bags.

Each checkout will be equipped with a large cupboard, into which we will slide our specially designed trolley. A collection of scanners will zap everything in the trolley, from every direction, hitting every bar code, no matter how badly we've piled stuff in the trolley. It will then, automatically, print out every item on a register tape to tell us the total. Our credit card will be debited while our trolley slides out the other end of the cabinet.

The entire process should take less than 30 seconds.

CHAPTER TEN

The Fixer

I don't see myself as a weapons dealer, but rather as a Clausewitz of retail. We develop the strategy and the tactics.

Paco Underhill

They had a problem at Bloomingdale's and no one there could figure out why.

One of the most famous department stores in the world, taking up an entire Manhattan block from 59th Street and Lexington Avenue to 60th and Third, the building is a hodge-podge of stairs and escalators, big galleries and smaller rooms, all connected with 'power aisles' – department store lingo for corridors that cut through the shopping floors to get you from one side of the building to the other.

In one of those power aisles, on the ground floor along the Third Avenue side where menswear is, there was a display counter with a tie rack on top of it. The powers that be noticed from their sales reports that this particular rack had a very low 'conversion ratio' – that is, sales as a percentage of the number of people passing by – but they didn't really know why. A best guess might be that most of the people walking by simply weren't interested in ties.

What no one seemed to fathom was that those people who

did stop to look at the ties discovered, to their displeasure, that the power aisle was too narrow to browse without getting 'butt-brushed'.

It took The Fixer to tell Bloomingdale's that all they had to do was move the tie rack out of the power aisle. They did. And within six weeks the increased volume of ties sold had paid The Fixer's fee.

They had a different kind of problem at Champs Sports – a sports gear outlet subsidiary of the Woolworth Corporation in the States – and no one there realized why, either.

The rear of each store where they sold weights and basketballs was underperforming. They knew they had a market for weights and basketballs, but people weren't buying enough of them. And yet the front of the stores was doing good business.

So Woolworth's director of research made a call. It didn't take long before The Fixer struck again.

He concluded that the culprit was the cash register on the far wall. Customers would queue where they were supposed to, but during busy periods the line stretched across the width of the store, literally blocking the way for anyone to get to or from the rear. The Fixer said, move the register. Champs did. And just like that they started selling a lot more weights and basketballs.

It left the bemused director of research to conclude, 'The obvious isn't always apparent.'

In 1974 Paco Underhill, a student at Columbia University, attended a lecture given by urban anthropologist William Whyte, the man who'd pioneered the use of time-lapse photography as an urban planning tool.

Two dozen years later, running his own company called Envirosell and using those same time-lapse film techniques, Underhill is the high priest of in-store consumer behaviour.

A 6 ft 4 in bearded man who once had a pronounced stutter, he says he realized as a child he was better off looking for answers rather than putting up with the humiliation that invariably came every time he tried to ask questions. Today, his stutter has largely disappeared, but forever instilled in him is the conviction that scrupulous observation can be a hugely powerful tool.

So what Underhill does is observe – 15,000 hours of time-lapse a year – and, on the basis of what he sees, he draws conclusions.

When he's called in by a client – the way he was with Bloomingdale's and Champs Sports, the way he has been with Levi's, Starbucks, Hallmark, McDonald's, Sony Music, RadioShack, Revco, Blockbuster, Wells Fargo Bank, Kinney Shoes, Waldenbooks, Brentanos, Burger King, Citicorp and Disney – he sets up cameras around the store. Six is the average. Then he puts his own people – referred to as trackers – into the store with clip boards to make even closer observations. Two, three, four days later he takes all of that tape and all of the trackers' notes and starts what turns out to be a laborious analysis process.

He goes through the footage frame by frame. It's soundless and grainy and people move in awkward spurts because the cameras shoot only one frame every four seconds, creating something that looks as if it's straight out of 'Cops', you know, where two guys come into a 7-Eleven and nervously make their way up to the counter.

Underhill has seen so much of this stuff that he knows exactly what he's looking for: what happens when we come into the store; what we do when we walk down the aisles; how we turn corners; where we look; what goes on when we're confronted by a display; what we do while we wait at the checkout; how we pay; where we put our trolleys; when we leave.

He categorizes his findings, breaking them down, mapping them out for each section of the store, aisle by aisle, counter by counter. After that, he compares what he's seeing here with what he's seen in 100,000 hours of other time-lapse images, so that he can go back to his client to say precisely what needs to be done in order to separate us more effectively from our money.

'We buy what we need,' he explains, 'but ergonomics, the study of human measures, is an important factor. What do we see? How do we touch it? How do we move around the shop? Generally speaking, it is a question of accessibility and comfort. That's why it is so critical to observe customers in the trenches. Once you know why they act the way they do, you can begin to sell them a lot more.'

It was by observing customers in the trenches that he discovered the butt-brush factor. 'The more a browser is bumped against while looking at merchandise, the less likely that browser is to be converted into a buyer. It is especially true of female shoppers. Women are much more sensitive to physical jostling than men.'

It was by observing customers in the trenches that he came up with his theory of the 'invariant right'. According to him, we walk the way we drive. We tend to keep to the right in North America and most of Europe, and to the left in Britain and Ireland. We do it, almost unconsciously, on pavements, in shopping malls, on escalators and in store aisles. But, regardless of the side of the street we walk on, when we step into a store we almost always automatically turn to the right, because most of us are right handed. So, he tells retailers, put your displays on the right.

But not just anywhere on the right.

When we step inside a store, it takes a few seconds before our eyes fully adjust to the change in light. During those few seconds, we've taken 10–15 steps, covering an area he calls 'the decompression zone'. The change in light critically affects what we see, or in this case what we don't see. Which is why he tells retailers, never put anything of importance inside the decompression zone. Putting displays at the rear of the decompression zone, and then to the right, increases awareness by at least 30%.

Next, he tells his clients, no one will read a 12-second message because the public are going to spend only two seconds looking at it. What's more, while most merchandising designers are in their twenties and thirties, a lot of the public are 40-plus. So, unless the type font is large enough and the message is simple enough, it's wasted.

He also advises retailers never to open a store next to a bank.

Watching people stroll along a pavement has shown him that we take a surprisingly long time to slow down when we decide to look in a display window. It can be anywhere from 12 to 25 feet. Because banks don't have display windows, there's nothing to look at, so we keep walking. That means we don't slow down fast enough to see the next-door retailer's window.

'Twenty years ago,' he says, 'retail was about finding and serving new markets. Today it's about breaking into existing markets. It's about stealing someone else's customer.'

He believes that, while traditional market research can indeed generate valuable information, it's never anything more than a window into consumer attitudes. It is both physically and emotionally removed from where the actual decisions are made.

'The way we've learned some very important lessons is by observing the behavior of real consumers in a real store. And many of those lessons are contrary to conventional wisdom.'

For instance, retailers assume we look at a package head-on. But from observation he's confirmed that most of us approach displays from an angle. So he gets retailers to adjust their selling messages accordingly. And when they do, sales increase.

For instance, stores looking to spawn impulse sales should position displays between where we finish our shopping but before we get to the checkout – because it's at the end of our shopping, not at the beginning, that we're most willing to consider other options. We are also, at that point, moving slower. Then, he says, retailers must never forget that a display at 9 a.m. is not the same as a display at 5 p.m. In other words, they must think about what the display will look like at the end of a rainy Saturday afternoon when thousands of people have come by it, touched it, moved it, spilled some of it on the floor.

For instance, every sign in a store should be designed and placed with one and only one customer in mind – a middle-aged person who has a bad back and needs glasses but left the glasses at home. If the sign works for that customer, it will work for everyone else.

For instance, the days when women were the primary shoppers are gone. But men shop differently from women. If a man can't find something in 45 seconds, he loses interest. Getting him to where he wants to be in under that time can generate a sale. To that, he adds, a real revolution has taken place in the past 15 years because more and more men are buying their own underwear. Yet in-store displays for men's underwear are still aimed at women.

Utterly convinced that, in order to generate sales, retailers must establish a congruous relationship between design, operations and marketing, he is constantly reminding them to fine-tune that relationship because it is an ongoing process.

'Shoppers are a moving target. They're becoming more complicated, and retailers need to know more about them simply to keep pace. As consumers' needs are better understood and better catered for, earnings increase. Often, though, the issues are painfully simple. What we tell clients is that we're just selling them a pair of glasses.'

He describes himself as a typical male shopper – 'Men tend to be more impulse-driven than women in grocery stores and shop less often with a list' – but even when he's shopping he's still observing.

'I'm tickled by things that are working well, just as I am fascinated by things that are working poorly. It's like being an engineer and walking into a factory. There are times when I'm glad to be very tall and very big, because when I walk around a store I can get away with stuff that other people might not be able to. I ask to see behind the register, or to take a quick look in the back room. I'm in stores all over the world all of the time. I'm shameless about being aggressive to acquire information.'

What he learns he remembers, adding what he's stored in his knowledge base to any new information he can sell to his next client.

'I was in a record store and I couldn't get over the fact that their primary market is CDs for teenagers. Except their racks were too high for many teenagers to reach.'

He agrees that it should have been manifestly evident to the retailer. But if retailers weren't making mistakes, they would not need him to fix them.

'There are so many little things that should be so obvious. If you walk down the block to Union Square, you'll find The Wiz' – a big discount electronic goods store – 'and, over the course of the day, maybe 200 Spanish-speaking tourists go through that store buying personal stereos, answering machines, cameras, whatever. Now, I've stood there and watched what's going on and by looking at the people working on the floor, I'd bet 20% of them speak Spanish. Yet there's nothing that The Wiz gives them to identify them as having that language skill. It strikes me that if the right sales person met the right customer whose credit cards were humming in their pocket, they could move someone up from being willing to spend two hundred bucks to actually spending a thousand.'

The closer that the management's decision-making gets to the store, he reckons, the more their cash registers will ring.

'Too many companies are still seeing it from the top down rather than the bottom up. I believe with Messianic fervour that one of the fundamental problems in marketing today is the distance from the boardroom conference table to the trenches where the battle is fought. That all of us in twenty-first-century business culture do a hell of a lot of talking about strategy and yet an overwhelming majority of people in positions of power don't know Jack-shit about tactics.'

Which is why so many people in positions of power are willing to pay large fees for his advice. Included in his general guidelines to them is the need for retailers to pay more attention to children. Their influence in the way we spend is increasing all the time and he says that retailers need to 'child proof' themselves by adding kid-friendly features. That's what he told AT&T when they were setting up their Phone Center Stores after he noticed that in one of their designs they'd inadvertently included a blatant invitation for trouble – merchandise sitting right in the middle of the shop at 2-year-old eye level.

'School-age children make incessant demands for toys and food. Toddlers quickly learn that they can affect their parents' behavior in stores. Even the smallest infant can cause a frazzled parent to abandon a shopping trip by throwing a tantrum in the middle of a supermarket.'

According to Underhill, one in eight people who walk through the door of a suburban bank is under the age of 10. Clearly, the child is not there to do business, but his or her restlessness can put a quick stop to a transaction. To give bank officers enough time to make a sales pitch and keep kids from getting in the way of their parents spending money, he advises them to reduce 'the whine factor'.

Put another way, the jar of lollipops on the loan manager's desk has nothing to do with being friendly.

At the same time, something as common in banks as a rope and stanchion to keep customers in line becomes a toy to a 6 year old and a distraction to adults who might otherwise be reading promotional materials.

Underhill cites the example of Britain's HFC Bank when they opened a series of newly designed offices. The offices were elegant. But a step in front of the door denied easy access to parents with pushchairs or to anyone in a wheelchair. Parents either had to leave their child outside – with all the built-in risks and distractions that entails – or carry them into the bank, causing themselves great inconvenience.

'It's simple. Customers are not willing to put up with inconvenience. And they will take their business elsewhere in a flash. They are especially likely to do this at the precise moment when they are most valuable – that is, when they are considering new products and services.'

Thanks to Underhill, all sorts of retailers, not just banks, are beginning to think about these things, coming to the conclusion that there is indeed truth in the old adage: It's always more cost-effective to sell something new to current customers than it is to find a new customer. In fact, according to the Customer Service Institute, it costs five times as much to get that new customer as it does to keep the old one. When the Wells Fargo Bank figured this out they published their own corporate colouring book for kids so that their parents could take care of business. A branch of Citibank went even further by turning a vacant office into a playroom, for exactly the same reason.

Thanks to Underhill, retailers are also beginning to discover that mothers are better than fathers at saying no. It's known in the trade as 'advocacy' – that is, what happens when a 4 year old goes over and grabs something the store has conveniently put there to tempt him and then demands that it be purchased.

If you're the parent, you have a problem.

If you're the store, you do whatever you can to create that situation. You do it by trying to separate mothers and fathers when they walk in – cosmetics and clothes on one side, tools and toys on the opposite side – always keeping in mind that you want the kids to stay with dad.

*

Many people consider shopping to be a leisure activity.

Accordingly, retail square footage has more than doubled in the past two decades to accommodate them. Yet we are in effect spending around 15% less time per shopping visit today than we did just five years ago. Retailers are, understandably, keen to reverse that trend. And the world according to Paco is helping them do that. Even if he isn't responsible for making all the changes, The Fixer has fired the first shots in the new war on our wallets.

Airports. These days they are designed, or rebuilt, specifically with our money in mind. They are little more than shopping malls with flying-bus stations attached, where planes pick us up and drop us off, and on our way from the check-in to the gate we are confronted with fast food joints, shoe stores, luggage stores, camera stores, clothes stores, newsstands and Duty Free shops that have been tantalizingly stocked with chocolate, alcohol, tobacco, toys, souvenirs, electronic goods and perfume. Ever mindful of traffic flow – they've got it all worked out and know which side of this shopping mall we will walk along – they sell space to gift shops on that side and fast food places on the other. As shrewd as it sounds, their reasoning is simple. Studies reveal we are more willing to cross a lane of pedestrian traffic to get something to eat than we are to buy a postcard, film or a magazine.

Supermarkets and convenience stores. They've discovered that beer is not just sold by brand name but that a major factor is how cold it is. Even though beer buyers have told in-store survey takers that they won't be drinking the beer for a day or two, they still want it cold and have been observed checking to make certain it is cold by holding the cans up to their face. So now supermarkets and convenience stores keep their beer coolers filled, even in winter.

Big department stores and mass merchandisers. They're becoming more and more aware of 'senior' customers because there is a pocket of wealth there and, like children, they are relatively easy prey. WalMart is one chain that found they could make older customers feel more welcome by hiring other seniors as greeters. At the same time, many stores have realized they need to set aside areas with comfortable chairs for their older clients. A nice gesture on the surface but, below it, a neat marketing gimmick. By giving the man a place to wait, they separate husband and wife so she has time to shop without his impatience getting in the way.

Pet shops. Putting puppies and cats in the window is the most blatant of manipulative strategies. It is so obvious, and yet it almost never fails to draw parents with children into the store. Once they get a family in, pet shops move them through it, past all the other pets, by putting the big family compromise item along the rear wall – No, you can't have a dog, but, okay, we'll buy you a goldfish.

Drugstores and pharmacies. An increasing number of us are reading labels on the back of packages and at pharmacies where that's been observed and understood they are selling more goods. Again, with seniors in mind, stores, like the Ekerds Drugstore chain in south Florida, realized that small type presents a problem, so they've placed magnifying glasses on chains at the over-the-counter drug section. Given the choice of a store that helps them read the labels and one that doesn't, older clients go to the place with the magnifying glass. Some newspapers in south Florida have also responded to the economic power of an ageing population by upping the size of their classified ad font.

Department stores. Crowd control is one of many ways to manipulate us. Store managers have noticed, for example, that sales at the fragrance counters often come in sprints. Over the course of an hour there may be six sales. For 50 minutes nothing happens. But then there are two five-minute sequences where three things sell. Somebody sees one person shopping, it catches their eye so they go over to the counter to buy something. When the counter reaches critical mass, say a third person, no one else goes there, so sales drop. Crowds can attract crowds but they can also repel them. So department stores are looking for ways to smooth out those long empty moments at the fragrance counters and create a more even flow, always keeping in mind that they can use crowds to attract. They're also sprucing up those areas and aisles that can create discomfort, such as bargain basements. The idea is that they no longer look as if the store itself has bought bargain decorations, lighting and displays.

Clothes retailers. More and more of them are using our sense of touch to sell clothes, a manipulation technique beautifully exploited at places like The Gap.

Thirty years ago The Gap was a San Francisco jeans store where they also sold rock albums. It got its name because those were the days when people spoke about the 'generation gap'. From there it evolved into a discount sportswear chain. By the time the mid-1980s arrived, it had gone the Benetton route – several thousand stores spread across several dozen countries – selling egalitarian-chic.

Nondescript clothes worn by descript people – their ads featured Nicolas Cage, Spike Lee and Henry Rollins – promised that nondescript people could become descript by wearing Gap. It worked. They branched out to Gap Kids and Baby Gap, bought the Banana Republic and have since opened the Old Navy/Gap Warehouse chain.

What made them pioneers was that, early on, they realized they could sell more sweaters by laying them out on big wooden tables so people could fondle them. Touching becomes the sales pitch but the secret ingredient is the table. They tapped into an inner association that we make between tables and food. We eat at tables. We touch food. We derive satisfaction from eating. We associate that satisfaction with tables.

So at The Gap – and other retailers that now grasp how

effective this can be – there are all those big wooden tables piled high with clothes to touch.

'I believe there are three categories of purchases,' Underhill says. 'There is what's on the list. Then there is what we're reminded of in-store which is not on the list. You know, you see something that you're out of and you decide to buy it because it's on sale. Is that impulse? I would argue no. That's a purchase that's been triggered by a memory connection made on the floor. The third category is the pure impulse purchase. That's when you walk down an aisle and see a bottle of salsa-flavoured ketchup and say to yourself, that looks really good I think I'll try it. So when you speak about that 60% impulse buying figure, you're speaking about the difference between what's on the list and what ends up in the basket. It's those two categories of stuff that are unplanned but not necessarily impulse.'

It's those two categories of stuff that Underhill helps his clients to target.

'Stores are getting better at what they're supposed to do. But there's a lot of room for improvement in areas such as package design. Today, a package in the retail setting is fundamentally different than it was even 10 years ago. When someone built a store 10 years ago, 65% of it was public area and 35% of it was storage. Today it's more typical to have 85% public space and only 15% storage. Public area has been turned into storage. Packaging has become a billboard in the store for the product. Whether it's toys or Uncle Ben's Rice, a designer looking at a package as a single entity doesn't make sense. He's got to see how it looks when there are six of them, or twelve of them, or stacks of them from floor to ceiling. Good designers are thinking that way. But the smoke and mirrors of packaging haven't changed a lot.'

On the other hand, the use of point of purchase as a promotional tool has changed radically, going from a sleepy $6 billion industry to becoming a worldwide, very robust $30 billion industry.

'The problem is that the money now being put into point of purchase has come out of package design and media advertising. You want to talk about manipulation? Consider the fact that shelving, point of purchase and package design, the three main images you see on the floor, are run by three separate companies. That's not manipulation, that's just ludicrous.'

It may be true in supermarkets, but there are certain businesses where the main images we see are not run by different companies or, if they are, at least they're tightly controlled by one. That's the essence of the theme store. Sometimes called the 'entertainment retail experience', at other times called 'adventure shopping', it's a rapidly evolving section. It's the Disney store. It's the Warner Brothers store. It's the Coke store. It's Nike Town.

Particularly cautious what he says here, because some of those stores are his clients, Underhill has observed people entering the Disney store with a big 'wow' on their lips because the retailer has made the experience of being there an especially enjoyable one.

'The more pleasant the experience is for the consumer, the more effective the consumer's visit is for the retailer. One of the things the concept does very well is take a lot of what are, in some ways, very ordinary products, and merchandise them beautifully. They get a lot of these products marching out the door. Although I have to think that there must be people walking around today with Tweety Bird button-down Oxford shirts, who, after the third or fourth time, start wondering, why the hell am I wearing this?'

The answer might well be, the power of manipulation. But he isn't sure he wants to commit himself to that.

'When Vance Packard wrote *The Hidden Persuaders,*' Underhill says, 'the notion that the ad men of the world had the ability to manipulate us and understand everything from our sexuality to our urbanimetrics, and that somehow there was a cabal of conspiracies to get us into a store, well, that was a largely accurate vision. But it's now 40 years later. I think we are a lot wiser and a lot more cynical and older as consumers. The idea that a 30-something-year-old marketing executive or a 27-year-old *wunderkind* at Saatchi and Saatchi somehow has the power to pull the wool over our eyes in a variety of different ways . . .' He shakes his head. 'I think it fallacious. And for a wide combination of circumstances. Maybe it's the fragmentation of media. Maybe it's the broadening of truly world cultures, the way London–Milan–New York governs what fashion is. Advertising may lead and influence but it certainly doesn't control.'

The real power of advertising today, he decides, is reinforcing predispositions. 'A customer walks into a store intending to buy one brand, but walks out with another. Time and time again we've watched people walk down the aisle, past the famous brands, to buy something simply because it's being offered on a deal. Those people may be utterly convinced, and probably are because of advertising, that what they originally intended to buy was better. But that's when they're outside the store.'

If that's proof that advertising reinforces predispositions, then it is also proof that both advertising and in-store promotion can be highly effective when it comes to pushing buttons.

'There definitely are buttons being pushed. And some people do it with exquisite skill. But what made perfect sense in 1955 didn't make any sense in 1997. What makes sense today, I don't think will make sense even two years from now. We're seeing marketing dollars chase an increasingly complex consumer in ways that we never could have imagined. Yet we do not have an integrated marketing presence that includes brand identity, package, media, print, in-store and shelf. Each of those six steps, which goes from advertising to the point where the rubber hits the road, which is sales, are ultimately controlled by six different companies.'

What would happen then if one day they somehow all got together? Would that then be Packard's dream come true?

'No,' he says right away. 'But it would sure streamline the marketing process. The problem here becomes, who's driving the boat? The advertising agencies see themselves driving the boat. The irony is that the advertising agency is the farthest away from the actual sale of the product. On the other hand, I sure as hell wouldn't want the boat to be driven by the packaging designers, or the point-of-purchase men. There needs to be another entity here that runs the show.'

Until someone comes along and becomes that, Paco Underhill will keep fixing what he can. Time-lapsing. Observing. Studying. Learning.

And preaching.

'You know, I just saw a very poignant exchange at Tower Records. A young French tourist came up to the security guard with a CD in his hand and asked, will this CD work in my CD player in France? The security guard looked at him with that expression on his face as if to say, don't you realize that a CD is a CD anywhere? But something else was going on in the French guy's head. He was thinking, here I am at Tower Records and this CD is priced at $11.99 and I just bought the same CD at FNAC and I paid 140 francs for it. There's a disconnect here. I recognize it because I go to Europe and find stores haphazardly designed and totally lacking in service. Clients must always have the impression that they're welcome, and this is often not the case in Europe. So then I watch Europeans coming here buying masses of CDs and jeans and because the stuff here only costs a third or half as much as what they would have to pay for it in Europe, they can't help but have the impression of being cheated back home.'

He pauses to let that sink in, then shrugs, 'It got me thinking that consumers in Europe and the US chase value differently. Sainsbury's in Britain, for instance, and all the other supermarkets there have built their house brands. At the same time, stores in the States have focused on everyday low prices. We see on our videos that people in the States are making comparisons by taking two packages, turning them around and studying them. Are the majority of people doing that? Absolutely not. But we have a certain very savvy, very focused consumer in America who isn't buying the classic brand spiel. Oddly enough, that consumer isn't the cash-strapped person who's madly trying to stretch his dollar. He's often the wealthy person who says I am not going to spend my money frivolously.'

The reason that same savvy consumer doesn't show up as much in Europe – and his absence gives British, French and German retailers a manipulating advantage – is not because European consumers are necessarily less savvy than Americans, but because the very structure of European retailing is, by design, more manipulative.

'One of the fundamental differences between Europe and the US is that in the US, across the three major retail categories – I'm talking here about supermarkets, mass merchandisers and drugstores – we have no national players. The closest we have is WalMart. And while they're heavy in some markets, they are also, for all practical purposes, non-existent in others. But look what happens in Europe. In Britain there's Sainsbury's, in France there's Coop, in Germany there's Bilte. There's national control and that changes the chemistry between the retailer and the consumer.'

Does this mean the European consumer should start to worry?

In many ways, he believes, it may already be too late. He figures the one who should be starting to worry is the European retailer.

'In the US, we've stayed focused on value. Go back to the French guy with the CDs. It is absolutely amazing the value we have been able to extract from the distribution chain and the retail experience, and still make money. Let me tell you, if I were a European manufacturer or a European retailer, I'd be scared shitless going into the twenty-first century. Because one of these days WalMart and the other big American retailers are going to max-out here. And when they do, they're going to start focusing their juices on Europe.'

CHAPTER ELEVEN

Selling Us Back Ourselves

Fashion is only an induced epidemic.

George Bernard Shaw

The famous designer takes over a hotel ballroom, has his personal 'show producer' construct a catwalk, fills what floor space is left with folding chairs, then puts a few slightly unpleasant young women on the doors to make certain that no one can get in without a ticket. Unless you happen to be someone who is starring in your own television show, or has been in a movie recently enough that your face is worth having in the crowd.

Making it tough to get in helps build up the idea that, once we are inside, we've joined the privileged people.

The catwalk is little more than very low scaffolding covered in some sort of carpeting – an upmarket version of Astro Turf – but the huge speakers that sit at all four corners are part of a serious sound system. At the far end, there are two Greek columns supporting a rippled curtain.

At the back of the room, young men with microphones attached to earphones sit in front of lighting desks and sound desks, making ready for the moment to begin. Backstage, a dozen very skinny young women, with legs up to their bottoms, are in various stages of undress, unconcerned about the men rushing through their changing room, caught up in the excitement.

The famous designer flits back and forth, hurrying everyone along, soothing egos bruised by a hairdresser who's not curled a strand just right, urging a seamstress to fix a zip yesterday because 'the world is waiting'.

Then, suddenly, the house lights go out, the spots flash on, the music booms, the crowd makes ready and the first young woman comes onto the catwalk with all the assurance of a major star commanding a Vegas nightclub.

Walking perfectly, with perfect posture and sparkling eyes, she moves to the end of the catwalk. Then another woman appears, and following her, there is a third.

Women move up and down the catwalk, winking at the men in the audience – most of whom were waiting for one of them to trip because with dresses that short they're certain there must be a glimpse of something to see under them – and nodding at the women in the audience, especially the ones with their own television shows, to tell them, you can look like this too.

Flashbulbs follow their every step.

So they play to the photographers too.

It goes on like this, never stopping, building up excitement with the music and the lights and the smiles and the nodding, for nearly an hour.

Then there's a model in a wedding gown – very short and very sexy – and no sooner has she strolled cockily down the catwalk than HE appears.

The audience cheers.

The other models follow him out, applauding and hugging him. He comes down the catwalk, applauding too, to thank the audience, blowing kisses, then taking the models in his arms and swinging them about.

And just like that, he's gone. And so are the models. And

the house lights come on.

An hour's parade of souvenirs to create instant identity.

And after the applause, after the lights come on and after the models go away and after the photographers pack up their gear, many people still mingle. They know what they'd just seen. They know why they'd been invited. They know what is now expected. No one has ever hid it or said that it doesn't exist. They come here as willing participants and continue to mingle here as willing participants. It makes them feel better. Which is fine.

Whatever the cost of putting the label on the outside, it's probably still a moderate price to pay for therapy.

All the usual rules of manipulation take second place to the dictum that has always governed the fashion industry – 'Sustain the Myth' – because there is simply too much money at stake, at every level, for anyone in the business to see it evaporate into the same thin air from which it came.

With that in mind, fashion is forever disproving the old adage that we get what we pay for. Instead, we pay for what it cost a designer to discover our own insecurities and then sell them back to us.

Much of it has to do with our apparent need to cover our bodies with logos and signs. T-shirts, belts, shoes, ties, hats, underwear, anything and everything with a name, logo or symbol on the front becomes a removable billboard – YSL, Maschino, Polo, USMC, Cheerios, love, hate, mother, I Survived the Voodoo Tour, Expensive But Worth It, You're Never Alone With Schizophrenia – it's no longer the medium that's the message, we are the message.

Designers not only have understood our need to tell the world who we are and what we believe in, but have given us the opportunity to do it with clothing and accessories while, at the same time, building into the exercise all the excuses we need to think we're really paying for something else.

Case in point, jeans.

There are those people in the business who would have us believe that jeans are not just jeans, despite the fact that some fit very well at £20. But for £200, they will assure us, the cut is special, the seams are perfect and the craftsmanship is exemplary. Except, this is not about getting denim to slide more easily over hips. It's about Maslow's fourth-level needs – esteem, recognition and respect. The real difference between Wranglers, Levi's and Armani is the status that Armani has built into his jeans, and the confidence that comes with believing in that status.

That's why they've made certain the label is no longer on the inside.

We're not buying jeans, we're renting the designer's name. If the label isn't seen then there is no message. If the label isn't recognized, then there is no way to say, I am a member of this particular club.

The fact that anyone can join the club simply by spending whatever it costs to buy the jeans or the shirt or the sweater or the shoes or the dress is neither here nor there. Because, in the end, price is a deterrent. Nor would everybody who has it want to spend it. And anyway, those aren't necessarily the people the label is speaking to. The idea is to get in touch with the other people who can spend it, or would spend it, or are already wearing it. Other people in the market for a billboard. In that case what the label says is, we're both unique.

'Fashion is a code,' notes Umberto Eco, who when he's not writing bestselling novels is actually a world-class authority on semiotics, the meaning of symbols. 'Armani or Krizia, they tell how to compose, and the informed, cultivated person uses them as advisors, while the uncultivated person invents styles by him- or herself. Blue jeans for both, but one has a small, private network of advisors.'

But fashion as a code defines many different worlds, and not just the cultivated and the uncultivated. It also defines the material world – no pun intended – which is represented by the cloth itself, and the symbolic world, represented by the label.

Consider the tale of the humble t-shirt.

Marlon Brando wore one in *A Streetcar Named Desire* and James Dean wore one in *Rebel Without a Cause*, and until they did that, t-shirts were underwear. They were what working-class men wore at home. But Brando's t-shirt was a macho statement. Dean's was a protest. Using an undergarment that way fired the imaginations of a generation of young middle-class men who decided they too wanted to be macho, and they too wanted to be angry. So the material definition gave way to a symbolic definition.

Today, we can buy plain cotton shirts off the rack in every colour imaginable, printed with just about every message imaginable.

San Francisco 49ers. Beethoven. James Joyce. My Parents Went to Athens and All I Got Was a Lousy T-Shirt. Kissing Instructor. Drink Coke. Property of Alcatraz. Baby Under Construction. Life is a Beach. Your Name Here. $E=MC^2$.

Off-the-rack macho. Off-the-rack anger. Off-the-rack mirror of social relationships.

The logical extension of the t-shirt is the sweatshirt and the baseball hat.

Tommy. Armani. Giorgio.

Budweiser. Goodyear. NY.

The logical extension of sweatshirts and baseball hats – clothing promoting products – is products promoting clothing.

Marlboro. Nike. Reebok. Adidas. Wilson. They've all gone into the ready-wear business. First we buy stuff with their logos on it pretending that there is some association. Now they say, hey, the association doesn't have to be illusory, and sell it right back to us.

Whatever it takes to sustain the myth.

*

Fashion advertising can loosely be divided into three areas, defined by the degree of myth implied by the label.

Downmarket they have to tell us what it is they're selling, how many different colours it comes in, what sizes are available, how much it costs and how stylish they'd like us to think it might be. That's what the mail order corduroy slacks catalogue is all about. Rugged guys and outdoorsy women standing around looking rugged and outdoorsy, promising that we can look just as good in dark red, bright blue, mud brown, Swiss gold, Hawaii sand, midnight black and banana yellow, too.

At the very top of the market the ads just have to look extraordinary. The glossiest magazines run the most powerful photos with the most beautiful models in the most exotic settings and with the fewest words. Often the only word on the page is the designer's name. Some people see that message as, 'If you don't know what we're talking about, you're not our kind of customer.' In reality, it's closer to, 'All you have to do to join those people who do understand, and make everyone else think you understand too, is buy this.' Hermes, for example, doesn't have to say anything more than Hermes because years of hard work have successfully burned that brand and the image of a certain quality into our minds.

It is, however, in the middle of the myth market where advertising must accomplish two things simultaneously. Firstly, it must attract attention. If no one sees it, it can't possibly work. Secondly, it must create some sort of feeling for the label.

This is where shock is at its very best.

The British-based company French Connection did it with the word 'FCUK'. As in, French Connection UK. They put their four-letter word first on t-shirts and shopping bags, then on billboards and in magazines. Often the ad was nothing more than the top of a woman's head and the words 'FCUK

Advertising'. Needless to say, it attracted a lot of attention. It also made a statement about fashion advertising. For anyone who bothered to look closely, in very small print at the bottom were the words, 'FCUK is a registered trade mark of French Connection UK.' And that was the problem with the campaign. You had to look too closely to figure out who was selling what.

With Benetton the ads are more shocking and there is no doubt about who is selling what.

The company have for several years used photographs – usually visual metaphors – to sell their name through in-your-face social consciousness.

A black horse mounting a white horse. A black woman nursing a white baby. A priest kissing a nun. An arm tattooed with the words HIV POSITIVE.

Believing that it is important for companies to take a stance on controversial issues, the man who runs the show, Luciano Benetton, says he wanted to find a way to make good on a decidedly haughty promise to 'produce images of global concern for global customers'. He opted for beautifully photographed, carefully shocking images, with no copy, just the Benetton logo somewhere to identify it.

'They do not show you a fictitious reality,' is the official company claim, 'in which you will be irresistible if you make use of our products. They do not tell anyone to buy our clothes, they do not even imply it. All they attempt to do is promote a discussion about issues which people would normally glide over if they approached them from other channels, issues we feel should be more widely discussed.'

Shrugging off the controversies he's provoked, Benetton insists, 'As more and more people understand our position and the urgency of these issues, we hope to become the vehicle for discussion and not its focus.'

Who do these messages appeal to? How about 18–34-year-old women who are aware and socially active, at least when it comes to trendy issues – AIDS, Bosnia, condoms, abortion and the death penalty. All themes in the ongoing campaign.

And who are the average Benetton customers? How about 18-34-year-old women who are aware and socially active, at least when it comes to trendy issues – like AIDS, Bosnia, condoms, abortion and the death penalty.

Now the message becomes: Buy the clothes and, at the same time, buy into social awareness.

Adult men are the easiest to fool.

Inside every man there is a little boy screaming to get out. Equally evident, inside that little boy there is a warrior trying to prove himself a man.

Male sexuality and identity are wrapped around visions of riding a white charger to rescue the beautiful damsel and – because fairy tales say it is possible, therefore it must be – to live happily ever after. As male fantasies are really little boys' fantasies, it doesn't pay to sell anything at all to the man because the one doing most of the buying is the little boy warrior.

—'Get in touch with your masculine side' – Jim Beam whiskey.

—'A few individuals know how to keep their heads, even when their necks are on the line' – J&B Scotch.

—'For the man who lives on the edge' – Karl Lagerfeld's KL Homme cologne.

—'Life is more adventurous when you feel like a New Man' – New Man sportswear.

—'What you carry says as much about you as what you put inside it' – Hartmann luggage.

The little boy warrior as a loner is just as good as the little boy warrior as a lover, because both involve winning and conquest. That's why Ralph Lauren and Rolex both picked up on polo, not exactly the most played game in the world, but one where ads offer images of a man alone, apart from the team, rugged, elite and on horseback. That's why Hilfiger picked up on ice hockey – big, baggy team TOMMY shirts suitable for aggressive high sticking, body checking and slap shooting – and also picked up on yachting. The little boy warrior on the deck, alone against the elements. Hilfiger actually did a collection designed to look like those heavy yachting waterproofs one wears in the middle of a stormy America's Cup, albeit with a huge TOMMY stretched across the front.

The most telling in this category, however, was probably the series of ads Nike ran during the 1996 Olympics. Criticized for being unsportsmanlike – talk about manipulation, this about a company that have done so much to build up their own myth that some inner-city kids sell drugs just to get the money to buy themselves the latest style – they went straight to the warrior's heart by saying out loud what so many little boys know but aren't supposed to say, that winning is indeed everything.

'You don't win silver, you lose gold,' was the way Nike put it. And just so that no one could doubt their intentions, an athlete comments, 'If I say I'm just thrilled to compete, blame my interpreter.'

Polo, yachting, Rolex, £200 running shoes, it's obvious that, as boys become men, their toys simply become more expensive. *Playboy* magazine – a kind of male (*sic*) order catalogue for toys – used to run a one-page ad inside every issue selling itself under the heading 'What Sort of a Man Reads Playboy.' The photo would show some dashing 29 year old in a $3000 suit, stepping out of a Lear Jet, with a knock-out blonde carrying his attaché case, while he checked his Gold Rolex Oyster before climbing into a nearby Maserati to take her, presumably, to the nearest hot-sheet Motel-6.

The impression Hugh Hefner wanted to give was, advertisers needing to reach this guy should be advertising in *Playboy* because this is the guy who reads his magazine.

That he said it is one thing. To believe it is a stretch. More likely, the fellow didn't have time to read *Playboy*, he was too busy keeping up payments on his toys. Anyway, what the ad was really about was 'embarrassment insurance'. Hefner's attempt to soothe the insecurities of 19-year-old college guys, who were forever insisting they only read *Playboy* for the articles and 45-year-old preachers who needed, somehow, to convince themselves that this was a good way to keep in touch with the youth of today so that they'd have something to rant and rave about on Sunday mornings. For both groups, being reassured that the blade in the picture read *Playboy* made it less embarrassing to buy a copy each month from the old lady at the station newsstand. Other than that, the 19 year old and the 45 year old share the same fantasies because the 45 year old hadn't changed since he was 19. Except now, presumably, his fantasies are finally over the age of consent.

Proof comes with the very narrow image of female beauty that is still used to pique male fantasies when someone wants to sell them something.

It is based on perfect bodies that are perfectly unobtainable.

If women in ads looked like everyone's fourth-year teacher – Mrs Whoever, with the sensible shoes and thick-ankle waddle – the little boy warrior wouldn't waste the candle on shoeing his white charger. But if it's Miss October saying, I'm yours if you buy this aftershave, he's saddling up.

Clearly, the adult man who is carrying this little boy inside him knows, intellectually, that Miss October isn't going to show up just like that. However, an ersatz Miss October might. And, the moment he starts thinking that way, the little boy warrior reassures the older version of himself that ersatz is better than nothing.

This is where modern feminists have a field day. Many of them see advertising as a weapon used by men to get back at women. Others argue that the use of unobtainable women creates a standard, not only by which men judge women but, worse, by which women are being asked to judge themselves.

They may both be right. But this kind of marketing didn't create the woman-as-object mentality – the little boy warrior learned that first – it merely exploits what's already inside the grown-up man's head.

Playing to the little boy warrior has, in fact, created a whole new category of automobile, ingeniously disguising the white charger as a fashion accessory.

It's called an off-road utility vehicle.

Cars have not always been about the warrior. They were once about getting from one place to another and often about the person who made them. That's why they were named after people called Ford, Daimler, Rolls, Morris, Chevrolet and Mercedes. But once Detroit got smart, and the rest of the world followed suit, cars became Mustangs, Mavericks, Cougars, Thunderbirds, Broncos and Tornadoes. And just in case someone wanted to fight his battles in romantic places, they also became Monte Carlo and Le Mans and Seville.

They were even advertised for the warrior. Ads talked about speed and horsepower, road-holding and being in control. Maserati used the line, 'Power corrupts. Absolute power corrupts absolutely.' Chrysler sells Le Baron, not La Baronne.

Then along came this whole new category. Safari jeeps for people who never get closer to a wild animal than the image of a tiger at the petrol pump. Big tyres. Sitting high. Macho lines. Hooks on the front to drag an elephant out of the mud. Rear-wheel drive to get through the bush and back to camp. Spotlights.

Here is Wrangler and Patrol and Trooper and Maverick and Grand Cherokee. The same kind of male toy that the pick-up truck used to be. The four-wheel drive equivalent of Brando's t-shirt.

In the beginning, they advertised to the little boy warrior. Since then, they've got smarter. Because little boys don't buy expensive toys without getting someone's approval, the manufacturers called in the researchers and discovered that, in the majority of sport utility purchases, a woman either drove the car or heavily influenced the decision to buy it. For them, the issue wasn't ground clearance, gear ratio or engine compression, it was safety. So now the manufacturers still advertise in men's magazines to the little boy warrior. But these days they're also advertising in women's magazines. Playing up safety and reliability. Playing up to mum so she'll give the little boy permission to have one.

Women can also be fooled – and are constantly being fooled – but not as overtly as men. Women don't tend to buy sex, but they do spend for security and expectations.

Case in point, cosmetics.

As early as the 1950s, manufacturers of lipstick, nail polish, creams, powders, soaps and lotions realized that the woman who paid 25p for a bar of soap to get herself clean would just as willingly pay £2.50 for skin cream to make herself beautiful. The lesson was, women will buy promise. And that is still the basis of the modern cosmetics trade.

'In the factory,' noted Charles Revson, the founder of Revlon, 'we make cosmetics. In the drugstore we sell hope.'

Cosmetics have since become less and less about skin care and more and more about fashion. To all intents and purposes, at least from the middle to the higher end of the market, the two businesses have merged – fashion is a logical ploy of the cosmetics houses and cosmetics are a logical extension of the fashion houses.

There's every reason to suspect that a £10 skin care cream will probably work just as well as a £100 skin care cream, but the pricier version comes with much better packaging and a lot more money being spent behind it to convince us that there is a difference. One of the ways they do that is with buzz-words – highlighting current fads – and bragging about how their product is made with things such as 'natural plant extracts'.

Well, according to the US Food and Drug Administration, the word 'natural' can mean anything. There is no accepted definition for it. Cosmetics manufacturers can, therefore, do nothing more than wave some plant extract over the jar and still have the right to put the word 'natural' on the label. In the case of at least one major player, while their 'natural' line does indeed use plant extracts, the base formulas are the same in both their natural line and their conventional products.

Of course, the prices aren't the same.

In fact, there are no officially recognized definitions for a lot of the buzz-words used in the beauty industry. 'Hypo-allergenic' doesn't mean that the ingredients won't cause allergic reactions, simply that they are less likely to do so. 'Fragrance' means any substance, natural or synthetic, which produces an odour. But 'fragrance-free' doesn't mean the opposite. Some so-called fragrance-free products do contain small amounts of fragrances in order to hide whatever unpleasant odours came along with other ingredients, such as animal fat in soap.

It is almost an unwritten rule that the cosmetics department of any department store should be close to the main entrance. That's so we will have to walk past the extremely high-margin – and profitable – perfume counters on the way in and again on the way out. Then, the aisles are often staffed by young women handing out samples – spraying us as we walk by, or offering a free bath towel with the purchase of two small atomizers or one large-size bath gel plus a medium-sized sleep cream – doing whatever they can to get us to stop. The theory is that a woman who is curious will be tempted if accosted by a product that could interest her and a man who is not otherwise curious might take a moment if pleasantly accosted by a young woman offering to make conversation.

In the past, except for those women in the aisles, the rest of the cosmetics department staff usually operated from behind an enclosed counter. These days that's seen as a restrictive barrier, so counters are being opened with space set aside behind them for a woman to feel as if she has entered a less crowded world. There are more easily accessible displays for someone who already knows what they want and, in some cases, a make-up area where a woman can sit down, away from the department store aisles, to experiment with different shades of lipstick.

An even more manipulative minefield that women are asked to navigate is the category of clothes called mass-designer.

This is not *haute couture*. This is not Karl Lagerfeld designing a gown expressly for Princess Caroline or Catherine Deneuve. This is the commercial by-product of *haute couture*. This is Lagerfeld and Klein and Armani and everyone else who can somehow lay claim to 'the world of high fashion' mass producing what residual glamour they can beg, borrow or steal from *haute couture*. It is the mass-design of an idea that is somehow supposed to represent the world of Caroline and Catherine.

At this level, myth turns into cult.

The cult of the designer. How else can anyone explain why newspapers around the world devoted their front pages to the murder of an Italian tailor named Versace.

The cult of the beautiful people. That's why Hermes call it the Grace Kelly bag.

The cult of the catwalk model. How else can anyone explain the rise to international stardom of Claudia, Kate, Elle, Cindy and Naomi. And the fact that they are identifiable, just like that, first names only.

In *haute couture*, someone is buying a designer's cut.

In mass-design, we're buying the name on the label.

The myth is sustained by keeping that name visible. When everybody is seen wearing YSL, everybody else wants to wear YSL. When no one is seen wearing Guess, Kookai or DKNY any more, no one will be seen wearing Guess, Kookai or DKNY.

In addition to being seen at all the right carousals, the designer's name is made even more visible by branching out into all sorts of related areas, much the way shrapnel from a hand grenade goes in all directions when it explodes.

From whatever hype made the designer big in the first place, they quickly head off into sleepwear, underwear, eye glasses, jewellery, tennis head-bands, sheets and pillow cases, picnic hampers, socks, beach towels, luggage, breakfast trays, portable telephones and fragrances. The really clever ones do their 'sundries' as licensing agreements with leading companies in that specific field. They may, as Hilfiger did, look to Pepe to develop their jeans business, Estée Lauder to develop their fragrances line, and Jockey Shorts to develop their underwear line. It doesn't matter much to the customer – because they're buying Tommy and that's what the label outside says – but it matters a lot to the designer when he tries to get store space for something the store might not have known he was even involved with.

The really clever ones also lock themselves into a healthy relationship with department stores. Not only are the department stores frequently found in malls, where an important section of the mass-design target audience hangs out, but also, because the younger segment of that target audience can't yet get a line of credit with Amex, Visa or MasterCard. They have to depend on cards where conditions are easier to meet – like department store cards with their 'instant credit'.

For the store it's a good deal because they keep the line of credit low, protecting themselves against bad debt while keeping the interest rates high. They also pocket the 4–5–6% they would otherwise have to hand over to Amex, Visa and MasterCard. For that section of the mass-design target market who need the department store for credit, it's a good deal too because they can have the latest designer hockey jersey as soon as it comes out.

Mass-designer is also showing up, very regularly, along

with jewellery and cosmetics on television shopping channels.

The electronic version of mail order catalogues, it's a good bet that it won't be long before QVC, the Home Shopping Channel and the others actually replace catalogue shopping. Mass-design has been quick to move into television because home shopping is proving a very successful way to sell to people who are looking for reassurance.

It's also about winning.

We're asked to get on the phone to buy a Pierre Cardin belt, and as we dial we can watch how many belts have been sold. That means we've got to get our bids in early. If we're really lucky, one of the presenters will take our phone call and make us think we've won something. Otherwise, the operator who takes our order will. Now we see the belts-sold counter go from 102 to 103 – hey, that was us – and we've not only bought into mass-design, we've also found ourselves at the leading edge of technology. Wow, we're on television!

The final stage in the mass-design cycle is when the designers build themselves a network of retail emporia. Today there are temples to their egos all along Fifth and Madison Avenues, in the smartest parts of London and Paris and, in fact, in most major cities.

Theory dictates that the longer any retailer can keep us in their store, the greater the chance of our spending money at the till. That's why stores selling to men use more metal, darker woods and slightly louder music – because most men will feel more comfortable in that environment – whereas stores selling to women use softer colours, softer music and softer lighting. That's especially important because softer lighting can make a woman's complexion look better when she's standing in front of a mirror checking the fit, wondering whether to buy or not.

Because men are more easily distracted, they are given less choice than shops selling to women. They'll have 6 different styles of sweater in 6 colours, rather than 20 styles in 20 colours.

Signs are also larger in men's stores than in women's stores because men don't necessarily like to ask where things are. Ties are next to shirts, and belts are next to trousers. Displays match colours for men, something they are less likely to do for women, because most men are less sure of themselves in these areas.

In stores where they sell to both sexes, resourceful planners make sure that the route between the men's counters and the changing rooms are embarrassment free, because men are less likely to try something on if they first have to steer themselves past piles of ladies' underwear.

It is also a characteristic of the fashion business that the higher up the food chain you go, the less user-friendly the fashion outlet becomes, on purpose. Anyone can stroll into Gap or Benetton. It's deliberately made more difficult simply to wander into Polo and Armani. The entrances to Gap, Benetton, Banana Republic and Levi's are, by design, large and often left open to the street. The entrances to Polo, Armani, Versace, Chanel, Gucci and the others are, by design, usually small, left closed, often guarded and decidedly less inviting.

The message from the first bunch is, we're all welcome.

The message from the second is, this is exclusive territory so if we don't belong, we'll have to get up our nerve to walk in.

That barrier serves two purposes.

For someone wishing to show off, it provides the opportunity of a grand entrance. For someone who needs the courage to walk in, it means they then need to find a way to get out.

Once past that barrier, the temperature of the reception is totally dependent on the prospect of a purchase. 'Just browsing' keeps the relationship decidedly chilly. 'I'll have six of these' raises it to very warm.

The woman who made the grand entrance now needs to find a grand exit, which is difficult to make empty handed.

The woman who needed to find the courage to walk in, now needs to find the courage to walk out, which is more easily accomplished by making a purchase.

We all want to be liked. Mass-design provides that possibility at every turn. All it takes is money.

In Ventimiglia, the first town on the Italian side of the border from the French Riviera city of Menton, there's a huge Friday morning market where every fashion house with an instantly recognizable name is represented by a pasty-faced sales representative who walks around searching for tourists to ask, 'Psst, wanna buy some stolen stuff?'

If you say no, or if you don't speak Italian, French or at least broken English, Pasty-face shrugs, adjusts his rip-off Ray-Bans and walks away in pursuit of a tourist who does. But if you are interested, and many people who show up at the Ventimiglia market seem to be, he motions you aside and tells you that he has a cousin who lives in Birmingham.

You ask, 'Alabama or England?'

He answers, 'Yes.'

After checking to make sure the coast is clear, he rolls up his sleeve to show you a dozen watches – 'Piaget? Rolex? You like Cartier?' – and opens his coat to reveal as many Hermes scarves, and out of his pocket he pulls a handful of Ray-Ban sunglasses in pouches that look exactly like the real thing. 'Luggage? I got Vuitton. You know Vuitton? Handbags? I got Prada. Latest model. Chanel too. You know Chanel?'

You say, 'Piaget? Rolex?'

Immediately the sunglasses disappear and the scarves do too. Now he rolls up his other sleeve and there are a lot more watches. 'Very good price. Stolen. Shhh. For you, only $100.'

You hesitate. 'How much?'

'Okay,' he says, '$75.' He pats your shoulder. 'You from

227

Birmingham? My cousin lives there. How about $50?' He grins, '$40? How much you give me? Guaranteed to be stolen. The real thing.'

Manipulation comes in many different forms.

The same scene is played out in most major cities. In New York, on Fifth Avenue, just around the corner from Tiffany's. In London, on Oxford Street, just in front of Selfridges. In Paris, on the Champs-Elysées, within walking distance of the Rue du Faubourg Saint Honoré, where the major fashion houses sell the real thing for real prices. Probably in Birmingham too – Alabama and England – where Pasty-face's cousin runs that side of the business.

It's not just Rolex watches, Hermes scarves, Vuitton luggage, Ray-Ban sunglasses and Prada or Chanel handbags, it's also CK perfume, Armani jeans, Versace t-shirts, Gucci jewellery, Oasis CDs, Ralph Lauren sweatshirts, Dior jackets, YSL jogging gear, Lacoste tennis clothes, Mont Blanc pens, Microsoft computer software and Nike running shoes.

None of it has been stolen. It has all been manufactured somewhere – very likely in Italy – as knock-offs that offer a fake label which looks like a real label. There isn't much quality. But this isn't about quality. It's about paying a bargain price for a counterfeit label that, you hope, no one will realize is a counterfeit. Of course, the sale of counterfeit goods is against the law – as well it should be – and costs the designer houses a fortune each year. Some fight it, the way Rolex did several years ago, forcing the Italian police finally to break up a counterfeit gang, then sending a message to the world through the publicity stunt of literally bulldozing a mountain of fake Rolexes. Others take a more pragmatic view.

Yves Piaget, who runs the watch company of the same name, has gone on record as saying that, when he first saw counterfeit Piagets being openly sold in markets like Ventimiglia, he was disappointed. 'It's a nuisance,' he conceded, but then added, 'yet the people who know our watches are not likely to buy one off the street. Do you really think someone who buys a $50,000 watch, or a Rolls-Royce, is likely to buy anything at all off the street?'

Sadly, the answer is yes.

At a large summer party in Paris, the manufacturer of a famous designer label – instantly recognizable – greeted his guests, many of them also instantly recognizable, with all the warmth of the perfect host.

Until one arrived wearing the manufacturer's label.

Except it was in a colour the manufacturer never made.

Sometimes living the myth requires more effrontery than money.

CHAPTER TWELVE

Imitation and Subterfuge

Show me the money.

From the film Jerry Maguire

Advertising has two prime objectives. One is to increase the number of customers who will buy the product. The other is to increase the amount of product those customers will buy. Anything and everything in between, no matter how it is stated, is a merely a variation on these two themes.

One of the most traditional techniques that advertisers have used to intensify a marketing campaign relies on what can only be called our indoctrinated respect for authority.

From the first time we are told as children not to do something, and for the rest of our lives, we are shuffled back and forth through a maze of power structures wherein various people, at various times, have some command over us. It might be imposed, such as when a traffic cop puts his hand up and orders us to stop. Or it might be commissioned, such as when we have hired a doctor to tell us what we have to do to cure an ailment.

While imposed authority often brings with it a backlash – a stubborn refusal to be told what to do – commissioned authority is more easily accepted because we can reassure ourselves that it was our idea. That is what makes commissioned authority a useful tool in advertising.

When it is superimposed over a sales pitch, the advertiser is hoping that we will confuse his message with an opinion we might otherwise respect. The announcer says, with great confidence, two out of three doctors recommend Bayer Aspirin, and a certain credibility is shifted from the commissioned authority image of a doctor and onto the product.

Obviously, had the same ad suggested that two out of three plumbers recommend Bayer Aspirin, it wouldn't have the same effect. But because they're talking about doctors and because most of us have been raised to believe that doctors know about such things, the advertiser doesn't have to worry that we will, *en masse*, demand to know: where are those doctors? And, who are those doctors? And, recommend Bayer Aspirin instead of what?

A variation on commissioned authority is hero worship. For whatever reason, fans of Arnold Schwarzenegger and Barbra Streisand sometimes listen to what they have to say about politics. In 1992, he campaigned actively for George Bush. That same year, she was asking people to vote for Bill Clinton. It goes without saying that both are entitled to their opinions. But why should anyone share their views just because one can flex and the other can sing?

The answer is, because we buy the products we like and finding someone we respect who also likes them makes us feel more secure in our own opinions. How else can anyone explain an Omega watch ad that features the headline, 'James Bond's Choice'? It has the added benefit of making us believe that we have something in common with that person. In a way, it's like finding out that your best friend bought the same pair of shoes.

Endorsements do just that.

They allow us to wear the same shoes as our best friend and the same watch as a British spy who doesn't really exist.

Imitation is not just the sincerest form of flattery, it is also one of the safest ways of forming opinions. I like George because Arnie likes George or I like Bill because Barbra likes Bill, so don't argue with me, go argue with them.

Imitation transfers certain qualities from the hero-worshipped to the hero-worshipper. In the late 1950s, when Brigitte Bardot was the world's biggest star, just about every teenage girl in France wore red and white checked dresses, the way she did. They also sat around cafés pouting, the way she did. And, in some cases, they refused to rationalize away their own sexual awareness, the way she did.

By dressing like her and looking like her and acting like her, they were hoping to share the public endorsement of her. It is no different today when young girls dress like the Spice Girls; teenage boys wear football jerseys with their favourite player's number on the back; or grown-ups vote for someone because an actor asks them to.

In healthy situations, imitation comes hand in hand with a certain suspension of disbelief.

Except in Japan.

For whatever reason, the Japanese are especially receptive to American and British stars selling products that those same stars might not want to be seen dead selling at home. Michael J. Fox has flogged tea and fishing tackle there; Whoopie Goldberg has sold chewing gum; Harrison Ford has been photographed in a sauna, sweating, to sell beer; Dennis Hopper has been photographed in a bathtub, with a little rubber duck, to sell Japanese bath salts; Sylvester Stallone has sold canned ham, which seems oddly appropriate; while none other than Ringo Star has endorsed Japanese apple juice. As the story is told, 'ringo' in Japanese means apple juice, so someone at a Tokyo ad agency decided that made him the perfect company spokesman. They got Ringo the drummer to pose with a bottle of ringo the apple juice. Which sounded great, until they discovered – the hard way – that no one in

Japan recognized Ringo the drummer. So the second time around they had to add his name to the ad.

Paying Mikhail Gorbachev reportedly in excess of £100,000 to lend his name to Pizza Hut was a terrific coup. Not only did the company wind up with a startlingly effective commercial but, because it was Gorbachev, they also received tons of media coverage. It was even the subject of leaders in news-papers no less prestigious than the *Washington Post*. (Their opinion was that the 40-second spot was 'unappetizing and cruel' but served, nevertheless, to reinforce the association.) Somewhere there is a statistic that says, for every 1000 or 10,000 or 100,000 people who make that association, another pizza will be sold. By working out what it cost to reach those people, the company could reasonably estimate what their return would be. By double-bouncing the TV spot, using Gorbachev to turn it into a news story, their cost per pizza customer went down.

Perhaps the most interesting thing about the spot was where they showed it. The esteem in which Mr Gorbachev is held – a commodity that the company was looking towards as a new topping for their pizza – guaranteed sales in the West. But in Russia itself, where the actors in the commercial actu-ally criticize Gorbachev for the collapse of the old state system – despite the fact that they praise him for having brought Pizza Hut to Moscow – the company knew enough not to bother showing it there.

Back in the real world, Bill Cosby sells Jell-O. But no one in their right mind is going to think that if we buy Cosby's Jell-O, we'll wind up being as smart and funny as him. On the other hand, when there is no suspension of disbelief, John Hinkley shoots Ronald Reagan to win the affection of Jodie Foster. Even in minorly less healthy ways, disbelief manifests itself in stalking. Yet, if imitation wasn't such a powerful force, why on earth would anybody buy Michael Jordan's cologne?

Certainly not to smell like a basketball player.

Jordan is the epitome of a star who can move a product. Perhaps the best basketball player who ever played the game, his colossal skills in being able to put a ball through a hoop 10 feet off the ground have given him a worldwide audience that transcends race, age and sex.

Because a part of that audience would do just about anything to share some of his fame, when he asks them to buy sneakers or wear his after shave, they do. Sharing that with Jordan hints at a deeper kinship which, in turn, creates a certain level of self-esteem. In good years, his work for companies such as Gatorade, Nike, McDonald's, Rayovac, Sara Lee and others is worth, to him personally, upwards of $40 million. That's not counting what he was paid to act in *Space Jam*, a Warner Brothers film that tied back in to companies like Nike and McDonald's.

But then a lot of companies believe he's worth every penny of what they pay him, especially Nike, as the Air Jordan is the bestselling sneaker ever.

Nike and Reebok each spend nearly $100 million a year on sports marketing. In some ways, it's like the Americans and the Russians escalating stockpiles of nuclear weapons during the height of the Cold War. Every time one side got a fancier bomb, the other side needed two.

In this case the weapons are glamour and credibility in the form of athletes willing to stand in front of the world and say, this is the best. Reebok have at times paid Shaquille O'Neal, Emmitt Smith and Frank Thomas to say that. Nike have at times paid Anfernee Hardaway, Drew Bledsoe, Deion Sanders and Ken Griffey Jr to say the same thing. Reebok have commercial ties with the National Basketball Association and National Football League. Nike have commercial ties with the National Basketball Association and the New York City Marathon. Reebok shoed more than 3000 athletes competing at the 1996 Olympics in Atlanta. Nike shoe about half the players in professional baseball.

The particular genius of Nike is that they have been able to find athletes who are not only talented but have some kind of humanity to them that makes them admirable beyond their physical prowess. What's more, they seem to find these athletes when they're still in high school, before they're in the world trying to become celebrities. They found John McEnroe, Andre Agassi, Michael Jordan and Tiger Woods that way. It's a sort of farm system of people whom other people will like and feel good about.

Granted, Jordan is smart, charming and also one of the greatest athletes of all times. Larry King once said about him, 'I have never seen a smile like Michael Jordan's.' His charm and presence can sell most things. As long as they somehow tie in to what he does, which is, first and foremost, play basketball. It gets a little bogus when he holds up just any-thing, because endorsements need our collaboration. We are the ones who must connect the product with the fellow pitch-ing the offer.

It gets back to two out of three plumbers. If we don't com-plete the circuit, if we don't plug in the connection, it doesn't matter who's selling what, we won't buy.

The makers of Rayovac rechargeable batteries discovered that when they hired Jordan to sell batteries with the theme, here's technology that's good for the environment. Taken out of a context in which we are willing to accept him, he was as miscast as someone from Greenpeace selling basketballs. So no, not even Jordan's élan can sell just anything.

Weight Watchers in the States believed Fergie – the Duchess of York – could sell their product and paid her to do just that. The British branch were dubious and didn't use her. Still, the connection we have to complete is obvious. There's no doubt that the late Princess of Wales could have sold make-up or clothes. A Diana line of clothes would have, without any doubt, been worth a fortune. Both Diana and Fergie were certainly known quantities when it came to selling tickets for a charity event.

But glamour doesn't sell rechargeable batteries.

In much the same way, there are certain people who probably couldn't sell anything. It would be the epitome of bad taste, and therefore counter-productive, to have Hitler's image endorsing a product. Which, in fact, an Italian winery recently tried to do. They were using the names of some of the more luminous villains of the Third Reich to sell their otherwise unknown vintage. They got a flood of ensuing publicity but the joke value – if that's what it was – of bringing home a little, light Goebbels' *Liebfraumilch* was non-existent. And not without reason.

The same thing would almost certainly happen to any product associated with mass murderers Richard Dahmer, Myra Hindley and Charles Manson.

Perhaps not surprisingly, O. J. Simpson, one of the most visible pitchmen of the 1980s, is known to be seeking whatever endorsement deals he might be able to secure. He only got so far selling his video and his book, but he thinks he can sell something at some point. Admittedly he's up against huge obstacles. But, at least in the black community where many people still believe in his innocence, it is not inconceivable that his face and name will, before long, be used to sell something.

When a pitchman puts his own name on a product, it moves endorsements up a notch.

Enter, again, Michael Jordan.

Bijan Paksad, the Iranian-born, Los Angeles-based menswear designer whose company, Bijan, is perhaps best known for the oval-shaped perfume bottle with the whole in the middle, struck up a deal with Jordan to design a line of cologne. Bijan even allowed him into the creative process, coming up with five scents – one, supposedly, for each of Jordan's interests. A grasslike smell for a golf course. A pine smell for Jordan's native North Carolina. A leather smell for his two-year sabbatical from basketball to play pro baseball. A cedarleaf, grapefruit and lemon smell to evoke a beach. And a sandalwood and musk smell called Sensual perhaps to summon forth images of sports groupies.

The packaging carries Jordan's own logo – his head and shoulders silhouetted in black against a red background.

'We have captured the essence of Michael Jordan,' came the boast from Bijan. Putting his money where Jordan's nose is, Bijan backed the boast with $20 million worth of advertising. The campaign was called 'Going Inside', because, for the first time, commercials didn't have him dunking baskets or otherwise flying through the air. He was shown relaxing at home. The message was, for a bottle of cologne you also get the key to Michael Jordan's private world.

The marketing was clever. A 3.7 ounce bottle of Jordan's cologne spray, priced at $35, was shipped to department stores and men's shops where the price would be considered pretty standard. A considerably smaller bottle – 0.5 ounces and guilefully called the 'Deluxe Travel Size' to reassure buyers that they weren't opting for the cheapest, tiny size – was priced at $12 and went to sports shops, where $12 would be considered more than just a whimsical purchase. Then, to tie the price directly to Jordan, they came up with a size in the middle, 1.7 ounces, which they marketed wherever they could for $23 – because that's Jordan's basketball number.

'What people are buying when they buy something with Michael Jordan's name on it,' explains Leslie Savan of the *Village Voice*, 'is a sense of his power, a connection with him. A piece of Michael Jordan. The idea is not to smell like a basketball player, because he is beyond being a basketball player. Look at how other people are selling him. He's being sold as a God.'

Her reference is to a Nike commercial where Jordan is shooting baskets in slow motion. Shots of him are intercut with shots of a lot of people all over the world who stop whatever they're doing to see him on TV doing what he's doing. As he shoots, they go into freeze-frame. Michael Jordan stops their world.

'It is definitely the deification of Michael Jordan,' she says. 'That's the whole point of his colognes and beauty products. You buy it not because he uses it but because by using it you can get the essence of this God. Come on, this is a man who shaves his head and sells shampoo.'

Associating a star with a product in a commercial is one thing. Associating a star with a product in a commercial when we're not supposed to realize it's a commercial is something else.

In the 1987 movie *Wall Street*, Michael Douglas held up a copy of *Fortune* magazine and, in the character of the wheeler-dealer who believed that 'greed is good', proclaimed the magazine to be 'the Bible'. What the audience didn't know was that *Fortune* had won the right to the title by outbidding *Forbes*.

In the Kevin Costner film *Bull Durham*, there were no fewer than 50 specific brand name references. In a 100-minute film, that works out to one every two minutes.

In the Danny DeVito film *Other People's Money*, he did a soliloquy that began, 'If I can't count on Dunkin' Donuts, who can I count on?' That product then showed up in another six scenes.

In *Home Alone*, there were reportedly 31 different brand names mentioned. Kraft General Foods even had the script changed so that, instead of turkey, Macaulay Culkin's Christmas dinner would be Kraft macaroni and cheese.

In *Demolition Man* one of the characters made a joke about the Taco Bell restaurant chain, saying it will be the only one left in the next century. For the Japanese version of the film, the producers changed the reference to Pizza Hut. Both were owned by Pepsi.

In *True Lies*, Arnold Schwarzenegger hung out of a window at a Marriott hotel. Apparently, Holiday Inn weren't willing to pay enough to have him hang out of one of their hotels.

In *Independence Day*, Jeff Goldblum saved the world with an Apple PowerBook computer.

In Tom Cruise's first hit, *Risky Business*, Ray-Ban outfitted him with their latest Wayfarer model sunglasses. Within 30 days of the film's release, they'd moved 18,000 pairs, more than they'd sold in the previous three years. So they did it again in *Top Gun* and *Jerry Maguire*.

In *The Firm* – Tom Cruise again – Red Stripe beer took a lesson out of Ray-Ban's play book and got themselves onto film. The beer had been mentioned by name in the John Grisham novel on which the movie was based, but it had been left out of the script. Red Stripe supposedly paid the producers $5000 in product to get put in. When *The Firm* came out, Red Stripe sales jumped 50%. Mercedes also wound up in *The Firm*, by outbidding BMW to be Tom Cruise's car, in spite of the fact that BMW was the car mentioned in the book.

Product placement is the practice of associating specific goods with films and television for the mutual benefit of the manufacturer and the production company.

If an action hero needs a cellular phone – which The Saint did in the recent remake of the 1960s TV series – the producers and the Nokia company both agree it has to be worth something if the star uses a brand-new Nokia 9000 cellular phone and fax machine. So a deal gets struck. In return, the producers deliver a captive audience – us – to watch a commercial that we don't realize is a commercial, or that we wouldn't otherwise get to see or, for that matter, particularly want to see.

Among those companies already known actively to seek product placement deals are Heineken, Amstel and Murphy's beers; Ever Ready and Energizer batteries; Hiram Walker, Ballentine's, Courvoisier, Drambuie, Kahlúa, Beefeater and Canadian Club alcohols; and Butterfinger, Baby Ruth, Nestlé Crunch, Raisinets, Milk Duds, Good 'n' Plenty, Chuckles,

Whooppers and Goobers candies. Also on the list are, MasterCard, Baskin-Robbins, Dunkin' Donuts, Kawasaki, Schwinn, Spalding, TDK, USA Today, Lee, Philips, Beech, Intel, RCA, Taittinger champagne and Colgate Palmolive.

The modern age of product placement was born in 1982 and Steven Spielberg was the midwife. However, the idea of putting real products in films in exchange for some sort of compensation has been around for years. As far back as black and white films, for instance, a scene in an airport might take place at the American Airlines check-in desk. It was a way of paying American back for supplying tickets to help ease production costs. But that sort of thing was peanuts until Reese's Pieces came along.

Spielberg was making *ET* and wanted the friendly alien to eat earthbound candy. He approached M&Ms but, for whatever reason, they turned him down. Needing something, he settled on the then little-known Reeses' Pieces. The Reeses' people said sure, paid nothing for the appearance and overnight – thanks entirely to the success of the film – sales jumped five-fold.

That's when it began to dawn on the studios that they might be sitting on something very big.

Today, each major studio has what's called a Production Resources Department. Their job is to assist films in arranging products, props, costumes, set decoration and transportation. They get a list of requirements from the film's producers, and then go out to try to meet them.

Say a director insists that a character in his film must eat Quaker Puffed Rice. Production Resources contact Quaker and say we want to use one of your cereals. Will you give us permission to do that? Or a company may phone the studio to say, if you ever need a widget, we'd be delighted if you'd use ours. Or a call might come in from any of the growing band of product resource agents, who represent companies looking to get placement. Regardless of who instigates the contact, clearance is required because showing a product on camera is considered to be using a trademark, logo or design for commercial purposes. The only area where it might not need approval is a scene, say, in a supermarket where literally thousands of products are visible. If the camera is just panning across shelves the studios generally don't worry about clearance. But if suddenly the camera stops and focuses on a product – because an actor either reaches for it, or does some dialogue in front of it – then clearance is required.

The studios have to be particularly careful because cases pop up on a regular basis where someone forgot to get permission, or didn't think they'd need it, and the lawyers start filing suits.

There was a film a few years ago at Universal which had computer workstations in the background, and stuck on one of the computers was a little Post-it note printed with the image of Grant Wood's famous painting 'American Gothic', but with Bill and Hillary Clinton's faces on it. It was incidental background, but the artist who owned the image spotted it, contacted the producers and insisted on a settlement.

So everything gets cleared. Magazines. Newspapers. Photographs. Designs – such as architects' archways in unique buildings and even cars. If it's traffic on the street, that's one thing. But if the scene calls for a car to break down, or one of the tyres flies off, the lawyers are going to want to see clearance in writing before the scene gets released. If a character who hates Mercedes simply says as much, that might pass without clearance. But if he says it in front of the Mercedes logo, then Mercedes had better be asked for approval first, or writs will certainly fly afterwards.

That said, the car industry tends to be more lenient than most when it comes to supplying product. Almost all films have cars in them somewhere and, as long as the actor isn't going to stand in front of a Mercedes badge and say something like, 'This car is a piece of crap,' manufacturers are happy to play along. In *GoldenEye*, BMW launched their Z3 Roadster by making it the chosen car of James Bond – a throwback to the days when Aston Martin was Bond's car of choice. In both cases, car sales soared. Sparked by that success, Land Rover manoeuvred a deal with the producers of *The Horse Whisperer*, Chrysler got their Sebring convertible into *Speed 2*, Volvo showed up in *The Saint* and, long before *GoldenEye* made it onto video, BMW was back in the game, negotiating an appearance in the next Bond film, *Tomorrow Never Dies*. The only catch to car placement in a film is who'll be driving it. Understandably, the manufacturer's main interest is in promoting their latest model. They don't necessarily want to be the car of choice of fleeing drug dealers, or have their latest models involved in fatal accidents.

The tobacco industry also used to be a big player in product placement, but that's all changed now. And everybody is on the lookout for cigarette brands sneaking in through the back door.

When a film is using an actual event, cigarette ads in a stadium can inadvertently show up on screen. The film-makers are asked to shoot around the ads but, in the end, there is relatively little the studios can do about that. On the other hand, if the budget warrants it, film-makers can digitally enhance the scene, taking the real sponsorship ads out and putting generic ads in their place. However, this can get complicated because, contractually, the companies that sponsor the events have the right to be associated with them.

Years ago, a number of baseball parks had cigarette ads in the outfield, among them Ebbets' Field where the Brooklyn Dodgers played. There was a huge cigarette ad in right field, and whenever someone hit a home run, a puff of smoke would come out of the ad. If that's necessary for historical purposes in a film, they might go with it. But there is such heightened awareness about cigarette advertising these days, that it is equally likely they would use a generic brand, taking a minor liberty with historical accuracy, rather than duplicate the actual brand.

In the days when tobacco companies could come in through the front door, Philip Morris are said to have paid $350,000 to provide James Bond with cigarettes in *Licence to Kill* and Brown and Williamson are said to have struck a deal to get Sylvester Stallone to smoke their Kool brand in five films. The way that story is told, Stallone was to have been given a $100,000 car, an $80,000 horse and around $25,000 worth of jewellery. It didn't happen, and wound up in court. But, allegedly, the reason it didn't happen was not because the tobacco company or Stallone didn't want it to happen but because an agent got in the middle and fouled up the deal.

These days, if an actor smokes, you don't see the cigarette package. Or if you do, it's only a small corner of it and not the name on the front. Or if it is, the brand is a generic fabrication of the art department.

Because a film studio is a business, if Production Resources thinks they can get paid to put a product in a film – tobacco notwithstanding – they'll put a price tag on it. However, the Entertainment Resources Marketing Association, the official trade group for all sides of the product placement business, says that their best guess is money only ever changes hands 5–10% of the time. In most deals, the product is either donated or payment is made in kind.

Most studios try to downplay their product placement involvement. They don't particularly like to discuss it. Although in weaker moments they will concede that this is kind of a secretive corner of the entertainment industry. They claim that money only rarely changes hands, and then only for 'key' placements. In other words, a direct endorsement. But, they insist, the days of under-the-table payments and dumping off tons of product in exchange for visibility are long gone. Today it's all about strategic alliances, about partnerships, about big business. It's also all about perceived value. So the marketplace dictates who pays and how they pay and, if they pay, how much.

When money does change hands, manufacturers aren't necessarily going to admit it and film executives aren't going to ruin their chances of future deals by disclosing how much. Instead, both groups would have us believe that product placement is almost always a case of a manufacturer supplying product and maybe even throwing in a few extra as a goodwill gesture for the crew, just so that they can be associated with the film. That may be fine for sunglasses and Reeses' Pieces, but throwing in a few extra could get very expensive when you're talking about BMWs.

There is, it must be said, an innocent side to product placement. Say you have a scene in a kitchen. The prop master chooses whatever household products he wants and the studio gets permission to use them. No promises are made as to whether the products will appear or, if they do, how they'll appear. In any case, this is stuff that the production needs whether or not the manufacturer supplies it to the production for free. So, if they can get it free, that helps keep costs down.

But there is a second type of product placement that bothers some film-makers. And that's when a company tells a production they'll pay to have the product prominently featured in the frame and then start to dictate terms – dialogue about the product, close-ups, how long the logo must be in frame.

The Robert Redford hit *Sneakers* was shot at Universal Studios, which was then owned by Matsushita, which makes JVC and Panasonic. Matsushita's biggest competitor, Sony, happened to own Columbia. It was obvious that when the prop master went looking for computers, which play a major role in the film, they shouldn't have Sony monitors. So, just to make it fair, the prop guys were told by the director not to use JVC or Panasonic either. Instead, they went out and found a brand called Northstar. It was a statement of independence on behalf of the film-maker, although, interestingly enough, it did not go unnoticed by the Universal bosses. At the first test-screening of the film, a senior studio exec wanted to know, 'What the hell are those South Korean monitors doing in this movie?'

That many studios are now owned by companies with their own products available for placement presents its own problems. Columbia-Tri-Star have been known to suggest that Sony products should be placed where possible in their films. In the days when Coke owned Columbia, Pepsi didn't show up in films made there. Even Disney are said to have first right of refusal with Coke.

As long as Seagrams owns Universal, when whiskey is shown in a film, responsible drinking will always be an underlying theme. If a Seagrams label is shown somewhere, there won't be any drinking and driving. When someone grabs a bottle from a bar and breaks it across another actor's head, it won't be a Seagrams bottle. Instead, it comes from the same corner of the art department as the cigarettes. On the other hand, if there is a shot in a bar and the setting is right, and the booze will be shown in a favourable light, then Seagrams will be the first choice. What's more, because Seagrams has enough different brands to stock a scene, the audience will almost certainly never realize that the entire bar is only Seagrams brands.

As for what placement is worth, there are no rules. It depends on the product and how good the placement is. It's especially complicated because there are all sorts of placement. There's verbal, where the product is mentioned by name. There's an implied endorsement, where a character in a movie uses the product. There's the simple situations where there's simply a box of the stuff sitting on a shelf. If it's just a box of Puffed Rice on a table, the producers may be happy to get a few cases of it. If one character in the film says, please pass me the Puffed Rice and another says, okay, here's the Puffed Rice, and the first says, this Puffed Rice tastes great, then that will probably cost someone more than a few cases of cereal.

Computer companies are always early on the bandwagon, and in exchange for having the product on camera are willing to supply hardware and software for the production. Certainly in the case of expensive equipment, which can amount to a massive saving in production costs, the studios accept that's just as good as a fee. Being able to shoot on board an American Airlines 757, in exchange for showing the AA logo a few times, can mean a saving of several hundred thousand dollars in production costs. At the same time, the American Airlines logo is thrown onto movie screens around the world. When a script calls for the hero to wear Ralph Lauren, the studios are fast to ring Lauren, hoping to structure a deal. If he says no, and the director is willing to allow his character to be dressed by a designer other than Lauren, the studios aren't shy about ringing Calvin Klein and trying to make a deal with him.

In the end, if there is payment, it still usually works out to be much cheaper than a television commercial. It's true that a TV spot may last 30 seconds and any product's time on camera in a film may be only a couple of seconds. But when we watch a celebrity endorse a product on television, we naturally assume that the company has bought the celebrity's support. It's obvious someone is paying him to say what's being said. But when we see that same celebrity in a movie saying exactly the same thing, for some reason it seems to be more believable. As long as we can forget that Rocky is really Sylvester Stallone, we're more likely to accept his endorsement of Wheaties – in *Rocky III* he winds up on the 'Breakfast of Champions' package – as a seal of approval.

This sort of thing is about to become a very important issue because there are digital VCRs on the market right now that are capable of automatically editing out commercials. You tape a film on TV, and when you play it back the VCR automatically fast-forwards past the ads. Needless to say, that presents a huge problem for advertisers. The answer, as many of them see it, is getting the ad inside the film or programme so that it can't be fast-forwarded out.

Unlike the movies, statute prohibits fees from being paid for placement on TV. However, this doesn't apply to cable. Nor does it apply to films broadcast on terrestrial television because, even if a fee was paid to the film production company, it wasn't paid to the broadcaster.

The way it works, at least in the States, if a product is used as a prize in a quiz show, or is shown in a drama or on a sitcom, the manufacturer is given a credit for 'promotional consideration'. That's how Kodak X-ray machines and Häagen-Dazs ice-cream, for instance, both show up regularly on 'ER'. The manufacturers appreciate the exposure and, in this case, the producers save a little of the $9000 per episode they otherwise spend on set-dressing.

When Jerry Seinfeld's writers called for an episode that put him in conflict with his car mechanic – whose function in life was to nag him about taking better care of his car – Saab jumped at the chance to have one of their 900SE turbo convertibles star with him. So the show wound up with a new car. A Saab 900SE turbo convertible can retail for around $50,000. But a 30-second commercial on 'Seinfeld' retails for around $500,000.

There is now a new trend in Hollywood.

Rather than charge a fee for placement, or get payment in kind, studios are on the look-out for what's known as 'back-end' deals – that is, using manufacturers to help promote the film with their own tie-in product promotion. And this is where the industry has become very savvy.

In the minor sci-fi thriller *The Arrival*, Luxottica sunglasses dressed Charlie Sheen and, in exchange, Luxottica used pictures of Sheen in their in-store, point-of-purchase ads. *Batman and Robin* did $125 million worth of tie-ins with Apple

Computers, Kellogg's, Taco Bell and Frito-Lay. Disney's *Hercules* tied in with General Motors, McDonald's, Nestlé and Quaker Oats. *Casper* was commercially linked with Pepsi, Pizza Hut and Choice Hotels. *Batman Forever* had deals with McDonald's, Kellogg's, Six Flags and Sears. *Pocahontas* joined forces with Chrysler, Nestlé, General Mills and Burger King. *The Lost World – Jurassic Park* took in $250 million worth of backing from JVC, Burger King, Kodak, Mercedes, Timberland, General Mills and Tropicana. Ford also came in, becoming the chosen car to be eaten by a dinosaur. In another scene, the camera showed the Jurassic Park gift shop, which happened to be filled with actual Jurassic Park tie-in products.

And, of course, Ray-Ban outfitted Tommy Lee Jones and Will Smith with sunglasses for *Men in Black*, then spent $10 million on a tie-in point-of-purchase promotion, featuring cut-outs of Jones and Smith wearing the sunglasses, using Smith's reference to them in the film, 'I make this look good.'

Companies getting involved with any form of product placement are constantly being warned to insist on written contracts that spell out every aspect of the deal. Most do. What they're never supposed to do is pay for placement before the movie comes out. And here the story is littered with the bones of good intentions. When Hollywood phones Corporate America, the walls come down, the warning lights go off and otherwise intelligent businessmen stand there with their mouths and wallets open.

Everybody wants to be in the movies.

There was a time when even Reebok did.

The Tom Cruise film *Jerry Maguire* was made at Tri-Star. A story centred around a sports agent, and the original script contained references to Nike. The character played by Cuba Gooding Jr is an arrogant, cocky athlete who isn't getting any endorsements. Initially, at the beginning of the movie, the script called for him to criticize Nike, saying, essentially, screw them because they weren't showing him any respect by giving him endorsements.

When Nike saw the script, they turned it down. They didn't want that kind of publicity. But Reebok heard that Nike had dropped out and they said that, under certain conditions, they'd be willing to take it. The main condition was a neat little twist. They would allow Cuba Gooding Jr to say what he was going to say, if at the end of the film he was redeemed by making a Reebok commercial. That would be integrated into the film. Reebok would then take the commercial out of the film and use it as a real commercial.

Tri-Star apparently loved the idea and said let's do it. So they made the commercial and then they made the movie. Reebok were all set to use the spot on TV as soon as the movie was released. Except, by the time the film made it into the cinemas, there was no commercial in it. Artistic licence resting with the director, the commercial somehow wound up on the editing room floor. Reebok speed-dialled their lawyers. The only reference to them that was left in the movie was Cuba Gooding Jr's comment, 'Fuck Reebok.'

CHAPTER THIRTEEN

The Softest Target

We are strip-mining our children's minds and doing it for commercial profit.

Al Gore

In the world of manipulation, eight year olds are sitting ducks. They simply do not have the defensive skills to ward off the massive advertising attack thrown at them by highly skilled, highly educated, highly sophisticated adults – in stores, on television, in the movies, in the print media, even at school.

It has been estimated that, in the first six years of the average American or European child's life, they will have spent more hours watching television or playing video games than bonding with their father over the entire course of their lives. That means, the single largest chunk of input shaping our children during these critically formative years is delivered, not by parents, but by people with something to sell.

By the time our children reach 18, they will have spent approximately 12,000 hours in school. But they will also have spent some 17,000 hours watching television!

What is true in the adult world is even more evidently true in the child's world, that the only reason children's TV exists – the only reason anyone bothers to entertain them with

'Rugrats' or 'Beavis and Butt-head' – is to deliver an audience to advertisers.

That's television's job.

Kids are the merchandise.

And for all the things that television is – both good and bad – nowhere is its extraordinary power more evident than in its ability to burn products into our children's brains, intensifying normal feelings of self-doubt, then manipulating them to think that the only way they can ever become adequate is to own whatever is being sold.

Advertisers play directly to their self-confidence. And because children cannot yet differentiate between big lies and little lies, television reshapes their concept of truth. It creates a vocabulary deliberately designed to make it as difficult as possible for them to discriminate between the real world and the world that advertisers want us all to live in.

A survey by *Harper's* magazine pointed out that, over the past 50 years, the written vocabulary of the average American 6–14 year old has diminished from around 25,000 words to just about 10,000. Instead, words have been replaced by symbols and icons, the vocabulary of television.

Through television, advertising has invaded our children's minds, coloured their judgement and usurped the family's influence. What's more, it has starkly reduced parents to being little more than brokers with whom children must bargain if they want to watch more television, have more toys and become bigger players in the world of youthful consumerism that advertising promotes.

Not that manufacturers are commercially wrong to try. Children represent a market which, in North America and Europe alone, is worth in excess of £20 billion and said to be growing at up to 20% a year. They also directly influence several hundred billion pounds worth of family spending. Kids are no longer just a market for action figures and Mars bars. The older children get, the more they insist on the right to make their own decisions over the way they dress, what they eat and how they spend their time. Surveys show that, on average, girls start flexing their consumer muscles as early as the age of 4, and that most begin to insist on having a say in products bought for them by 6 or 7. It takes boys a little longer, usually at around 10 years old, before they become vocal about the same things.

Understanding this, advertisers focus first on girls in general and grooming products in particular. They encourage prepubescent independence by making things more readily available at the stage when the child begins to notice them. The films children want to see are promo'd on television, with tie-in toy merchandising available at McDonald's. Tie-in clothes merchandising is available in most high street stores – including, these days, Marks & Spencer. Coupons offering discounts on the price of admission to see the film are packed into cereal boxes; competitions to attend the première are offered on television; games off-shot from the film are available on the Internet; and more merchandising is sold in the cinema lobby.

A recent study at Texas A&M University revealed that most of the money 6–12 year olds have at their disposal is spent on food and beverages – which makes it all the more understandable why McDonald's, Burger King, Mars, Kellogg's and just about everybody else in the food and beverage industry has an interest in this group. They're followed closely by manufacturers and marketers of toys, clothes, films, music, sports and video games.

What they all have in common is their advertising appeal to young children through the use of rhyme and song. Commercials aimed at boys feature louder music and louder voices than commercials aimed at girls. Colours used in commercials for girls are the obvious pinks, purples and pastels. Colours used in commercials for boys are red, yellow and black. Appeals to older children and teenagers are made through the use of peer pressure.

You aren't cool if you don't have one of these.

There's no doubt that these advertisers know exactly what they're doing. And when they sink their teeth into a specific target group, their bite is lethal. Case in point: one out of every five cellphones sold in the United States is bought by a teenager.

Terrestrial TV around the world is filled with programmes for children every weekday afternoon as soon as school gets out and, traditionally, throughout Saturday mornings. But the real home of kids has become cable and satellite, where entire networks – among them Nickelodeon, Fox Kids, the Children's Channel and the Disney Channel – are exclusively devoted to delivering children to advertisers.

Born out of cartoon reruns, these 'kids only' networks have become huge outlets for shows that either couldn't find a place on national network television, or have been specifically designed for a cable audience. Nickelodeon, as an example, uses generous helpings of 'Ren and Stimpy', 'Rugrats', 'Doug', 'Clarissa Explains It All' and 'The Adventures of Pete and Pete', plus game shows – featuring good prizes for the winners and purple slime poured over the heads of the losers – to separate the commercials.

Long gone are endless reruns of Mickey, Donald and Bulwinkle Moose.

Today's cartoon fare is for kids of the millennium, with toys spun off the shows, so that once they see the cartoons they can buy the dolls, play the games, live with the posters and eat the breakfast cereal. Who pays for it? Among the top 10 brands advertising on cable and satellite are McDonald's, Burger King, Pizza Hut and Barbie Dolls.

Once the kids grow out of Nickelodeon, there's MTV.

That phenomenon came into the world in August 1981, an infant of cable and satellite, simply to sell music on television the way the Top 40 had been sold on commercial radio for nearly 60 years. But the powers-that-be misjudged the market. They believed that they could merely transfer radio to television in partnership with the big record companies. Music videos were never intended to be anything more than fancy commercials for a pop star's latest release, so if MTV were going to make money, they reckoned they might as well make a lot of money, which meant looking to the big record companies with budgets to help feed their stars to the public.

In those early video-only days, there was Madonna, Billy Joel and Bruce Springsteen. After a while there was Prince. Because the audience was largely white, middle class, suburban – black street kids didn't have cable then – the music was largely white, middle class, suburban. In those early days, Prince was about as far as they could stretch it. In those early days, Michael Jackson was not yet that.

It was rap that changed things.

Much to the amazement of those white, middle-class suburbans, rap became too big to ignore. In 1988, MTV conceded defeat and put on a programme called 'Yo!' A weekly rap video show, it was an instant success, and management – always sensitive to commercial potential – quickly transformed it into a daily event. Three years later, the Madonnas, Joels and Springsteens had been pushed aside – relegated to VH-1, an off-shoot cable operation aimed at that original grown-up, white, middle-class audience – and new bands were given more attention. At first there was pop-metal, then there was Nirvana. Then there was Soundgarden, Pearl Jam and Alice In Chains.

It was no longer true that everyone over 30 was subversive. Suddenly, it was everyone over 22.

MTV made the world younger and noisier, all the more so when it pledged allegiance to electronic music. Today the station reaches an astonishing quarter of a billion people – many of them under 22 – and is no longer video-only.

It's hardly a coincidence that both Nickelodeon and MTV

are owned by the same corporation, Viacom. The only real difference is that, where MTV shows commercials disguised as music videos, Nickelodeon shows programmes to separate the commercials.

In the so-called McLibel case, the longest-running court trial in British history, the verdict confirmed an especially salient point made by the defendants. Although they lost, the judge agreed they had satisfactorily demonstrated their claim that McDonald's advertising made 'considerable use of susceptible young children to bring in custom'.

It would have to be someone who'd been living on Jupiter for the past 25 years not to know that the McDonald's community relations programme revolves around children, child welfare and youth-related social issues. One of the world's most visible corporate images, the clown Ronald McDonald, promotes hamburgers through public appearances in, among other places, children's hospitals. Diverse cartoon characters, such as those featured in various Disney movies, are also used to promote Happy Meals. And while the judge in the McLibel case was fast to say that he did not believe McDonald's deliberately set out to deceive, there is clearly a manipulative element in the way they link hamburgers and fries with fun in the minds of children.

But then, McDonald's is hardly alone. One look around the world's high streets is all it takes to see that where you find McDonald's you also generally find Burger King, Pizza Hut, Taco Bell, Wendy's plus most of the also-rans in the fast food business.

McDonald's have the deepest pockets of all. Their annual advertising war chest – these days around $425 million – not only puts them on television and everywhere else kids might stumble across their ads, but also pays for their 10-year exclusive tie-in deal with Disney. The importance of that arrangement is two-fold. It establishes a link that children can easily make between their favourite Disney characters and McDonald's, in addition to guaranteeing that the same link will not be made to Burger King, from whose grasp, incidentally, McDonald's snatched the deal.

To keep the product new, fresh, desirable and therefore exciting, McDonald's go on regular invention sprees, as they did not long ago, coming up with a new hamburger sandwich called the 'Arch Deluxe'. Needing to respond, Burger King tried to make people understand through their advertising that they were 'Still the One'. Using television spots, they demonstrated how a McDonald's whopper was put together, superimposing over those images the words, 'McDonald's may try and romance you with a new burger. But there's nothing like an old flame.'

The hamburger war is mostly fought in plain view. Under the surface, however, like nuclear submarines stalking each other, there's another battle going on for the hearts, minds and thirsts of our children. This is 'Coke v. Pepsi – The Sequel'.

For a product to sell on the scale that both Coke and Pepsi do, they need a gigantic distribution network. Distribution is, by the way, one reason Coke has such a lead over Pepsi, particularly in the United States. Coke is the drink of choice in McDonald's, Burger King and Wendy's. Pepsi competes through Pizza Hut, KFC and Taco Bell, three chains which PepsiCo used to own. By holding title to those outlets, Pepsi inevitably opened the door to Coke to say to everyone else – including McDonald's and Burger King – why would you buy Pepsi when they're your direct competitors? To counter that, Pepsi decided to distance themselves from their own chains, spinning them off to a subsidiary. That, in turn, allowed the restaurants to negotiate with whichever soft drinks brand they want. The ploy is to put Pepsi in a position to go back to McDonald's and Burger King – where the serious money is – and say, we're no longer competing against you, we're now ready to compete against Coke in order to get into your outlets.

The results are not yet in and won't be for several years. This will be a long, protracted campaign. But then, with stakes this high, it's no wonder. If Pepsi can get just one out of every hundred kids to switch, they're looking at increased revenues in the tens of millions of dollars.

It's one thing for a child to watch television at home and see commercials for McDonald's, Burger King, Coke and Pepsi. It's another to see them in school.

Back at the end of the 1980s, a young entrepreneur in Tennessee named Chris Whittle had an idea. He believed that a great untapped market was the nation's schoolchildren, and that if he could find a way to bundle them together as a group – to corner them in the same place at the same time – advertisers would beat a path to his door.

It didn't take a lot of imagination to realize that this audience was already wrapped up in one neat package – it's called school – and that, thanks to satellite technology, the market was ripe for Whittle's plucking.

His problem was how to get satellite receivers into schools. He knew he couldn't go to schools and say, buy a dish, buy a bunch of televisions, buy a bunch of VCRs, and let me send programmes to your kids. Most schools were too strapped for resources. Many were already cancelling important things like sports and after-school activities. So he went to junior and senior high schools across the country and said here's $22,000 worth of free stuff – a 19' television set for every classroom, two free VCRs for every school, and a satellite dish which he promised to hook up and service. All he wanted in return was access to every student between the ages of 12 and 18 for 12 minutes a day.

He named the venture Channel One.

And 12,000 schools across the United States fell for it.

Having snatched the attention of 8 million students – it cost him $250 million to set up in 1990 – Whittle began broadcasting 10 minutes of soft news a day, together with 2 minutes of hard commercials.

Of the 10 minutes devoted to news, 2–3 usually report on current events. That leaves 7–8 minutes to devote to feature stories, some of which are product oriented, such as how Nike sneakers are made. Technically, the programming is slick. But those 2–3 minutes of hard news cover an average of around seven stories. The 2 minutes of commercials are devoted to 4 spot ads. In other words, each ad runs almost twice as long as each hard news story.

Everything is aimed at spotlighting those ads. Half a minute before a commercial break, music comes up out of the background to segue into the spot. The idea is obviously to make certain that everyone in the class is wide-awake for the ads.

The programming is professionally competent. But the commercials are nothing short of brilliant. One series, for Skittles sweets, features a newscaster beginning what appears to be another story when an announcer breaks in to 'interrupt this class for a temporary fun emergency'. He says, for the next 30 seconds we're only going to think of fun thoughts, like the fact that students in many foreign countries go to school on Saturday and Sunday. The kids laugh and Skittles sales increase.

It's when the laughter dies down that some educators can be heard raising genuine concerns. They feel that schools are allowing Channel One to sell sweets to teenagers when health education courses are trying to tell those same teenagers to cut down on sweets. Diet with children can be a real problem, especially where sugar has helped to create a wave of adolescent obesity. Now, here's a television programme beamed straight into classrooms – to a captive audience, forced to watch – saying, forget what they teach you in school about diet, go ahead and eat more sweets. The question then becomes, how wise is it for publicly funded schools to permit the private sector in, essentially, to undermine parts of the curriculum?

Some states have gone so far as to ban Channel One on the grounds that it is inappropriate for educational institutions to endorse advertisers. Others have tried to ban it but failed, while still managing to make the point that 12 minutes a day add up to one hour a week, time that might be put to better use developing reading and writing skills.

The argument in Channel One's defence is that it's bringing current events to children. That's backed up by surveys which have shown that its audience is, as a consequence, more aware of current events than non-Channel One kids. As for the advertising, Channel One argues that kids are seeing the same commercials elsewhere.

Put another way, they're saying that, because advertising sweets to kids isn't new, that makes it harmless, while editorial content is new and that makes it healthy.

Whittle ran into financial problems with Channel One – he'd overextended himself, having announced plans to set up other direct-targeted television, such as in doctors' waiting rooms – and in 1994 he sold out to K-III Communications. That company has, for years, supplied accessory materials to schools, including the *Weekly Reader, The World Almanac* and *Funk & Wagnall's Encyclopedia*. Unlike Whittle when he started, K-III already had a foothold in the nation's schools. Consequently, their presence is today more secure than Whittle's ever was. Getting them out, if anyone ever tries, will be that much more difficult.

It is also that much less likely to happen.

Economics have forced schools to look beyond public funding for ways to supplement various programmes. One school in Colorado has supposedly got so desperate that it's allowed advertising to go up in the corridors.

Not that school doors have, until now, been shut to companies. In the old days, companies that knew could always get in. What's changed is that, these days, the doors are purposely left open.

Ask Benetton.

The company that uses shock advertising to attract adults haven't been shy about doing soft-shock to attract kids. Under the banner of 'The United Colors of Peace', they've supplied 130,000 elementary school students and 16,000 of their teachers in Italy, Germany, France, Belgium and Spain with a peace-oriented educational programme consisting of books and posters, all of which are aimed at helping children to learn to respect cultural differences.

That those 130,000 elementary school students might just live within walking distance of a Benetton Kids store is no accident.

Before long, nowhere will be safe.

The final frontier for children is already populated with advertisers desperate to sell them things. The Internet – and, through that, the World Wide Web – is filled with sites luring children into the world of cyberspace with games and prizes. But, before they can play and possibly even win something, they have to supply the people on the other end with a lot of important information about themselves – their name, their age, their sex, sometimes their home address and phone number, always their e-mail address, their favourite TV shows, their favourite commercials, their favourite stars, and the names and e-mail addresses of their friends, so they too can 'join'.

Like supermarket loyalty programmes, web-site operators – include among them McDonald's, Disney, Nickelodeon, Oscar Mayer, Kellogg's, Frito-Lay – know who our kids are, what they like and where to find them. They already know how to get them interested in buying. But here they do it in special ways, such as by erasing any visible line between entertainment and advertising. Kids are invited to play a game that turns out to be little more than a hard sell for a product. Advertising characters are the hosts, so when kids are 'playing' at the Kellogg's web site they're interacting with Snap, Crackle and Pop. Everything the child does while visiting the web site is monitored. Eventually, a print-out arrives on some programmer's desk to say that kids will play longer with Snap than with Crackle, the result being predictable. Those print-outs also help a company to tailor the hard-sell message to the child, often including his or her name inside the message, repeating details that the child has, perhaps unknowingly, fed into the system. Finally, the company have a valuable database from which direct mail and other marketing pitches can be launched towards the child. Often included is the possibility of buying things on-line.

Those companies that have already established a substantial presence on the Web – and, at this point, those who haven't are rushing to get there because they realize they're coming late to the party – explain that all they're doing is providing on-line entertainment for kids. The way they see it, what they're doing is nothing more sinister than what they do on cable or satellite television. What they don't say is that, if they tried the same thing on television, they'd risk getting their hands slapped. Unlike the World Wide Web, television and radio have some in-place statutory safeguards to protect children against these same, manipulative techniques.

CHAPTER FOURTEEN

Future Shock

All great advertising has two things in common. It's effective. And it's always preceded by a meeting in which someone says, are you crazy?

Bob Kuperman, the Chiat/Day Agency

If Bill Gates and Boeing have their way, the earth will soon be ringed by 324 satellites which will do nothing but serve the Internet.

In a $9 billion deal announced in Spring 1997, their idea is to link every outpost on earth to the information superhighway, providing instant access, video-conferencing and any multimedia application that anyone can think of. If they pull it off – and they say they expect to by the year 2002 – they will have shrunk the world to a minute size.

At the same time, there are at least 14 other major conglomerate-sponsored plans to do much the same thing and, at least according to one space consultancy group, there are plans right now for more than 1700 satellites to be launched before 2005.

With literally hundreds of billions of dollars at stake, the Internet is almost guaranteed to become as commonplace in our lives as telephones, radios and televisions. In fact, the

Internet is almost certainly destined to take over all three, combine them, add in as yet unthought-of services, and become the single most determining factor in the way we live. It will be the second most dominating means of communication, surpassed only by speech itself.

So far, the Internet has proved highly effective at selling product tie-ins to kids and at delivering pornography to just about anyone of any age looking for it. One recent statistic claimed that 85% of all the images currently available on the World Wide Web are sexual in nature. But the Net is also electronic mail – connecting people around the world for, at most, the price of a local phone call – as well as forums and chat rooms. For the same local phone call, anyone can discuss any subject imaginable, and many that aren't easily imagined, with people they've never met.

In that respect, as a tool for communications, it is no more sinister than a telephone. Obscenities, in whatever form and by whatever definition, come from the people using the tool, not from the tool itself.

Its real potential remains as a tool. Included among the near-infinite uses for this tool is as a conduit for buying and selling stuff, and for reaching consumers in a way that, until now, has been only wild wishful thinking. When the Net as international shopping mall lives up to its promise, which it is beginning to, consumers' borders will reshape the globe. For better or worse, entire worlds will be created and made available to us without any input from politicians or governing authorities. Freedom of speech and freedom of thought will be taken to their outer limits. With that will come the never-ending debate about too much freedom. Thankfully, for people who believe that freedom of speech and freedom of thought are inalienable rights – ones that can never be defined in terms of too much, and certainly not something that should ever be defined by politicians – the debate will go nowhere. Anyway, it is, by definition, futile because cyberspace will not exist within boundaries of political control. Even the discussion of how to tame it is frivolous. It will not be domesticated – or nationalized, as some governments would hope – any more than politicians or governments could tame the oceans or the heavens.

But parts of cyberspace will be colonized and made habitable, and over the next 10 years more and more people will be working and playing inside artificial environments.

The roads to and from these new colonies will not be like the one-way route of the Canastoga Wagons westward, but will be multidimensional. Left by the wayside will be the innovations – such as television – that shaped the twentieth century. Those media will be confined to museums that will recall the dark ages when information travelled in only one direction.

We have already seen the birth of interactive media. But the future is not one new star, it is a galaxy of supernovas that will go far beyond modems and telephone lines – which are hardly more than the Ninas, Pintas and Santa Marias of this expedition – to a future of plural-active media. Simple desktop computers will accomplish a multitude of tasks at the same time, reaching out in thousands of directions simultaneously to fetch whatever it is we need, and bring it all back in easily digestible forms.

The entire globe is already a local phone call away. Long-distance is swiftly becoming yet another relic of the twentieth century. As it disappears, so must political boundaries. They may be the last to go, but they too will evaporate. Government, a system established to control territory and to decree laws which oversee the daily workings of society and which, all too often, attempt to manage the flow of information available to the people, will simply prove inadequate.

To all intents and purposes, digital technology, fibre optic cables and satellites will redefine our political structures, if not making them meaningless then at least making them impotent.

To all intents and purposes, within the next 10–20 years it will not matter where we live, as long as we live within the information technology boundary. It will be just as easy to conduct most businesses from a balcony overlooking the Mediterranean as from a glass-fronted skyscraper in New York, London or Hong Kong.

Such ease of movement, alone, will eradicate boundaries.

But ease of access to information – and the colossal amount of information that will come with the opening of the techno-logical floodgates – will also, unintentionally, divide our world into those with technology and those without.

Tragically, that division will bring with it incalculable costs. Consider the fact that, with hindsight, the British, Spanish and French should have realized that their definition of progress spelled decline for the native American tribes. Yet the cost to foreign civilizations has never stopped man from exploring.

Without foresight, we will repeat those same sins in cyber-space.

As boundaries evaporate and information empires take their place, products – that is, goods and services – will become what Esperanto was never able to become, the inter-national language. Just as consumer goods brought radio, then television into our homes, they will litter cyberspace with billboards. But those billboards will not look like road signs. The separation between entertainment and advertising will have finally disintegrated. We will, without any choice, be turned from passive collectors of information into creators of ideas, visions, worlds. We will all become publishers, to the detriment of monopolies of ideas. Wars will not be fought with tanks, because there will be no dividend in holding a mountain or defending a valley. They will be fought with bytes and megabytes, because there will be gigantic profit in trying to influence the flow of data.

Today, commerce over the Internet is minuscule, involving mostly books, compact discs, archives of magazines and newspapers, gambling and pornography. Tomorrow, it will be unrecognizable by today's standards. Computer speed and capacity are doubling about every 200 days. Fast computers designing faster computers to design faster-still computers have become the closest thing in the universe to perpetual motion. By the end of 1998, 15–18 million more American households will have come on-line, bringing the total above 50 million. In Europe – traditionally slower than the USA to accept these sorts of advancements, either because of governmental reluctance to cede communication power to the people or because of a lack of dedicated funding to hasten what is an inevitable transfer of that power – the pace is gaining velocity to the point of being ferocious. To the point where more computers will be sold than TV sets. To the point where the ratio of computers to TV sets is fast approaching parity.

It took 40 years for the telephone to reach 50 million users. It took the Internet just five. Modem-equipped computers will outnumber television sets within 5–10 years. By 2015, it is a good bet that the entire developed world will be on-line, and that most of the third world will be too. All of which begs the question: will the Internet create the second world and, more sharply than ever, separate those who are on-line, being the haves, from those who aren't on-line, being the have nots?

And then what?

It is absolutely beyond doubt that the diminutive cow path we see today as the Internet will become a 64-lane superhighway within 5–10 years. Competition in the global marketplace will not, by definition, be limited to domestic enterprises. A foreign manufacturer merely needs a web site. It will be of no consequence that someone is 6000 miles away. He or she will appear on our big-screen TVs or, even better, in virtual reality sitting in our own living room. At the same time, the digital revolution in television will change the way information and entertainment come into our homes. Instead of 5 or even 50 stations, there will be 1000.

Commerce on the Net will also multiply geometrically. If it was worth £2 billion in 1998, it will be worth 10 times that by the millennium. And 10 times that again two years later.

Companies that have spent billions off-line building brand equity – making certain that when we hear the word 'cola' we think of Coke and when we hear the words 'computer chips' we think of Intel – are now aiming their financial artillery at building brand equity in cyberspace. But this is a market that levels the playing field. A $25 billion conglomerate must compete with some fellow living in an 8x8 room in a country with an unpronouncable name, because on the Web – if he learns how to manipulate these tools – he can look like IBM.

Some companies are only now beginning to realize that if they don't get into the game they will be left too far behind. So they are rushing around, not only to ensure that they own their own brands, but also to buy up all the words that define their brands. This is Procter & Gamble registering domain names like *headache.com* and *diarrhoea.com* and *underarm.com*. Most companies haven't yet figured this out. Most have no clue that if they don't take Internet ownership of the words that they have spent billions on owning off the Net, someone else will take them.

Without those words, they will never be found.

One of the ironies of cyberspace is that, no matter how big a company's presence in the physical world, if their cyberspace site can't be found, they do not exist.

The digital revolution will ultimately meld telephones, television, fax machines, electronic mail and all other forms of communication into the Internet, creating a resource of still-unimaginable possibilities.

It is already starting to happen.

What's more, it is happening at blinding speed. Markets are globalizing. Information technology is feeding on itself to expand at the speed of light. Authority is being disconnected.

The information age economy is burgeoning. The result is that we are living through the twenty-first century's equivalent of the industrial revolution. And like Version I, 200–250 years ago, the effects on the way we live are fundamental.

The information technology available right now in every brand-new, medium-priced automobile is more complex, more powerful and more advanced than the information technology developed for NASA's first lunar-landers. We have come so far, in so short a time, that there are now inexpensive watches and cheap pocket calculators that have more computing power than most mainframe computers could muster when Apollo spaceships went to the moon. It is reasonable to project, therefore, that as the speed of information technology has increased geometrically over the past 30 years, it will increase multimillion-fold in capability over the next 30 years.

The world our children will inherit from us will be nothing like the one we inherited from our parents. Consequently, the world of tomorrow's manipulators will be as distant from ours as ours is from that of the caveman.

They will not speak of declining cost curves through mass marketing. Theirs will be a new language.

Today we are randomly exposed to advertising. The Internet is the first step in our actively seeking it. And the advertiser's trick will be in getting us to do just that.

The most likely way will be by providing some reward, perhaps through entertainment and information, but more likely by spoon-feeding us satisfaction for some need at the upper end of Maslow's hierarchy. As long as the media were directed at the masses, in the days when we, as consumers, had no choice but to accept the fact that networks had turned us into the product – that the only way we could watch their programmes was also to get their commercials – advertisers could do what they wanted with us. Our only defence was to turn off the set.

Welcome to the Maginot Line.

The sciences that will emerge – whether they're called 'mechatronics', which is the combination of mechanical and electronic engineering, or words not yet made up – will almost certainly produce everything from bionic human body parts to entire cybernetic civilizations. While such a future might sound as strange to us as submarines did to Jules Verne's readers when he first published *Twenty Thousand Leagues Under the Sea*, it's worth noting that submarines today can stay under water for a year, circle the globe without being detected, and carry enough scientific 'advances' to destroy the earth and all creatures living on it several hundred times over.

There was a time, not really all that long ago, when Tom Swift and Captain Video, and all of the other cartoon cut-outs who once inhabited the twenty-fifth century, spoke to each other over telephone wristwatches and had computers in their cars – which weren't cars, of course, but flying vehicles – that directed them from point to point. Today even grandmothers carry cellphones and anyone who doesn't own a helicopter can have a computer system in their car, linked to satellites, to guide them accurately along streets they've never driven down before.

Futurologists, looking now merely a decade or two ahead, see a world where currency is global and entirely electronic, where subliminal learning – going to sleep with a language tape playing under your pillow and waking up with some fluency in that language – has been perfected, where electronic shopping is an everyday affair, where most newspapers are delivered electronically and where products of all kinds are customized to suit individual requirements.

Back in the 1980s, western manufacturers hitched onto the Japanese doctrine of 'just-in-time'. The idea was that assembly lines were driven, not by production goals but by orders. Stock rolled off the lines and was immediately shipped, reducing the costs of inventories and stock taking. Ten years later, computer giants Dell and Gateway 2000 realized that they

could add personalization to just-in-time, not simply manufacturing to order but manufacturing specifically to suit individual customers. One computer gets built with 32 meg of
RAM and a 12-speed CD-ROM unit, the next gets 16 meg of
RAM and no CD-ROM unit. That idea has since spread across
all sorts of industries, for instance car manufacturers, which
are gearing up to offer literally hundreds of variations for each
model, customized for individual buyers on the assembly line.
Today we can order a bicycle over the Internet from a subsidiary of Matsushita, which will be made to our specific
requirements. And we can order shoes to pedal that bicycle
from a company on-line that will upload to our computer the
necessary graphics program so that every design combination
is possible.

The inevitable outcome is a world where everything is
customized, including the advertising that comes to us.

Mass manipulation will one day be called 'precision-
strafing'.

Companies looking to reach us with pinpoint accuracy will
turn to hundreds of millions of narrow windows, each of them
on offer on-line, through which each of us can be reached.
Instead of trying to define who we are *en masse*, advertisers
will already know who we are as individuals, and will target
their appeals directly to us. It is the futuristic electronic version of what we've come to accept as personalized junk mail.

Just as letters from companies looking to sell stuff address
us by name and then sprinkle our name throughout the body
of the letter – as if we're supposed to believe they're actually
writing to each of us personally – digital communications will
do that too in more subtle, and more sinister, ways.
Furthermore, it will be done so slickly that most of us will
believe it is true.

This will be advertising targeted to each one of us as a mass
of individuals. Advertising so precisely aimed that Coke
drinkers will see ads only for Coke and Coca-Cola will be able

to ensure that their followers will never see ads for Pepsi.

This will be our next-door neighbour watching the same programme as we do but getting different commercials.

This will be two people in the same house watching the same sporting event in two different rooms and seeing different advertising signs on the stadium walls.

This will be two of us in the same room having advertising directed to us, as a pair, that would have been different had one of us been alone.

Tomorrow's manipulators will use the world being created by us today to return to us a world where, despite media diffusion, our choices will be severely limited to what they have decided we think we want to see. The only divergence will be what those fanatics among us – those of us who learn to scavenge – can somehow, mostly by chance, find.

It is not that Big Brother will have won.

It is, rather, that we will have become Big Brother.

Bibliography

Selected quotations from

Columbia Dictionary of Quotations, Columbia University Press, New York, 1993.

Contemporary Quotations, Vail-Ballou Press, Binghamton, NY, 1964.

Crown's Book of Political Quotations, Crown Publishing, New York, 1982.

Crown Treasury of Relevant Quotations, Crown Publishing, New York, 1978.

Dictionary of Canadian Quotations, Stoddart Publishing, Toronto, 1991.

Fitzhenry & Whiteside Book of Quotations, Fitzhenry & Whiteside Limited, Canada, 1993.

International Dictionary of Thoughts, Ferguson Publishing, Chicago, 1969.

International Thesaurus of Quotations, Thomas Y. Crowell, New York, 1970.

New York Public Library: Book of Twentieth-Century American Quotations, Stonesong Press, New York, 1992.

Ocford Dictionary of Modern Quotations, Oxford University Press, New York, 1991.

Oxford Dictionary of Quotations, Oxford University Press, Oxford, 1992.

Routledge Dictionary of Quotations, Routledge & Kegan Paul, London, 1987.

Stein & Day Dictionary of Definitive Quotations, Stein & Day Publishing, New York, 1983.

Selected Books

Advertising Age, *How It Was in Advertising – 1776–1976*, Crain Books, Chicago, 1976.

Albion, Mark S., *Advertising's Hidden Effects*, Auburn House, Boston, 1983.

Albion, Mark S. and Farris, Paul, *The Advertising Controversy*, Auburn House, Boston, 1981.

Alexander, George J., *Honesty and Competition – False-Advertising Law and Policy Under FTC Administration*, Syracuse University Press, Syracuse, 1967.

Ansolabehere, Stephen and Iyengar, Shanto, *Going Negative – How Attack Ads Shrink and Polarize the Electorate*, Free Press, New York, 1995.

Applegate, Edd, *The Ad Men and Women – A Biographical Dictionary of Advertising*, Greenwood Press, Westport, CT, 1994.

Atwan, A., McQuade, D. and Wright, J.W., *Edsels, Luckies, & Frigidaires – Advertising the American Way*, Dell Publishing, New York, 1979.

Backer, Bill, *The Care and Feeding of Ideas*, Times Books, New York, 1993.

Backman, Jules, *Advertising and Competition*, University Press, New York, 1968.

Baker, C. Edwin, *Advertising and a Democratic Press*, Princeton University Press, Princeton, NJ, 1994.

Baker, Samm Sinclair, *The Permissible Lie – The Inside Truth About Advertising*, World Publishing Company, Cleveland, OH, 1968.

Baker, Stephen, *Advertising Layout and Art Direction*, McGraw-Hill, New York, 1959.

Barnouw, Eric, *The Sponsor*, Oxford University Press, New York, 1978.

Barry, Thomas E., *Children's Television Advertising*, American Marketing Association, Chicago, 1977.

Barthes, R., *Mythologies*, Paladin, London, 1986.

Barton, Bruce, *The Man Nobody Knows – A Discovery of the Real Jesus*, Bobbs-Merrill, Indianapolis, 1925.

Baudrillard, Jean, *Revenge of the Crystal – Selected Writings on the Modern Object and Its Destiny*, Pluto Press, London, 1990.

Baudrillard, Jean, *Simulations*, Semiotexte, New York, 1983.

Baudrillard, Jean, *For a Critique of the Political Economy of the Sign*, Telos, St Louis, 1981.

Bauer, Raymond A. and Greyser, Stephen A., *Advertising in America*, Cambridge, 1968.

Bedell, Clyde, *How to Write Advertising That Sells*, McGraw-Hill, New York, 1952.

Berger, Arthur Asa, *Media Research Techniques*, Sage Books, Newbury Park, CA, 1991.

Berman, Ronald, *Advertising and Social Change*, Sage Books, Beverley Hills, CA, 1981.

Birren, Faber, *Light, Color and Environment*, Schiffer Publishing, New York, 1988.

Birren, Faber, *Creative Color*, Reinhold Publishing, New York, 1961.

Bocock, R., *Consumption*, Routledge, London, 1993.

Boddewyn, J. J. and Marton, Katherine, *Comparison Advertising*, Hastings House, New York, 1978.

Bogart, Leo, *Strategy in Advertising*, Harbinger, New York, 1976.

Book, Albert C. and Cary, Norman D., *The Radio and Television Commercial*, Crain Books, Chicago, 1978.

Boorstin, Daniel, *The Image*. Harper & Row, New York, 1962.

Borden, Neil H., *Economic Effects of Advertising*, Irwin, Chicago, 1947.

Borden, Neil H., *Problems in Advertising*, McGraw-Hill, New York, 1937.

Bourdieu, P., *La Distinction*, Editions de Minuit, Paris, 1979.

Brewer, J. and Porter, R., eds, *Consumption and the World of Goods*, Routledge, New York, 1993.

Brian, Rigby, *Popular Culture in France, A Study of Cultural Discourse*, Routledge, London, 1991.

Brown, A., *Roland Barthes – The Figures of Writing*, Clarendon Press, Oxford, 1992.

Brozen Y., ed., *Advertising and Society*, New York University Press, New York, 1974.

Burnett, Leo, *Communications of an Advertising Man*, University of Chicago Press, Chicago, 1961.

Burton, Philip W., *Advertising Copywriting*, Grid, Columbus, OH, 1978.

Buzzi, Giancarlo, *Advertising – Its Cultural and Political Effects*, University of Minnesota Press, Minneapolis, 1968.

Calvet, J.-L., *Roland Barthes – Un Regard politique sur le Signe*, Payot, Paris, 1973.

Campbell, C., *The Romantic Ethic and the Spirit of Modern Consumerism*, Basil Blackwell, Oxford, 1989.

Caples, John, *Tested Advertising Methods*, Prentice-Hall, Englewood Cliffs, NJ, 1974.

Cherington, Paul Terry, *The Consumer Looks at Advertising*, Garland, New York, 1985.

Clark, Blake, *The Advertising Smoke Screen*, Harper Brothers, New York, 1944

Clark, Eric, *The Want Makers – Inside the World of Advertising*. Penguin Books, New York, 1988.

Colley, Russell H., *Defining Advertising Goals for Measured Advertising Results*, Association of National Advertisers, New York, 1961.

Comanor, William S. and Wilson, Thomas A., *Advertising and Market Power*, Harvard University Press, Cambridge, MA, 1974.

Cone, Fairfax, *For All Its Faults – A Candid Account of 40 Years in Advertising*, Little, Brown and Company, Boston, 1969.

Cook, Guy, *The Discourse of Advertising*, Routledge, London, 1992.

Creel, George, *How We Advertised America*, Harper Brothers, New York, 1920.

Cross, G., *Time and Money – The Making of Consumer Culture*, Routledge, London, 1993.

Cross, Mary, *Advertising and Culture*, Praeger, Westport, CT, 1996.

Csikszentmihalyi, M. and Rochberg-Halton, E., *The Meaning of Things – Domestic Symbols and the Self*, Cambridge University Press, Cambridge, 1981.

Culler, J., *Roland Barthes*, Fontana, London, 1983.

Davis, Howard and Walton, Paul, eds, *Language, Image, Media*, Basil Blackwell, Oxford, 1983.

De La Croix, A., *Barthes – Pour une éthique des signes*, Prism, Brussels, 1987.

Della Femina, Jerry, *From Those Wonderful Folks Who Gave You Pearl Harbor*, Pocket Books, New York, 1971.

Dittmar, Helga, *The Social Psychology of Material Possessions – To Have Is to Be*, St Martin's Press, New York, 1992.

Dixon, N.F, *Subliminal Perception – The Nature of a Controversy*, McGraw-Hill, London, 1971.

Doob, Leonard, *Propaganda – Its Psychology and Technique*, Henry Holt and Company, New York, 1935.

Douglas, M. and Isherwood, B., *The World of Goods – Towards an Anthropology of Consumption*, Penguin, London, 1979.

Doyal, L. and Gough, I., *A Theory of Human Needs*, Macmillan, London, 1991.

Dreyfuss, H., *Designing for People*, Simon & Schuster, New York, 1955.

Dunn, Watson, *International Handbook of Advertising*, McGraw-Hill, New York, 1964.

Dyer, Gillian, *Advertising as Communication*, Routledge, London, 1982.

Easthope, A, *Literary into Cultural Studies*, Routledge, London, 1991.

Eco, Umberto, *Travels in Hyper Reality*, Harcourt Brace, San Diego, 1986.

Ellul, Jacques, *Propaganda – The Formation of Men's Attitudes*, Vintage Books, New York, 1965.

Enid, Verity, *Color Observed*, Van Nostrand Reinholt Company, New York, 1980.

Evans, Ralph M., *An Introduction to Color*, John Wiley & Sons, New York, 1948.

Ewen, Stuart, *All Consuming Images*, McGraw-Hill, New York, 1988.

Ewen, Stuart, *Captains of Consciousness*, McGraw-Hill, New York, 1976.

Ewen, Stuart and Ewen, Elizabeth, *Channels of Desire – Mass Images and the Shaping of American Consciousness*, University of Minnesota Press, Minneapolis, 1992.

Featherstone, M., *Consumer Culture and Postmodernism*, Sage, London, 1991.

Festinger, L., *A Theory of Cognitive Dissonance*, Stanford University Press, Stanford, CA, 1957.

Fine, B. and Leopold, E., *The World of Consumption*, Routledge, London, 1993.

Fisher, Joseph C. and Cook, Peter A., *Advertising, Alcohol Consumption, and Mortality – An Empirical Investigation*, Greenwood Press, Westport, CT, 1995.

Fiske, J., *Understanding Popular Culture*, Unwin Hyman, Boston, 1989.

Forty, Adrian, *Objects of Desire*, Thames & Hudson, London, 1986.

Foster, H., *Postmodern Culture*, Pluto Press, London, 1985.

Fowles, Jib, *Advertising and Popular Culture*, Sage Books, Thousand Oaks, CA, 1996.

Fox, Richard Wightman and Lears, T. Jackson, *The Culture of Consumption*, Pantheon, New York, 1983.

Fox, Roy F., *Harvesting Minds – How TV Commercials Control Kids*, Praeger, Westport, CT, 1996.

Fox, Stephen, *The Mirror Makers*, Vintage Books, New York, 1984.

Frey, Albert W., *The Advertising Industry*, Association of National Advertisers, New York, 1958.

Garvey, Ellen Gruber, *The Adman in the Parlor*, Oxford University Press, New York, 1996.

Gensch, Dennis, *Advertising Planning*, Scientific Publishing, Amsterdam, 1973.

Goffman, Erving, *Gender Advertisements*, Harper, New York, 1979.

Goldman, Robert, *Reading Ads Socially*, Routledge, London, 1992.

Goldman, Robert and Papson, Stephen, *Sign Wars – The Cluttered Landscape of Advertising*, Guilford Press, New York, 1995.

Goode, Kenneth M, and Powel, Harford Jr, *What About Advertising?* Harper Brothers, New York, 1928.

Goodrum, Charles A. and Dalrymple, Helen, *Advertising in America – The First 200 Years*, Harry Abrams, New York, 1990.

Gundladi, E. T, *Facts and Fetishes in Advertising*, Consolidated, Chicago, 1931.

Haberstroh, Jack, *Ice Cube Sex – The Truth about Subliminal Advertising*, Cross Cultural Publications, Notre Dame, IN, 1994.

Haineault, Doris-Louise, *Unconscious for Sale – Advertising, Psychoanalysis and the Public*, University of Minnesota Press, Minneapolis, 1993.

Harris, Richard, *Information Processing in Advertising*, Lawrence Erlbaum Associates, Hillsdale, NJ, 1983.

Harvey, D., *The Condition of Postmodernity – An Enquiry into the Origins of Culture*, Basil Blackwell, Oxford, 1988.

Haug, W. F., *Commodity Aesthetics, Ideology & Culture*, International General, Paris, 1987.

Haug, W. F., *Critique of Commodity Aesthetics – Appearance, Sexuality & Advertising*, Polity Press, Cambridge, 1986.

Hebdige, D., *Hiding in the Light – On Images and Things*, Comedia, London, 1988.

Hebdige, D., *Subculture, The Meaning of Style*, Methuen, London, 1979.

Heelas, P. and Morris, P., eds, *The Values of Enterprise Culture – The Moral Debate*, Routledge, London, 1992.

Higgins, Dennis, *The Art of Writing Advertising – Conversations with Masters of the Craft*, NTC Business Books, Lincolnwood, IL, 1987.

Hobbs, Whit, *I Love Advertising*, Adweek Books, New York, 1985.

Hollingworth, Harry Levi, *Advertising and Selling, Principles of Appeal and Response*, Appleton, New York, 1920.

Hopkins, Claude C., *My Life in Advertising*, Crain Books, Chicago, 1976.

Hopkins, Claude C., *Scientific Advertising*, Crown, New York, 1966.

Hornung, Clarence Pearson, *200 Years of American Graphic Art – A Retrospective Survey of the Printing Arts and Advertising since the Colonial Period*, G. Braziller, New York, 1976.

Hotchkiss, George B., *An Outline of Advertising*, Macmillan, New York, 1950.

Hotchkiss, George B., *Advertising Copy*, Harper, New York, 1949.

Houck, John W., *Outdoor Advertising – History and Regulation*, University of Notre Dame Press, Notre Dame, IN, 1969.

Hovland, Roxanne and Wilcox, Gary B., *Advertising in Society – Classic and Contemporary Readings on Advertising's Role in Society*, NTC Business Books, Lincolnwood, IL, 1989.

Howard, John A. and Hulbert, James, *Advertising and the Public Interest*, Crain Communications, Chicago, 1973.

Hower, Ralph Merle, *The History of an advertising Agency – N.W. Ayer & Son at Work, 1869–1949,* Harvard University Press, Cambridge, MA, 1939.

Hummel, William and Huntress, Keith, *The Analysis of Propaganda,* William Sloane Associates, New York, 1949.

Institute for Propaganda Analysis, *The Fine Art of Propaganda.* Harcourt Brace, New York, 1939.

Institute for Propaganda Analysis, *Propaganda Analysis,* Columbia University Press, New York, 1938.

Jamieson, Kathleen Hall, *Packaging the Presidency – A History and Criticism of Presidential Campaign Advertising,* Oxford University Press, New York, 1984.

Jenks, C., *Culture,* Routledge, London, 1993.

Jewler, A. Jerome, *Creative Strategy in Advertising,* Wadsworth, Belmont, CA, 1981.

Jhally, Sut, *The Codes of Advertising – Fetishism and the Political Economy of Meaning in the Consumer Society,* Routledge, New York, 1990.

Jones, John Phillip, *When Ads Work, New Proof That Advertising Triggers Sales,* Lexington Books, New York, 1995.

Judd, Deane B., *Color in Business, Science, and Industry,* John Wiley, New York, 1952.

Keat, R. and Abercrombie, N., eds., *Enterprise Culture,* Routledge, London, 1991.

Keat, R. and Whiteley, N., *The Authority of the Consumer,* Routledge, London, 1994.

Kenner, H. J., *The Fight for Truth in Advertising,* Advertising Federation of America, New York, 1936.

Kern, Montague, *30-Second Politics – Political Advertising in the Eighties,* Praeger, New York, 1989.

Kern-Foxworth, Marilyn, *Aunt Jemima, Uncle Ben, and Rastus – Blacks in Advertising, Yesterday, Today, and Tomorrow,* Greenwood Press, Westport, CT, 1994.

Key, Wilson Bryan, *The Age Of Manipulation – The Con in Confidence, The Sin In Sincere,* Holt, New York, 1989.

Key, Wilson Bryan, *The Clam-Plate Orgy and Other Subliminal Techniques for Manipulating Your Behavior*, Signet, New York, 1980.

Key, Wilson Bryan, *Media Sexploitation*, Prentice-Hall, Englewood Cliffs, NJ, 1976.

Key, Wilson Bryan, *Subliminal Seduction*, Signet, New York, 1972.

Kirkpatrick, Jerry, *In Defense of Advertising – Arguments from Reason, Ethical Egoism, and Laissez-Faire Capitalism*, Quorum Books, Westport, CT, 1994.

Klein, Richard, *Cigarettes Are Sublime*, Picador, London, 1995.

Kleinman, Philip, *Saatchi & Saatchi – The Inside Story*, NTC Business Books, Lincolnwood, IL, 1989.

Kleppner, Otto, *Advertising Procedure*, Prentice-Hall, Englewood Cliffs, NJ, 1966.

Kufrin, Joan, *Leo Burnett – Star Reacher*, Leo Burnett Company, Chicago, 1995.

Lasch, C., *The Culture of Narcissism*, Abacus, London, 1979.

Lasker, Albert, *The Lasker Story – As He Told It*, NTC Business Books, Lincolnwood, IL, 1987.

Lavers, A., *Roland Barthes – Structuralism and After*, Macmillan, London, 1982.

Leachman, Harden Bryant, *The Early Advertising Scene*, Garland, New York, 1985.

Leak, A., *Roland Barthes – Mythologies*, Grant & Cutler, London, 1994.

Lears, Jackson, *Fables of Abundance – A Cultural History of Advertising in America*, Basic Books, New York, 1994.

Lears, T. Jackson and Fox, Richard Wightman, eds, *From Salvation to Self-Realization – The Culture of Consumption – Critical Essays in American History, 1880–1980*, Pantheon Books, New York, 1983.

Lee, M. J., *Consumer Culture Reborn – The Cultural Politics of Consumption*, Routledge, London, 1992.

Leiss, William and Kline, Stephen, *Social Communication in Advertising*, Nelson Canada, Ontario, 1990.

Leiss, William, Kline, Stephen and Jhally, Sut, *Social Communication in Advertising – Persons, Products, and Images of Well-Being*, Methuen, New York, 1986.

Levenson, Bob, *Bill Bernbach's Book – A History of the Advertising That Changed the History of Advertising*, Villard Books, New York, 1987.

Leymore, V. L., *Hidden Myth*, Basic Books, New York, 1975.

Lipstein, Benjamin and McGuire, William J., *Evaluating Advertising*, Advertising Research Foundation, New York, 1978.

Longman, Kenneth, *Advertising,* Harcourt & Brace, New York, 1971.

Lorimer, Rowland, and McNulty, Jean, *Mass Communication in Canada*, McClelland & Stewart, Scarborough, Ontario, 1990.

Lowenthal, Leo and Guterman, Norbert, *Prophets of Deceit*, Pacific Books, Palo Alto, CA, 1970.

Lucas, Darrell B. and Britt, Steuart H., *Measuring Advertising Effectiveness*, McGraw-Hill, New York, 1963.

Luckiesh, M., *The Language of Color*, Dodd, Mead, New York, 1920.

Lunt, Peter K. and Livingstone, S. M., *Mass Consumption and Personal Identity*, Open University Press, London, 1992.

Maas, Jane, *Adventures of an Advertising Woman, Ballantine Books*, New York, 1986.

McAllister, Matthew P., *The Commercialization of American Culture, New Advertising, Control and Democracy*, Sage Publications, Thousand Oaks, CA, 1996.

McCracken, G., *Culture and Consumption*, Indiana University Press, Indianapolis, 1988.

McGann, Anthony F. and Russell, John T., *Advertising Media*, Irwin, Chicago, 1981.

McGuigan, J., *Cultural Populism,* Routledge, London, 1992.

McLuhan, M., *Culture Is Our Business*, Ballantine Books, New York, 1970.

McNeal, James U., *Kids as Consumers – A Handbook of Marketing to Children*, Lexington Books, New York, 1992.

Maddock, Richard C. and Fulton, Richard L., *Marketing to the Mind, Right Brain Strategies for Advertising and Marketing*, Quorum Books, Westport, CT, 1996.

Mannes, Marya, *But Will It Sell?*, Lippincott, New York, 1964.

Marchand, Roland, *Advertising the American Dream – Making Way for Modernity, 1920–1940*, University of California Press, Berkeley, 1985.

Marra, James L., *Advertising Creativity – Techniques for Generating Ideas*, Prentice-Hall, Englewood Cliffs, NJ, 1990.

Martineau, Pierre, *Motivation in Advertising*, McGraw-Hill, New York 1957.

Mayer, Martin, *Whatever Happened to Madison Avenue? Advertising in the '90s*, Little, Brown, Boston, 1991.

Mayer, Martin, *Madison Avenue USA*, Pocketbooks, New York, 1958.

Miller, Clyde, *The Process of Persuasion*, Crown Publishers, New York, 1946.

Miller, D., *Material Culture and Mass Consumption*, Basil Blackwell, Oxford, 1987.

Miller, F., *Music in Advertising*, Amsco Publications, New York, 1985.

Moog, Carole, *Are They Selling Her Lips? Advertising and Identity*, William Morrow, New York, 1990.

Morgan, Richard, *J. Walter Takeover – From Devine Right to Common Stock*, Irwin, Chicago, 1991.

Moskin, J. Robert, *The Case For Advertising*, American Association of Advertising Agencies, New York, 1973.

Murphy, John H. and Cunningham, Isabella C. M., *Advertising and Marketing Communication Management*, Dryden Press, Orlando, 1993.

Neelankavil, James P. and Stridsberg, Arthur B., *Advertising Self-Regulation*, Hastings House, New York, 1980.

Nicosia, Franco, *Advertising Management and Society*, McGraw-Hill, New York, 1974.

Norins, Hanley, *The Compleat Copywriter*, McGraw-Hill, New York, 1966.

Norris, James D., *Advertising and the Transformation of American Society 1865–1920*, Greenwood Press, New York, 1990.

O'Toole, John, *The Trouble with Advertising*, Chelsea House, New York, 1981.

Ogilvy, David, *What's Wrong with Advertising*, NTC Business Books, Lincolnwood, IL, 1990.

Ogilvy, David, *Ogilvy on Advertising*, Crown Publishers, New York, 1983.

Ogilvy, David, *Confessions of an Ad Man*, Atheneum, New York, 1963.

Packard, Vance, *The Waste Makers*, Penguin, Baltimore, 1960.

Packard, Vance, *The Hidden Persuaders*, McKay, New York, 1957.

Palda, Kristian S., *The Measurement of Advertising's Cumulative Effects*, Prentice-Hall, Englewood Cliffs, NJ, 1964.

Pate, Russ, *Adman – Morris Hite's Methods for Winning the Ad Game*, E-Heart Press, Dallas, 1988.

Pease, Otis A., *The Responsibilities of American Advertising*, Yale University Press, New Haven, CT, 1958.

Percy, Larry and Woodside, Arch, *Advertising and Consumer Psychology*, Lexington Books, Lexington, MA, 1983.

Perrin, Wes, *Advertising Realities – A Practical Guide to Agency Management*, Mayfield Publishing, Mountain View, CA, 1992.

Petty, Ross D., *The Impact of Advertising Law on Business and Public Policy*, Quorum Books, Westport, CT, 1992.

Pope, Daniel, *The Making of Modern Advertising*, Basic Books, New York, 1983.

Postman, Niel, *Amusing Ourselves to Death*, Penguin Books, New York, 1985.

Pratkanis, Anthony and Elliot, Aronson, *Age of Propaganda – The Everyday Use and Abuse of Persuasion*, Freeman, New York, 1991.

Presbrey, Frank, *The History and Development of Advertising*, Greenwood Press, New York, 1929.

Preston, Ivan, *The Tangled Web They Weave – Truth, Falsity and Advertisers*, University of Wisconson Press, Madison, 1994.

Preston, Ivan, *The Great American Blow-up – Puffery in Advertising and Selling*, University of Wisconsin Press, Madison, 1977.

Randazzo, Sal, *The Mythmakers – How Advertisers Apply the Power of Classic Myths and Symbols to Create Modern Day Legends*, Probus Publishing, Chicago, 1995.

Reeves, Rosser, *Reality in Advertising*, Knopf, New York 1961.

Richards, Jef I., *Deceptive Advertising – Behavioral Study of a Legal Concept*, Lawrence Erlbaum Associates, Hillsdale, NJ, 1990.

Ries, A. and Trout, J., *Positioning – The Battle For Your Mind*, McGraw-Hill, New York, 1986.

Roman, Kenneth and Maas, Jane, *How to Advertise*, St Martin's Press, New York, 1976.

Rothenberg, Randall, *Where the Suckers Moon – An Advertising Story*, Knopf, New York, 1994.

Rotzoll, Kim B., Haefner, James E., and Sandage, Charles H., *Advertising in Contemporary Society – Perspectives Toward Understanding*, South-Western Publishing, Cincinnati, 1986.

Rowell, George P., *40 Years an Advertising Agent*, Franklin Books, Palisade, NJ, 1926.

Rust, Roland, *Advertising Media Models – A Practical Guide*, Lexington Books, Lexington MA, 1986.

Sampson, Henry, *A History of Advertising from the Earliest Times*, Chatto & Windus, London, 1974.

Samtag, Nicholas, *How Business is Bamboozled by the Ad Boys*, Heinemann, New York, 1966.

Sandage, Charles H., *Promise of Advertising*, Irwin Books, Homewood, IL, 1961.

Sandage, Charles H., *The Role of Advertising*, Irwin Books, Homewood, IL, 1960.

Sargent, Hugh W., *Frontiers of Advertising Theory and Research*, Pacific Books, Palo Alto, CA, 1972.

Saussure, F. de, *Cours de linguistique Générale*, Payot, Paris, 1949.

Savan, Leslie, *The Sponsored Life – Ads, TV and American Culture*, Temple University Press, Philadelphia, 1994.

Schmalensee, Richard, *The Economics of Advertising*, North-Holland Books, New York, 1972.

Schudson, Michael, *Advertising, the Uneasy Persuasion – Its Dubious Impact On American Society*, Basic Books, New York, 1984.

Schultz, Don E., Martin, Dennis, and Brown, William P., *Strategic Advertising Campaigns*, NTC Business Books, Lincolnwood, IL, 1987.

Schwartz, Tony, *The Responsive Chord*, Anchor Books, New York, 1974.

Scott, Walter Dill, *Psychology of Advertising*, Dodd Mead, New York, 1931.

Scott, Walter Dill, *The Theory of Advertising – A Simple Exposition of the Principles of Psychology in Their Relation to Successful Advertising*, Small, Maynard & Amp, Boston, 1907.

Seiden, Hank, *Advertising Pure and Simple*, Macmillan, New York, 1963.

Shields, R., *Lifestyle Shopping – The Subject of Consumption*, Routledge, London, 1992.

Silva Martins, Maria Cristina da, *Humour & Eroticism in Advertising*, San Diego State University Press, San Diego, 1995.

Simon, Julian, *Issues in the Economics of Advertising*. University Press, Urbana, IL, 1970.

Sinclair, J., *Images Incorporated – Advertising as Industry and Ideology*, Croom Helm, London, 1987.

Sissors, Jack Z. and Surmanek, Jim, *Advertising Media Planning*, Crain Books, Chicago, 1976.

Smith, George H., *Motivation Research in Advertising and Marketing*, McGraw-Hill, New York,1954.

Solomon, Jack, *The Signs of Our Times*, Jeremy P. Tarcher, Los Angeles, 1988.

Spero, Robert, *The Duping of The American Voter – Dishonesty and Deception in Presidential Television Advertising*, Lippincott & Crowell, New York, 1980.

Stabiner, Karen, *Inventing Desire*, Simon & Schuster, New York, 1993.

Staniszewski, Mary Anne, *Seeing is Believing – Creating the Culture of Art*, Penguin Books, New York, 1995.

Starch, Daniel, *Measuring Advertising Readership and Results*, McGraw-Hill, New York, 1966.

Starch, Daniel, *Advertising Principles*, A. W. Shaw, London, 1923.

Sterling, C. and Kittross, J., *Stay Tuned – A Concise History of American Broadcasting*, Wadsworth Publishing, Belmont, CA, 1990.

Storey, John, *An Introductory Guide to Cultural Theory and Popular Culture*, Harvester Wheatsheaf, London, 1993.

Swingewood, A., *The Myth of Mass Culture*, Macmillan, London, 1985.

Thum, Gladys and Thum, Marcella, *The Persuaders – Propaganda in War and Peace*, Atheneum, New York, 1972.

Tomlinson, A., *Consumption, Identity and Style – Marketing, Meanings, and the Packaging of Pleasure*, Routledge, London, 1990.

Turner, Ernest Sackville, *The Shocking History of Advertising*, Dutton, New York, 1953.

Twitchell, James B., *Adcult Usa – The Triumph of Advertising in American Culture*, Columbia University Press, New York, 1996.

Vestergaard, Torben and Schroder Kim, *The Language of Advertising*, Basil Blackwell, Oxford, 1985.

Wakeham, Frederick, *The Hucksters*, Rinehart, New York, 1946.

Watkins, Trevor, *The Economics of the Brand*, McGraw-Hill, London, 1986.

Wedding, C. Nugent and Lesler, Richard S., *Advertising Management*, Ronald Press, New York, 1962.

Weir, Walter, *Truth in Advertising and Other Heresies*, McGraw-Hill, New York, 1963.

Weir, Walter, *On the Writing of Advertising*, McGraw-Hill, New York, 1960.

Wernick, A., *Promotional Culture – Advertising, Ideology and Symbolic Expression*, Sage, London, 1991.

White, Percival, *Advertising Research*, Appleton, East Norwalk, CT, 1927.

Wicke, Jennifer, *Advertising Fictions – Literature, Advertisement and Social Reading*, Columbia University Press, New York, 1988.

Wight, Robin, *The Day the Pigs Refused to be Driven to Market*, MacGibbon Ltd, London, 1972.

Williamson, Judith, *Decoding Advertisements – Ideology and Meaning in Advertising*, Calder & Boyars, London, 1978.

Willis, P., *Common Culture – Symbolic Work at Play in the Everyday Cultures of the Young*, Open University Press, London, 1990.

Woods, Gail Baker, *Advertising and Marketing to the New Majority*, Wadsworth Publishing Co, Belmont, CA, 1995.

Woodside, Arch G., *Measuring the Effectiveness of Image and Linkage Advertising – The Nitty-Gritty of Maxi-Marketing*, Quorum Books, Westport, CT, 1996.

Wright, John S. and Mertes, John E., *Advertising's Role in Society*, West Books, St. Paul, MN, 1974.

Wright, John W., *The Commercial Connection – Advertising and the American Mass Media*, Dell Publishing, New York, 1979.

Young, James Webb, *How to Become an Advertising Man*, NTC Business Books, Lincolnwood, IL, 1989.

Zukin, L. A., *Landscapes of Power, From Detroit to Disney World*, University of California Press, Berkeley, 1991.

Selected Magazines and Journals

Advances in Consumer Research

d'Astous, A., Maltais, J. and Roberge, C., Compulsive Buying Tendencies of Adolescent Consumers, 1990.

Hoch, S. and Rook, D., Consuming Impulses, 1985.

Schindler, R., Consumer Recognition of Increases in Odd and Even Prices, 1984.

Schindler, R., Berbaum, M. and Weinzimer, D., How an Attention-Getting Device Can Affect Quick Choice among Similar Alternatives, 1987.

Shugan, S., Displays and Advertising – A Theory Seduction, 1981.

Advertising Age

Phone Now, Said CBC Subliminally, But Nobody Did, 10 February 1958.

Subliminal Advertising – Today It's Just Historic Flashback for Researcher Vicary, Danzig, F., 17 September 1962.

Another Look at Subliminal 'Facts', Weir, W., 15 October, 1984.

Advocate

Ouellette, Laurie, Whoops for Whittle Communications and Deconstructing Channel One, 1993.

America magazine

State of the Question, 14 December 1957.

American Psychologist

Greenwald, A. G., New Look 3 – Unconscious Cognition Reclaimed, 1992.

Vokey, J. R. and Read, J. D., Subliminal Messages – Between the Devil and the Media, 1985.

American Quarterly
Ributto, L, Jesus Christ as Business Statesman, 1981.

Atlantic Monthly
Leighton, T., The Art of Corporate Iconology, 1986.

British Journal of Social Psychology
Dittmar, Helga, Gender Identity-related Meanings of Personal
   Possessions, 1989.

Business Ethics
Crisp, R., Persuasive Advertising, Autonomy, and the
   Creation of Desire, 1987.

Cognitive Psychology
Marcel, A. J., Conscious and Unconscious Perception –
   Experiments on Visual Masking and Word Recognition,
   1983.

Consumer Reports
The Cola Wars – The Battle for Your Brain, 1991.

Culture and Society
Kellner, D., Critical Theory, Commodities and the Consumer
   Society Theory, 1983.

Discount Merchandiser
Nichol, D. A., The Future of Private Brands, 1993.

Educational Leadership
Tiene, Drew, Channel One – Good News or Bad News for Our
   Schools? 1993.

European Journal of Marketing
Uncles, M. D. and Ellis, K., The Buying of Own Labels, 1989.

Morris, D., The Strategy of Own Brands, 1979.

Graphics Art Monthly
Griffin, G, Advertising's Greatest Challenge, 1993.

Harvard Business Review
Quelch, J. A. and Hardinger, D., Brands versus Private Labels
 – Fighting to Win, Jan.–Feb. 1996.

Institute of Retail Management
Laaksonen, H., Own Brands in Food Retailing across Europe,
 1994.

Institute for Retail Studies
Burt, S., Retailer Brands in British Grocery Retailing, 1992.

International Journal of Retail & Distribution Management
Omar, O. E., Retail Influence on Food Technology and
 Innovation, 1995.
Omar, O. E., Comparative Product Testing For Own Label
 Marketing, 1994.

International Journal of Retailing
Davies, K. and Gilligan, C., The Development of Own Label
 Product Strategies in Grocery and DIY Retailing in the
 United Kingdom, 1986.

Journal of Advertising Research
Bellenger, D., Robertson, D. and Hirschman, E., Impulse
 Buying Varies by Product, 1978.
Cook, W., Lurking behind the Ice Cubes, 1993.
Rogers, M. and Seiler, C., The Answer Is No – A National
 Survey of Advertising Industry Practitioners and Their
 Clients about Whether They Use Subliminal Advertising,
 1994.

Rogers, M. and Smith, K., Public Perceptions of Subliminal Advertising – Why Practitioners Shouldn't Ignore This Issue, 1993.

Journal of Communication
Greenberg, Bradley S. and Brand, Jeffrey E, Television News and Advertising in Schools – The Channel One Controversy, 1993.

Journal of Consumer Policy
d'Astous, Alain, An Inquiry into the Compulsive Side of 'Normal' Consumers, 1990.
Dittmar, Helga, The Functions of Favourite Clothes and Clothing (Dis)Satisfaction – A Gender Analysis among British Students, 1995.
Elliott, Richard, Addictive Consumption – Function and Fragmentation in Postmodernity, 1994.
Scherhorn, G., Reisch, L. and Raab, G., Addictive Buying in West Germany – An Empirical Investigation, 1990.

Journal of Consumer Research
Beatty, S. E., and Smith, S. M., External Search Efforts – An Investigation across Several Product Categories, 1987.
Bettman, J. R. and Kakkar, P., Effects of Information Presentation Format on Consumer Information Acquisition Strategies, 1977.
Bettman, J. R. and Park, C. W., Effects of Prior Knowledge and Experience and Phase of the Choice Process on Consumer Decision Processes, 1980.
Bloch P. H., Sherrell, D. L. and Ridgeway, N. M, Consumer Search – An Extended Framework, 1986.
Davis, H. L., Decision Making within the Household, 1976.
Deighton, J., Romer, D. and McQueen, J., Using Drama to Persuade, 1989.
Hoch, S., Who Do We Know – Predicting the Interests and

Opinions of the American Consumer, 1988.

Hoch, S. and Young-wonha, Consumer Learning – Advertising and the Ambiguity of Product Experience, 1986.

Marmorstein, H., Grewal, D. and Fishe, R. P. H., The Value of Time Spent in Price Comparison Shopping – Survey and Experimental Evidence, 1992.

O'Guinn, Thomas C. and Faber, Ronald J, Compulsive Buying – A Phenomenological Exploration, 1989.

Richins, Martha and Dawson, S., Materialism as a Consumer Value, 1992.

Shugan, S., The Cost of Thinking, 1980.

Simonson I., Choice Based on Reasons – The Case of Attraction and Compromise Effects, 1989.

Urbany, J. E., Dickson, P. R. and Wilke, W. L., Buyer Uncertainty and Information Search, 1989.

Wallendorf, Melanie and Arnould, E. J., My Favourite Things – A Cross-Cultural Inquiry into Object Attachment, Possessiveness and Social Linkage, 1988.

Journal of Consumer Satisfaction, Dissatisfaction and Complaining Behavior

Schindler, R., The Role of Ego-Expressive Factors in the Consumer's Satisfaction with Price, 1988.

Journal of Economic Psychology

Braun, O. L. and Wicklund, R. A., Psychological Antecedents of Conspicuous Consumption, 1989.

Dittmar, H., Beattie, J. and Friese, S., Gender Identity and Material Symbols – Objects and Decision Considerations in Impulse Purchases, 1995.

Hanley, A. and Wilhelm, I. W., Compulsive Buying – An Exploration into Self-Esteem and Money Attitudes, 1992.

Journal of Economics and Management Strategy
Mills, D. E., Why Retailers Sell Private Labels, 1995.

Journal of Experimental Psychology
Debner, J. and Jacoby, L., Unconscious Perception – Attention, Awareness, and Control, 1994.
Payne, J. W., Bettman J. R. and Johnson, E. J., Adaptive Strategy Selection in Decision Making, 1988.

Journal of Industrial Economics
Connor, J. M. and Peterson, E. B., Market-Structure Determinants of National Brand-Private Label Price Differences of Manufactured Food Products, 1992.

Journal of Marketing
Burke, M. C. and Edell, J. A., The Impact of Feelings on Ad-Based Affect and Cognition, 1989.
Bruner, G. C., Music, Mood, and Marketing, 1990.
Hoch S. and Deighton, J., Managing What Consumers Learn from Experience, 1989.
MacInnis, D. J. and Jaworski, B. J, Enhancing and Measuring Consumers' Motivation, Opportunity, and Ability to Process Brand Information from Advertisements, 1991.
Moore, T. E., Subliminal Advertising – What You See Is What You Get, 1982.
Murray K. B., A Test of Services Marketing Theory – Consumer Information Acquisition Activities, 1991.
Stern, A., The Significance of Impulse Buying Today, 1962.

Journal of Marketing Research
Kollat, David T. and Willet, Ronal P., Customer Impulse Purchasing Behavior, 1967.
Sujan, M., Bettman, J. R., and Baumgartner, H., Influencing Consumer Judgments via Autobiographical Memories, 1993.

Journal of Mind and Behavior
Bornstein, R. F., Subliminal Techniques as Propaganda Tools
– Review and Critique, 1989.

Journal of Personality and Social Psychology
Wilson, T. D. and Schooler, J. W., Thinking Too Much –
Introspection Can Reduce the Quality of Preferences and
Decisions, 1991.

Journal of Retailing
Hoch, S., Dreze, X. and Purk, M., Shelf Management and
Space Elasticity, 1994.

Journal of Social Behaviour and Personality
Kamptner, N. L., Personal Possessions and Their Meanings,
1991.

Management Science
Jeuland, A., Brand Choice Inertia as One Aspect of the Notion
of Brand Loyalty, 1979.

Marketing and Research Today
Kapferer, J., Stealing Brand Equity – Measuring Perceptual
Confusion between National Brands and Copycat Own-
Label Products, 1995.

Marketing Science
Hauser, J. and Shugan, S., Defensive Marketing Strategies,
1983.

Marketing Week
Mitchell, A., Own Label Suppliers at High Noon, 1995.
Murphy, C. and Klerman, P., Countering the Own-Label
Brigade, 1993.

Memory and Cognition
Russo, J. E. and Rosen, L. D., An Eye Fixation Analysis of Multi-Alternative Choice, 1975.

Ms.
Steinem, G., Sex, Lies & Advertising, 1990.

Newsweek
Dumber Than We Thought, 20 September 1993.
Advertising, Devilish? 14 October 1957.
Inside the Consumer, 10 October 1955.

Open magazine
Dery, Mark, Culture Jamming – Hacking, Slashing and Sniping in the Empire of Signs, pamphlet.

Perception
Young, A. W. and Deregowski, J. B., Learning to See the Impossible, 1981.

Progessive Grocer
Mathews, R., Tough Talk on Store Brands, 1996.
Rose, J., The Decade of the Private Label? 1995.
Raphel, M. and Raphel, N., Use Your Imagination – Use Radio, 1993.
What the Buyers Say, 1994.

Psychology and Marketing
Deighton, J. and Schindler, R., Can Advertising Influence Experience? 1988.
Moore, T. E., The Case against Subliminal Manipulation, 1988.

Psychology Bulletin
Payne, J. W., Contingent Decision Behaviour, 1982.

San Jose Mercury-News
Watson, A., Channel One Used Ethnic Divisions to Win Customers, 13 December 1992.

Skeptical Inquirer
Auday, Bryan C., Subliminal Tapes – Controlled Tests, 1992.
Creed, Thomas L., Subliminal Deception – Pseudoscience on the College Lecture Circuit, 1987.
Moore, T. E., Subliminal Perception – Facts and Fallacies, 1992.
Pratkanis, A., The Cargo Cult Science of Subliminal Persuasion, 1992.

Sloan Management Review
Hoch, S., When Do Private Labels Succeed? 1993.

Social Science and Medicine
Goldman, R. and Montagne, M., Marketing Mind Mechanics – Decoding Drug Advertisements in Medical Journals, 1986.

Social Text
Goldman, R., We Make Weekends – Leisure and the Commodity Form, 1984.

Theory, Culture & Society
Goldman, R., Marketing Fragrances – Advertising and the Production of Commodity Signs, 1987.

USA Today magazine
Pratkanis, A. R. and Aronson, E., Subliminal Sorcery – Who Is Seducing Whom? 1991.

US News & World Report
Leo, John, Hostility among the Ice Cubes, 1991.

Village Voice
Savan, L., The Rock Stars Belong to Michelob, 1988.

Yale Law Journal
Branscomb, A., Anonymity, Autonomy, and Accountability –
  Challenges to the First Amendment in Cyberspace, 1995.

Index